Investment im Iran | Investment in Iran | سرمایه‌گذاری در ایران

Esmaeil Karimian • M. Saleh Jaberi •
Saeed Soltani • Michael Lorenz

Investment im Iran | Investment in Iran | سرمایه‌گذاری در ایران

Ein Praxishandbuch für die Zeit nach den
Sanktionen auf Deutsch, Englisch und Farsi –
A Practical Guidebook for the post-sanction
era in German, English and Farsi –

کتاب راهنمایی کاربردی به زبان آلمانی، انگلیسی و فارسی

Springer Gabler

Esmaeil Karimian
ESK Law Firm,
Teheran, Iran

Saeed Soltani
ESK Law Firm,
Teheran, Iran

M. Saleh Jaberi
ESK Law Firm,
Teheran, Iran

Michael Lorenz
Lorenz & Partners Co., Ltd.
Bangkok, Thailand

ISBN 978-3-658-14432-6   ISBN 978-3-658-14433-3 (eBook)
DOI 10.1007/978-3-658-14433-3

Die Deutsche Nationalbibliothek verzeichnet diese Publikation in der Deutschen Nationalbibliografie; detaillierte
bibliografische Daten sind im Internet über http://dnb.d-nb.de abrufbar.

Springer Gabler
© Springer Fachmedien Wiesbaden GmbH 2017

Gedruckt auf säurefreiem und chlorfrei gebleichtem Papier

Springer Gabler ist Teil von Springer Nature
Die eingetragene Gesellschaft ist Springer Fachmedien Wiesbaden GmbH
Die Anschrift der Gesellschaft ist: Abraham-Lincoln-Strasse 46, 65189 Wiesbaden, Germany

Investment im Iran

Ein Praxishandbuch für die Zeit nach den Sanktionen
auf Deutsch, Englisch und Farsi

© Springer Fachmedien Wiesbaden 2017
E. Karimian, M. S. Jaberi, S. Soltani, M. Lorenz,
Investment im Iran | Investment in Iran | سرمایه‌گذاری در ایران
DOI 10.1007/978-3-658-14433-3_1

Inhaltsverzeichnis

Abkürzungsverzeichnis

ADR	Alternative Dispute Resolution (Alternative Streitbeilegung)
BIP	Bruttoinlandsprodukt
BOT/BOOT	Build-Operate-Transfer / Build-Own-Operate-Transfer (Begriff aus dem Anlagenbau)
DBA	Doppelbesteuerungsabkommen
EPC	Engineering, Procurement and Construction (Begriff aus dem Anlagenbau)
ESCWA	Economic and Social Commission for Western Asia (Wirtschafts- und Sozialkommission für Westasien der Vereinten Nationen)
FEAS	Federation of Euro-Asian Stock Exchanges (Vereinigung der europäisch-asiatischen Aktienmärkte)
FIPPA	Foreign Investment Promotion and Protection Act (Ausländerinvestitionsgesetz des Iran)
GMT	Greenwich Mean Time (Zeitzone)
GUS	Gemeinschaft unabhängiger Staaten
ICGN	International Corporate Governance Network
INTA	Iranian National Tax Administration (die iranische Finanzverwaltung)
IOR/EOR	Improved Oil Recovery / Enhanced Oil Recovery
IPC	Iran Petroleum Contract (Vertragsart in der iranischen Erdölindustrie)
IRR	Iranischer Rial (Währung Irans)
JVC	Joint Venture Company
LAPFI	Law on the Attraction and Protection of Foreign Investment
MENA	Region des Mittleren Ostens und Nordafrika
OIC	Organisation of Islamic Cooperation
OIETAI	Organisation for Investment, Economic and Technical Assistance of Iran (iranische Investitionsbehörde)
OTC	Over-the-counter
PPP	Purchasing Power Parity (Kaufkraftparität)
SAARC	South Asian Association for Regional Cooperation (Südasiatische Vereinigung für regionale Kooperation)
SSF	Single Stock Features
TSE	Tehran Stock Exchange (Teheraner Börse)
UNECE	United Nations Economic Commission for Europe (Wirtschaftskommission für Europa der Vereinten Nationen)
VAT	Value Added Tax (Mehrwertsteuer)
VATA	Value Added Tax Act of Iran (Mehrwertsteuergesetz Irans)
WFE	World Federation of Exchanges (Weltverband der Börsen)
WIPO	World Intellectual Property Organization (Weltorganisation für geistiges Eigentum)

1.   Einführung

1.1   Geografische Lage und Bevölkerung

Die Islamische Republik Iran hat eine Fläche von 164.819,6 km², eine Bevölkerung von 81 Mio. und liegt in Südwestasien. Das Land grenzt im Westen an die Türkei und den Irak, im Osten an Afghanistan und Pakistan, im Norden an Armenien, Aserbaidschan, Russland, Kasachstan und Turkmenistan, und im Süden durch den Persischen Golf und das Omanische Meer an Kuwait, Saudi-Arabien, Katar, Bahrain, die Vereinigten Arabischen Emirate und Oman.

Iran ist daher ein strategisches Land mit Grenzen zu Mitgliedsstaaten der Wirtschafts- und Sozialkommission für Westasien der Vereinten Nationen („ESCWA", *Economic and Social Commission for Western Asia*) im Süden und Westen, Mitgliedsstaaten der Südasiatischen Vereinigung für regionale Kooperation („SAARC", *South Asian Association for Regional Cooperation*) im Osten und Staaten der Gemeinschaft unabhängiger Staaten („GUS") sowie der Wirtschaftskommission für Europa der Vereinten Nationen („UNECE", *United Nations Economic Commission for Europe*) im Norden. Iran hat seit Langem eine geostrategische Bedeutung aufgrund seiner zentralen Lage in Eurasien und Westasien, sowie aufgrund seiner Nähe zur Straße von Hormus.

Das Land gilt als eines der an Kohlenwasserstoff-Reserven reichsten Länder, und ist daher weltweit das Land mit den zweitgrößten Gasreserven und -exporten sowie der zweitgrößte Exporteur von Rohöl. Laut Berichten von internationalen Institutionen wie der Weltbank liegt die Islamische Republik Iran mit einem Bruttoinlandsprodukt („BIP") von mehr als 425 Mrd. US$ an 18. Stelle der 20 herausragendsten Nationen, und ebenfalls an 18. Stelle bezüglich Kaufkraft (*Purchasing Power Parity, PPP*). Mit einem Binnenmarkt

von über 81 Mio. Einwohnern und geplanten Großinvestitionen des Staates wird dieser
Anteil weiter wachsen.

1.2   Wirtschaftliches Umfeld

Laut Weltbank ist Iran die zweitgrößte Wirtschaftsnation in der Region des Mittleren
Ostens und Nordafrika („MENA") mit einem geschätzten BIP von 425 Mrd. US$ in 2014.
Irans Wirtschaft ist gekennzeichnet durch einen starken Rohstoffsektor, Kleinlandwirt-
schaft und einen Dienstleistungssektor, sowie einer starken staatlichen Präsenz im Pro-
duktions- und Finanzsektor. Iran steht weltweit an zweiter Stelle in Bezug auf Gasvorkom-
men und an vierter Stelle in Bezug auf nachgewiesene Rohölvorkommen. Das BIP und
Staatseinkommen hängen – nach wie vor – stark von Erlösen aus dem Ölgeschäft ab und
sind daher sehr volatil.

Öl und Gas sind zwei der wesentlichen natürlichen Rohstoffe Irans, die Investitionen
und Handel fördern. Iran ist zu einer der größten Wirtschaftsnationen in Asien und insbesondere im Mittleren Osten herangewachsen. Das Land bietet unzählige Investitionsmög-
lichkeiten für lokale und internationale Investoren und zieht Handel an durch die zahlreichen Freihandels- und Sonderwirtschaftszonen (*Free Zones* und *Special Economic Zones*)
im ganzen Land, die lukrative Anreize anbieten. Derzeit gibt es mehr als 20 Free Zones und
Special Economic Zones im Iran, die je nach Region verschiedene Vorteile bieten, sodass
Investoren die für sie am günstigsten Optionen wählen können.

1.3   Investitionen und Geschäftsmöglichkeiten

Überblick:
– Die diversifizierte Wirtschaft und breite Industriebasis mit mehr als 40 an der Tehera-
  ner Börse gelisteten Branchen ist der Kernmarkt der MENA-Region.
– Ressourcenreichtum
– Junge und gebildete Bevölkerung
– Großer Binnenmarkt
– Der Mittlere Osten ist Hauptabsatzmarkt für Irans Exporte außerhalb des Ölsektors.
– Der zunehmende Ausbau von Infrastruktur und Humankapital bildet die Grundlage
  für eine wissensbasierte Wirtschaft.

Seit 2006 hat die U.S. Regierung Sanktionen gegen Iran verhängt sowie gegen Geschäfte
mit dem Iran. Dies hat dazu geführt, dass ausländische Unternehmen sich von Großpro-
jekten (wie z.B. der Erschließung des South Pars / North Dome Erdgasfeldes) zurückge-
zogen haben oder weitere Investitionen verschoben haben. Ausländische Finanzierungen
sind seitdem weitgehend nicht mehr verfügbar. Iran hat sich daher stärker den eigenen
Ressourcen und inländischen Investoren und Unternehmen zugewandt und bspw. den

Pars Investment Fund eingerichtet, um Anteile an der South Pars / North Dome Erschließung im Wert von 3,5 Mrd. US$ auszugeben.

Die Sanktionen gegen Iran wurden mittlerweile graduell abgebaut, was eine gute Möglichkeit für viele Unternehmen bietet, ihre Aktivitäten im Iran wieder aufzubauen bzw. neue Vorhaben anzugehen. Vor diesem Hintergrund sollten internationale Unternehmen unbedingt diese Änderungen und die aussichtsreiche Gelegenheit in Betracht ziehen.

Das Ausländerinvestitionsrecht Irans, der *Foreign Investment Promotion and Protection Act* („FIPPA"), wurde in 2002 vom Parlament verabschiedet. Einige der wesentlichen Verbesserungen, die durch den FIPPA eingeführt wurden, können wie folgt beschrieben werden:

1. Erweiterung der für ausländische Investoren zugänglichen Bereiche, inkl. Infrastrukturprojekte

2. Erweiterung des Begriffs der ausländischen Investition, der nun alle Arten von Investitionen abdeckt, von direkten Auslandsinvestitionen zu verschiedenen Arten der Projektfinanzierung, inkl. Joint Ventures, Rückkaufvereinbarungen, Gegengeschäften und diversen BOT-Arten

3. Gestrafftes und schnelles Lizenzierungs- und Genehmigungsverfahren für Investitionen

4. Schaffung einer zentralen Anlaufstelle der Investitionsbehörde, das sog. *Center for Foreign Investment Services*, um zielgerichtete und effiziente Unterstützung für Investitionsvorhaben im Iran zu gewährleisten

5. Mehr Flexibilität und Vereinfachung der Regulierungen in Bezug auf Zugang zu ausländischem Kapital und Kapitalfluss für ausländische Investoren

6. Gemäß Art. 12 – 15 des FIPPA hat jeder ausländische Investor, der seine Investition im Iran unter dem FIPPA registriert, das Recht, Kapital und Dividenden ins Ausland zu überweisen:

   Art. 12: *„Der zum Zeitpunkt des Import oder Exports von ausländischem Kapital geltende Fremdwährungswechselkurs sowie der Wechselkurs für sämtliche Fremdwährungstransfers soll, im Falle eines einheitlichen Wechselkurses, derselbe Wechselkurs wie der des Bankenwesens des jeweiligen Landes sein; anderenfalls soll der anwendbare Wechselkurs der von der Zentralbank der Islamischen Republik Irans sein."*

Internationalen Unternehmen, die Geschäfte im Iran betreiben möchten, bietet sich eine Vielzahl von Möglichkeiten. Abgesehen von einfachen Handelsbeziehungen über Handelsvertreter besteht für viele Unternehmen ein deutlicher Vorteil darin, eine eigene Präsenz vor Ort zu haben. Dies erleichtert es, Marktmöglichkeiten zu erforschen, Kontakte zu knüpfen, sich mit Kunden auszutauschen und die Einzelheiten von Geschäften zu begutachten.

Eine eigene Präsenz zu haben, ist auch im Zusammenhang mit der Geschäftskultur des Mittleren Ostens wichtig. Geschäftsleute und -inhaber in der Region bevorzugen es, mit jemandem Geschäfte zu machen, den Sie kennen und dem sie durch den Aufbau einer persönlichen Beziehung vertrauen. Ein weiterer regionaler Faktor, der zur Bedeutung einer physischen Präsenz beiträgt, ist, dass das Kaufverhalten mancher von Iran bedienter Länder unvorhersehbar ist, was eine Marktkenntnis aus erster Hand umso wichtiger macht.

1.4   Politisches System

Iran ist eine Islamische Republik, deren politisches System auf der Verfassung von 1979, der sog. *Qanun-e Asasi*, dem iranischen Grundgesetz, basiert. Der Staat besteht aus verschiedenen Regierungsorganen, die teils demokratisch gewählt sind, teils aus Religionsvertretern bestehen.

Das einzigartige politische System kombiniert Elemente einer parlamentarischen Demokratie mit einer religiösen Theokratie, die vom iranischen Klerus unter Leitung des einflussreichen Obersten Geistlichen geführt wird.

Die iranische Verfassung sieht Gewaltenteilung in drei Bereiche vor, namentlich die Exekutive, Legislative und die Judikative. Die drei Gewalten sind wie auch in anderen Ländern ausgestaltet.

Iran ist eine multikulturelle Nation, die aus zahlreichen ethnischen und linguistischen Gruppen besteht, wobei die meisten Einwohner Schiiten sind. Die Landessprache Persisch (Farsi) wird flächendeckend gesprochen, während Englisch die zweite Sprache des Iran ist.

1.5   Währung

Die Währung des Iran ist der Iranische Rial (IRR, ريال). Der häufigste Währungswechsel erfolgt zwischen IRR und US$.

1.6   Geschäftszeiten / Zeitzone

Die iranische Arbeitswoche geht von Samstag bis Donnerstag; Freitag ist der wöchentliche Feiertag. Ministerien haben donnerstags geschlossen. Die normalen Geschäftszeiten von Behörden sind zwischen 8.00 und 14.00 Uhr. Banköffnungszeiten sind für gewöhnlich samstags bis mittwochs von 7.30 bis 13.30 Uhr und donnerstags von 7.30 bis 12.30 Uhr. Geschäfte und Märkte sind in der Regel von 8.30 bis 20.30 Uhr geöffnet, außer freitags.

Iran liegt in der Zeitzone GMT + 3,5 Std., sodass eine gute geschäftliche Anbindung sowohl nach Europa als auch nach Asien besteht.

1.7   Iranische Feiertage 2016

Datum	Anlass
20. – 23. März	Nowruz (Neujahr)
31. März – 1. April	Nationalfeiertag, Ende von Nowruz
21. April	Geburtstag von Imam Ali
5. Mai	Eid-e-Mab'ath
22. Mai	Geburtstag von Imam Mahdi
4. Juni	Khordad Aufstand
27. Juni	Martyrium von Imam Ali
6. Juli	Eid-e-Fitr
7. Juli	Eid-e-Fitr
30. Juli	Martyrium von Imam Sadeq
12. September	Eid-e-Qorban
20. September	Eid-e-Ghadir
11. Oktober	Tasua
12. Oktober	Ashura
20. November	Arbaeen
28. November	Martyrium von Imam Hasan und Muhammad
30. November	Martyrium von Imam Reza
17. Dezember	Geburtstag von Muhammad und Imam Sadegh

1.8   Länderinformation im Überblick

Hauptstadt	Teheran
Landessprache	Persisch
Hauptreligion	Shia Islam
Währung	ریال Rial (IRR)
Fläche	1.648.195 km²
Bevölkerung	2014 Schätzung: 80,8 Mio.
Internationale Vorwahl	+98

2.   Ausländische Investitionen im Iran

Nach beinahe 48 Jahren wurde im Jahre 2002 das neue Ausländerinvestitionsrecht, der
Foreign Investment Promotion and Protection Act („FIPPA"), vom Parlament verabschie-
det. Der FIPPA hat damit das *Law for the Attraction and Protection of Foreign Investment*
(„LAPFI") aus dem Jahre 1955 abgelöst. Der FIPPA hat gegenüber dem LAPFI die rechtli-
chen Rahmenbedingungen und operativen Gegebenheiten für ausländische Investoren im
Iran weiter verbessert.

2.1   Arten von ausländischen Investitionen

Der FIPPA unterscheidet gemäß Art. 3 zwischen den folgenden beiden Arten von ausländischen Investitionen:
1. Ausländische Direktinvestitionen – nur im privaten Sektor erlaubt.
2. Ausländische Investitionen im Rahmen eines Joint Ventures, Rückkauf- oder
    Build-Operate-Transfer (BOT) Projektes, bei denen Ertrag und Gewinn aus-
    schließlich aus dem Betrieb des Projektes stammen, in das investiert wird, wobei
    Ertrag und Gewinn nicht von einer Garantie der Regierung, eines Staatsunterneh-
    mens oder von Banken abhängig sein sollen – in allen Sektoren erlaubt.

2.1.1   Ausländische Direktinvestitionen
Ausländische Direktinvestitionen sind eine Art von grenzübergreifender Investition in
eine geschäftliche Unternehmung durch eine natürliche oder juristische Person in einem
anderen Land mit dem Ziel, langfristig Gewinne zu erwirtschaften. Bei dieser Art von
Investition liegen Kontrolle und Leitung des Unternehmens meist vollständig oder zum
Teil in den Händen des ausländischen Investors. Gemäß dem FIPPA können ausländische
Direktinvestitionen wie folgt erfolgen:
1. Durch eine ausländische Investition in eine neue iranische Gesellschaft oder durch
    den Erwerb der Anteile an einer bereits bestehenden Gesellschaft durch den aus-
    ländischen Investor.
2. Durch vertragliche Abreden zwischen den Parteien, entweder mit oder ohne
    Gründung einer Gesellschaft.
    Ausländische Direktinvestitionen im privaten Sektor sind selbstverständlich nur unter
Einhaltung der vom FIPPA vorgeschriebenen Verfahren zulässig. Des Weiteren ergibt sich
aus Art. 3 des FIPPA und den entsprechenden Regulierungen, dass ausländische Investitionen in Wirtschaftsbereichen, in denen der Staat eine Monopolstellung hat, nur erlaubt
werden, wenn der Ertrag und Gewinn ausschließlich aus der wirtschaftlichen Betätigung
des Investitionsprojekts stammt und nicht auf Garantien des Staates, eines Staatsunter-
nehmens oder von Banken beruht. Art. 3 des FIPPA regelt die Kriterien für ausländische
Investitionen im privaten und öffentlichen Sektor der iranischen Wirtschaft.
    Art. 44 der Verfassung der Islamischen Republik Iran besagt Folgendes:

„Die Wirtschaft der Islamischen Republik Iran soll aus drei Sektoren bestehen, namentlich dem staatlichen, dem kooperativen und dem privaten Sektor, und soll auf systematischer und sinnvoller Planung beruhen.

a) Der staatliche Sektor soll alle Groß- und Schlüsselindustrien beinhalten, sowie Außenhandel, Rohstoffe, Banken- und Versicherungswesen, Stromerzeugung, Staudämme, große Bewässerungssysteme, Radio und Fernsehen, Post, Telegraphen- und Telefondienste, Luftfahrt, Schifffahrt, Straßen- und Schienenverkehr, etc.; all diese Bereiche stehen im Eigentum und unter der Verwaltung des Staates.

b) Der kooperative Sektor soll kooperative Gesellschaften und Unternehmen beinhalten, deren Aufgabe die Produktion und der Vertrieb ist, sowohl im städtischen als auch im ländlichen Bereich, unter Einhaltung der islamischen Kriterien.

c) Der private Sektor beinhaltet die Bereiche Landwirtschaft, Tierzucht, Industrie, Handel, sowie Dienstleistungen zur Ergänzung des staatlichen und kooperativen Sektors.

Das Eigentum in allen drei Sektoren ist durch die Gesetze der Islamischen Republik geschützt soweit das Eigentum im Einklang mit den übrigen Vorschriften dieses Kapitels steht, nicht gegen islamisches Recht verstößt, und zum wirtschaftlichen Wachstum und Fortschritt des Landes beiträgt und die Gesellschaft nicht schädigt. Der Umfang aller drei Sektoren sowie die Regelungen und Bedingungen bezüglich ihres Betriebes werden durch Gesetz festgelegt."

Abschnitt „A" der allgemeinen Grundsätze von Art. 44 der Verfassung der Islamischen Republik Iran besagt:

„Investitionen in und die Leitung von den unter Art. 44 fallenden Sektoren ist nicht-staatlichen Unternehmen und öffentlichen Einrichtungen sowie den kooperativen und privaten Sektoren wie folgt erlaubt:

a) Groß- und Schlüsselindustrien (inkl. Downstream Öl- und Gas-Schwerindustrie) und Minen-Schwerindustrie (außer Öl und Gas)

b) Außenhandelsaktivitäten in Einklang mit den Handels- und Fremdwährungsgrundsätzen des Landes

c) Bankwesen durch nicht-staatliche Unternehmen und öffentliche Einrichtungen, Kooperativen in öffentlicher Hand und Joint Stock Companies, sofern die Gesellschafterstruktur den gesetzlichen Vorschriften entspricht

d) Versicherungswesen

e) Stromversorgung, Erzeugung und Einfuhr von Energie für den Binnenverbrauch und Export

f) Sämtliche Post- und Telekommunikationsleistungen, außer dem Telekommunikations-Hauptnetz, Vergabe von Frequenzen und Hauptnetzwerke des Briefverkehrs, Zustellung und Abwicklung von Briefen und einfachen Postdienstleistungen

g) Straßen und Schienen

h) Luftfahrt (Lufttransport) und Schifffahrt (Seetransport)

Der optimale Anteil am staatlichen und nicht-staatlichen Sektor in der von der Präambel von Art. 44 erfassten Aktivitäten wird durch Gesetz geregelt unter Berücksichtigung der Souveränität und Unabhängigkeit des Landes, der sozialen Gerechtigkeit und wirtschaftlicher Entwicklung und Wachstum."

Unter Beachtung der Grundprinzipien des vom Obersten Geistlichen eingeführten Art. 44 kann der private Sektor in die entsprechend festgelegten wirtschaftlichen Bereiche investieren und diese leiten und besitzen. Demzufolge sind ausländische Direktinvestitionen in diesen acht Bereichen erlaubt.

2.1.2 Vertragliche Ausgestaltungen

Gemäß Art. 3 b) des FIPPA sind ausländische Investitionen in allen Bereichen erlaubt, sofern sie im Rahmen eines Joint Ventures, Rückkauf- oder BOT-Projektes erfolgen:

2.1.2.1 Joint Ventures

Der Begriff „Joint Venture" wird häufig im Zusammenhang mit Auslandsinvestitionen gebraucht, da dieser vertragliche Rahmen von Investoren in vielen Rechtssystemen für Investitionen genutzt wird. Aufgrund der Reduzierung von Risiko und Kosten der Investitionen ist das Joint-Venture-Modell seit jeher von Interesse für Investoren. Das Joint Venture unterliegt dabei allerdings den jeweiligen nationalen Gesetze und Regulierungen im Tätigkeitsland.

Unter Berücksichtigung der Gesetze und Regulierungen des Gastlandes, des Projektinhalts und der Leistungsanforderungen kann es empfehlenswert sein, das Joint Venture in Form einer eigenständigen Rechtsform durchzuführen, also ein sog. *„Corporative Joint Venture"* zu gründen. In anderen Fällen ist ein sog. *„Contractual Joint Venture"* vorzugswürdiger, also eine Kooperation ohne Gründung einer eigenständigen Rechtsform. Das Eingehen einer Partnerschaft ist dabei nicht Selbstzweck, sondern soll ausländischen Investoren zur Erreichung der im Businessplan festgesetzten Ziele verhelfen.

In verschiedenen Rechtsordnungen hat diese Investitionsform verschiedene Namen, wie z.B. „Joint Venture", „Partnerschaft", „Konsortium" oder „Gesellschaftervertrag". In manchen Rechtsordnungen können die einzelnen Begriffe in gewissen Aspekten voneinander abweichen, weshalb eine detaillierte Analyse der einzelnen Termini den Rahmen dieser Darstellung sprengen würde. In der Rechtsliteratur Irans ist die Rechtsform der Partnerschaft im Zivilgesetzbuch (Art. 501 – 606) und im Handelsgesetzbuch (Abschnitt „Gesellschaften") genannt sowie in der *Interest-Free Banking Regulation* (Art. 18) impliziert. Art. 3 des FIPPA nennt als Möglichkeit der Investitionen ebenfalls die zivile Partnerschaft, welche in Form eines Joint Ventures errichtet werden kann.

Bei einem korporativen Joint Venture gründen die Partner eine eigenständige Gesellschaft, die sog. *Joint Venture Company* („JVC"), in der jeder Partner einen bestimmten Anteil hält. In diesem Falle werden die Partner als Gesellschafter bezeichnet und die Gesellschaft ist für die Umsetzung des dem Joint Venture zugrunde liegenden Projekts verantwortlich. Im Gegensatz hierzu wird das Projekt bei einem rein vertraglichen Joint Venture, bei dem keine eigenständige Gesellschaft gegründet wird, unmittelbar durch die Partner auf der Grundlage ihres Vertrages umgesetzt.

2.1.2.2   Irans Erdölverträge

2.1.2.2.1 Rückkaufverträge

Die zweite in Art. 3 des FIPPA genannte Investitionsmethode sind sog. Rückkaufverträge. Diese Art der vertraglichen Investitionstechnik hat in den letzten Jahren eine wichtige Rolle in der Wirtschaft des Iran gespielt und ist vorwiegend bekannt für ihre Verwendung bei der Erschließung von neu entdeckten Öl- und Gasfeldern, aber auch in anderen Industrien.

Ein Rückkaufvertrag ist eine Art Gegengeschäft, das auch als „Hybridvertrag" eingestuft wird, und wird oftmals als Vertrag zwischen einem Käufer und Verkäufer definiert, bei dem der Verkäufer zustimmt, die Ware beim Eintreten eines bestimmten Ereignisses innerhalb einer bestimmten Frist vom Käufer zurückzukaufen, wobei der Rückkaufpreis üblicherweise auch im Vertrag festgelegt wird. Unter iranischem Recht hat der Rückkaufvertrag allerdings eine weitere Bedeutung erlangt: Gemäß Art. 2 der Ausführungsverordnung des Ministerrates ist ein Rückkaufvertrag eine Vereinbarung, bei der der Lieferant die zur Errichtung, Expansion, Rekonstruktion, Verbesserung oder fortlaufender Produktion erforderlichen Güter und Dienstleistungen zeitweise oder dauerhaft dem Produzenten zur Verfügung stellt.

Der Preis für die zur Verfügung gestellten Güter und Dienstleistungen wird, nach Abzug von eventuellen Vorauszahlungen oder sonstiger im Vertrag vereinbarter Beträge, an den Lieferanten in der Form von Gütern oder Dienstleistungen des Produzenten und/oder anderer im Iran produzierter Güter oder Dienstleistungen gezahlt. Aufgrund bestimmter Vorschriften in der iranischen Verfassung und im *Petroleum Act* werden Rückkaufverträge vorwiegend für die Erschließung von Öl- und Gasfeldern im Iran abgeschlossen.

Öl- und Gas-Rückkaufverträge, bei denen die Exploration Teil der angebotenen Leistungen ist, werden als *Risk Service Contract* mit zusätzlichem Zahlungsplan eingestuft. Bei diesem Vertragstyp schließt der Anbieter einen Vertrag mit der Regierung des Gastlandes und nutzt monetäre und nicht-monetäre Bestandteile des zur Verfügung gestellten Kapitals um Öl- und Gasfelder zu erschließen. Der Vertrag legt zudem verschiedene Kosten fest, wie z.B. die Vergütung des Anbieters, welche durch den Verkauf des produzierten Öls und Gases und durch ein *Long Term Crude Oil Sales Agreement* als Annex zum Rückkaufvertrag abgesichert ist.

2.1.2.2.2 Iran Petroleum Contract („IPC")

Heutzutage ist eine der wichtigsten Debatten in wissenschaftlichen und technischen Kreisen die Optimierung von Vertragsmechanismen für Upstream Öl- und Gasprojekte im Iran. Auf einem Teheraner Seminar im Februar 2014 wurden einige Regelungen der vom *Oil Contracts Revision Committee* entwickelten neuen Ölverträge unter dem Titel „*Iran Petroleum Contract (IPC)*" präsentiert. Dieser Vertragstyp wurde entwickelt, um Fehler und Lücken in verschiedenen Generationen von Rückkaufverträgen zu beheben und zu schließen, und stellt somit den Beginn einer Revolutionierung iranischer Ölverträge dar. Auch das iranische Parlament hat hierzu wesentlich beigetragen, indem es verschiedene Gesetze verabschiedet hat, insbesondere den *Act on the Duties and Powers of the Ministry of Petroleum* aus dem Jahre 2012.

Der IPC ist kein neuer Vertragstyp neben Konzessionsverträgen, Produktionsteilungsverträgen, Risikoverträgen oder Joint Ventures. Vielmehr ist er ein Mischvertrag, der
sowohl Merkmale von Joint Venture Verträgen (bezüglich der Durchführung des Ölpro-
jektes) als auch von Produktionsteilungsverträgen (bezüglich der Kostendeckungsmecha-
nismen) enthält.

In der Explorationsphase wird beim IPC vom Auftragnehmer und von der *National
Iranian Oil Company* eine Projektgesellschaft, die sog. *Oil Exploration Operations Company,* gegründet, durch die der Auftragnehmer die Exploration vornimmt und hierfür sein
eigenes Kapital nutzt und das Risiko trägt. Die *National Iranian Oil Company* fungiert
lediglich als technischer Partner und begleitet den Auftragnehmer, ohne jedoch Kosten
oder Risiken der Exploration mitzutragen. Falls die Exploration nicht zu einem kommerziell verwertbaren Vorkommen führt, werden die Kosten des Auftragnehmers nicht
erstattet. Wird jedoch ein kommerziell verwertbares Vorkommen entdeckt, so werden die
Explorationskosten des Auftragnehmers in die Entwicklungsphase übertragen und während der Amortisationsphase erstattet.

Nach der Entdeckung eines kommerziell verwertbaren Vorkommens und dessen
Bewertung tritt das Projekt in die nächste Phase ein. Für diese Erschließungsphase wird in
der Regel wiederum eine Projektfirma, die *Development Operation Company,* gegründet.

Wie in der vorangegangenen Phase trägt der Auftragnehmer sämtliche Kosten und
Risiken der Erschließungsphase und leitet die Operation. Die *National Iranian Oil Company* fungiert wiederum lediglich als technischer Partner und begleitet den Auftragnehmer, ohne jedoch Kosten oder Risiken der Erschließung mitzutragen. Sämtliche direkten
und indirekten Kosten der Erschließung, die dem Auftragnehmer und der *National Iranian Oil Company* entstehen, werden nach einem bestimmten Prozentsatz von der Projektgesellschaft getragen.

Als nächster Schritt folgt die Produktionsphase, die umfangreicher als die Explora-
tions- und Erschließungsphase ist. Im Wesentlichen sind die folgenden drei Ausgestaltun-
gen denkbar: (i) Die Produktion wird von der *National Iranian Oil Company* oder einem
ihrer verbundenen Unternehmen durchgeführt und der Auftragnehmer stellt finanzielle
und technische Unterstützung bereit. (ii) Die Erschließungsgesellschaft führt ebenfalls die
Produktion durch. (iii) Zur Durchführung und Leitung der Produktion wird eine weitere Projektgesellschaft, die *Production Operations Company,* gegründet und die Erschließungsgesellschaft leistet finanzielle und technische Unterstützung.

Gemäß den Ergebnissen des zuvor erwähnten Seminars soll die Produktionsgesellschaft
IOR/EOR[1] durchführen und der Erschließungsgesellschaft hierüber Bericht erstatten.

Der Ölvertrag endet am Ende des vereinbarten Zahlungszeitraums, welcher in der
Regel zwischen 15 und 20 Jahren beträgt.

---

[1] IOR (*Improved Oil Recovery*) und EOR (*Enhanced Oil Recovery*) meint die Implementierung
verschiedener Techniken um den Ertrag eines Ölfeldes zu steigern.

Das Seminar hat keine speziellen Gesellschaftsformen für die Exploration oder Erschließung vorgesehen; die Produktionsgesellschaft hingegen soll als sog. *Non-Profit Joint Operating Company* gegründet werden.

2.1.2.3 Build-Operate-Transfer (BOT) Verträge

Laut FIPPA ist eine weitere Vertragsform für Investitionen der *Build-Operate-Transfer (BOT) Vertrag.* Diese Form der Investitionen wird häufig für Infrastrukturprojekte genutzt, wie z.B. Kraftwerke, Telekommunikation, Flughäfen und Autobahnen, kann jedoch auch für Erholungsprojekte, wie z.B. Seilbahnen, genutzt werden. Bei BOT-Verträgen vergibt eine Regierungsstelle die Konzession für den Bau und Betrieb eines bestimmten Projektes an einen Auftragnehmer des Privatsektors, welcher dann für Finanzierung, Entwicklung, Bau, Prüfung und Betrieb des Projektes verantwortlich ist. Während der Betriebsphase nutzt der Auftragnehmer die Erträge des Projekts, um seine Kosten zu decken und Gewinne zu erwirtschaften. Am Ende der Betriebsphase wird das Eigentum an der Anlage schenkungsweise auf die Regierungsstelle übertragen.

Der BOT-Vertrag ist eine Art der öffentlich-privaten Partnerschaft, bei der eine Regierungsstelle oder Stelle des öffentlichen Sektors beschließt, ein Infrastrukturprojekt in Partnerschaft mit dem privaten Sektor zu realisieren. Die Erfahrung hat gezeigt, dass solche Partnerschaften eine deutlich schnellere und kosteneffizientere Durchführung von Infrastrukturprojekten ermöglichen. Die Auswahl eines geeigneten Partners aus dem Privatsektor (in der Regel ein Konsortium) erfolgt durch Ausschreibung und anschließenden Vertragsschluss zwischen öffentlichem Auftraggeber und Auftragnehmer.

2.1.2.4 Investitionen in Irans Bauprojekte

Irans Immobilienpreise übersteigen die von vergleichbar großen Nationen und in den vergangenen Jahren hat es einen Immobilienboom im Iran gegeben. Aufgrund des jungen demographischen Trends des Landes setzen Investoren zunehmend auf Investitionen in Immobilien, welche sich über lange Zeit als sichere Festanlage erwiesen haben. Gleichzeitig haben Bauunternehmer und Berater landesweit Möglichkeiten entdeckt, um sowohl Touristen als auch Einheimische, die moderne und komfortable Immobilien suchen, zu bedienen. Investoren sind ebenfalls gern bereit, in diese Projekte zu investieren, was den zukünftigen Bedarf decken und gute Renditen garantieren wird.

Auch die nationale Infrastruktur erfährt Wachstum. Die iranische Regierung und der öffentliche Sektor streben nach dem Bau bzw. der Renovierung von Infrastruktur im ganzen Land, was gute Möglichkeiten für Investoren bietet, in Form von öffentlich-privaten Partnerschaften (BOT, BOOT, Joint Venture, etc.) in diese Projekte zu investieren, da diese lukrative Renditen für Investoren bieten. In den vergangenen Jahren ist die Bauindustrie dank nationaler und internationaler Investitionen aufgeblüht und zählt mittlerweile zu einer der größten im Mittleren Osten.

2.1.2.4.1 Bauverträge

Welche Art von Verträgen in Irans Bauindustrie genutzt werden, hängt von der Position des Auftraggebers ab. Handelt es sich um eine Privatperson oder eine juristische Person des Privatsektors, sind jegliche Vertragsgestaltungen möglich, wie z.B. *Design-Bid-Build, Design and Build, EPC,* Verträge zur schlüsselfertigen Übergabe, etc. Handelt es sich beim Auftraggeber allerdings um eine Regierungsstelle oder Stelle des öffentlichen Sektors, besteht begrenzter Verhandlungsspielraum bei der Vertragsgestaltung, da diese an bestimmte, von der Regierung vorgegebene Vertragsarten bzw. -muster gebunden sind.

2.1.2.4.2 Auswahl des Auftragnehmers

Auftraggeber im Privatsektor Irans können direkt mit Auftragnehmern verhandeln, um so einen geeigneten Auftragnehmer auszuwählen, der über technisches Wissen und angemessene Ressourcen verfügt, um das Projekt zu verwirklichen. Regierungsstellen hingegen müssen ein förmliches Bieterverfahren durchführen, um einen Auftragnehmer zur Durchführung öffentlicher Projekte auszuwählen. Das Vergabegesetz Irans wurde in 2005 verabschiedet und besagt in Art. 1:

> *„Alle drei Gewalten der Islamischen Republik Iran sollen bei Ausschreibungen diesem Gesetz folgen; hiervon umfasst sind: Ministerien, öffentliche Einrichtungen und Institutionen, Gesellschaften und gewinnerzielende Institute der Regierung, öffentliche Finanzinstitute und Banken, öffentliche Versicherungsgesellschaften …"*

Das Vergabeverfahren staatlicher und öffentlicher Organisationen im Iran ist nicht frei zugänglich, sondern unterliegt einem Vorauswahlverfahren, nach der Bieter in die engere Auswahl kommen und eingeladen werden, für das jeweilige Projekt zu bieten. Art. 12 des Vergabegesetztes besagt insoweit:

> *„Im Vorauswahlverfahren soll Folgendes berücksichtigt werden: (i) Garantie der Qualität von Gütern und Dienstleistungen, (ii) Erfahrung und Fachwissen auf dem jeweiligen Gebiet, (iii) Bisherige Reputation, (iv) Arbeitserlaubnisse oder Qualitätszertifikate, sofern erforderlich, (v) finanzielle Leistungsfähigkeit des Bieters zur Durchführung, sofern erforderlich."*

2.1.2.4.3 Preisfindungsmethoden

Vertragsparteien im Privatsektor sind bei der Wahl der Preisfindungsmethode frei. Je nach Bedingungen des Projekts kann beispielsweise zwischen den folgenden Methoden gewählt werden: Pauschalpreis, *Cost Plus*, Preisanpassung, Stundenbasis, Schätzung etc. Im staatlichen und öffentlichen Sektor hingegen wird der Preis vom Auftraggeber anhand des sog. Stückpreises ermittelt. Bei dieser Vertragsart basiert der Preis auf der geschätzten Anzahl von Einheiten, die für das Projekt benötigt werden, und deren jeweiliger Stückpreis. Der Gesamtpreis ergibt sich somit aus der Gesamtzahl der für das Projekt benötigten Einheiten.

2.1.2.4.4 Streitbeilegung

Wie in der Baubranche vieler anderer Länder nehmen auch im Iran die meisten Bauverträge Bezug auf Alternative Streitbeilegungsmethoden (*Alternative Dispute Resolution, "ADR"*). Die Streitbeilegung beinhaltet in der Regel Güteverhandlung und Mediation, aber den Vertragsparteien steht es auch frei, den Streit an die Schiedsgerichtsbarkeit oder ordentliche Gerichtsbarkeit zu verweisen, sofern er nicht anderweitig beigelegt werden kann. Sofern der Auftraggeber jedoch aus dem staatlichen oder öffentlichen Sektor stammt, sind die Regeln zur Streitbeilegung bereits im Bauvertrag festgeschrieben und können nicht frei verhandelt werden. Solche Verträge sehen zwar in ihren Standardklauseln ADR-Methoden vor, jedoch variiert deren Durchführung von Vertrag zu Vertrag, weshalb es empfehlenswert ist, vor dem Abschluss von Bauverträgen professionellen Rat einzuholen.

2.1.3 Ausländisches Portfolio Investment

2.1.3.1 Die Iranische Börse

Die *Tehran Stock Exchange ("TSE")* wurde 1968 gegründet und ist der Hauptaktienmarkt Irans. 2005 wurde das neue Iranische Kapitalmarktgesetz vom Parlament verabschiedet und, wie von diesem Gesetz vorgesehen, wurde die TSE 2006 in eine Aktiengesellschaft mit über 6.000 Aktionären umgewandelt. Die TSE genießt seit ihrer Gründung einen guten Ruf für die Aufrechterhaltung eines geordneten Marktes und eines kosteneffizienten Handelsplatzes. Das 1994 eingeführte vollständig computergestützte System hat zum Handelsvolumen und zur Effizienz der Börse beigetragen. 2007 hat die TSE auf ein neues, leistungsstärkeres System (mit Unterstützung von Atos Euronext) umgestellt, um dem hohen Handelsvolumen zu begegnen. 2009 wurde der TSE die ISO9001-Zertifizierung verliehen und eine ISO27001-Zertifzierung für das IT-Sicherheits-Management-System ist derzeit geplant.

Die TSE hat in den vergangenen Jahren viele Reformen durchgeführt, um es in Einklang mit internationaler Praxis zu bringen und die Interessen von Investoren besser widerzuspiegeln. Die TSE plant auch weiterhin, Fortschritte in Richtung Liberalisierung und Internationalisierung zu unternehmen. Die TSE, mit ihrem voll automatisierten Handelssystem und Buchungsmechanismen, ist eine der aktivsten Börsen im Mittleren Osten. Ende März 2015 betrug die Marktkapitalisierung aller 314 an der TSE gelisteten Gesellschaften über 172 Mrd. US$. Das Verhältnis der Gesamtmarktkapitalisierung zum BIP betrug in 2015 etwa 60%. In diesem Jahr betrug das Gesamthandelsvolumen 180 Mrd. US$, was einer Marktumschlagsrate von 132,5% entspricht. Das Kurs-Gewinn-Verhältnis (*Price/Earnings (P/E) Ratio*) an der TSE betrug 5,4.

Um die Wettbewerbsfähigkeit der TSE zu verbessern und schneller Fortschritt in Richtung Liberalisierung und Internationalisierung zu machen, haben die Behörden auch die Einführung neuer Finanzprodukte und neuer Finanzinstitute gefördert, sowie zahlreiche Reformmaßnahmen durchgeführt, wie z.B. die Listung von *Single Stock Futures ("SSF")*, die Lockerung von Beschränkungen für ausländische Investitionen, die Vereinheitlichung der Registrierungsprozesse für Ausländer, sowie die Anpassung zahlreicher Handelssysteme und -mechanismen zwecks Anpassung an internationale Standards.

2.1.3.2   Ausländische Investitionen an der Teheraner Börse

Wie bei vielen aufstrebenden Börsen hat auch die TSE gewisse Beschränkungen für ausländische Investitionen gesetzt. Mit dem Wachstum der Iranischen Börse und der Entwicklung der Wirtschaft haben die Börsenaufsichtsbehörden diese Beschränkungen graduell abgebaut. Seit April 2010 gilt für Investitionen ausländischer Investoren nicht mehr das Zulassungs- sondern das Repatriierungssystem. Am 18. April 2010 hat der Ministerrat auf Empfehlung des *Ministry of Economic Affairs and Finance* und auf Grundlage von Art. 4 Abs. 3 des in 2005 verabschiedeten *Securities Market Law* die *Regulations Governing the Foreign Investment in the Exchanges and OTC Markets* verabschiedet. Dies hat zu einer Vereinfachung des Anmeldeverfahrens zur TSE für ausländische Investitionen geführt.

Gem. Art. 7 dieser *Regulations* gelten die folgenden Beschränkungen für den Aktienbesitz durch nicht-strategische ausländische Investoren an sämtlichen Börsen und *over-the-counter („OTC")* Handelsplätzen: Der Anteil der von allen ausländischen Investoren gehaltenen Aktien darf 20% der Aktien aller an der Börse oder dem OTC-Handelsplatz gelisteten Gesellschaften bzw. 20% einer einzelnen gelisteten Gesellschaft nicht übersteigen. Der Anteil je ausländischem Investor an einer gelisteten Gesellschaft darf 10% der Aktien der jeweiligen Gesellschaft nicht übersteigen.

Gemäß Art. 4 müssen Ausländer/ausländische Unternehmen die nötigen Informationen und Dokumente bei der *Securities Exchange Organization* in der von dieser vorgeschriebenen Form einreichen, um die Lizenz zu erhalten, an der jeweiligen Börse bzw. dem OTC-Handelsplatz zu handeln.

2.1.3.3   Kaufen und Verkaufen von Aktien

Die folgenden Schritte sind zu befolgen, um Aktien an der TSE zu handeln:
1. **Auswahl eines Brokers.** Bei der Auswahl eines Brokers (Privatperson oder Gesellschaft) sollte darauf geachtet werden, dass dieser ein Mitglied mit guter Reputation an der TSE ist. Eine vollständige Liste der TSE-Mitgliedsbroker findet sich in zahlreichen Publikationen sowie beim *TSE Membership Department*. Es ist wichtig, seinem Broker zu vertrauen und mit den erbrachten Dienstleistungen zufrieden zu sein. Brokerleistungen beinhalten Marktreports, Beratung bezüglich Auswahl von Aktien und Timing von Käufen und Verkäufen, Ausführung der Transaktion, pünktliche Zustellung wichtiger Dokumente – wie z.B. Bestätigungsschreiben – und andere handelsbezogene Aktivitäten, die der Kunde benötigt.
2. **Eröffnung eines Aktiendepots.** Sobald der Investor sich für einen Broker entschieden hat, ist ein Aktiendepot zu eröffnen. Dieses Depot erlaubt es dem Kunden, jederzeit Transaktionen (Kaufen und Verkaufen von Aktien) durchzuführen – ähnlich einem Bankkonto mit der Möglichkeit, Geld einzuzahlen, zu übertragen und abzuheben. Die Eröffnung eines Aktiendepots ist relativ einfach und dauert nicht länger als die Eröffnung eines Bankkontos. Eine Musterunterschriftenkarte muss ausgefüllt werden mit folgendem Inhalt: Name, Adresse (privat und geschäftlich), Telefonnummer(n), und insbesondere die Unterschrift des Kunden. Referenzen von Banken oder Geschäftspartnern müssen regelmäßig eingereicht werden. Sobald das Depot eröffnet ist, kann

der Kunde sofort mit dem Kaufen und Verkaufen durch entsprechende Anweisungen an den Broker beginnen. Solche Anweisungen variieren je nach dem Ziel des Investors – kurz- oder langfristig, minimales oder maximales Handelsvolumen (Handelslimit), etc. Alle Transaktionen werden vertraulich behandelt.

3. **Anweisung an den Broker.** Nach der Depoteröffnung wird dem Investor ein Makler zugeteilt. Ein Makler ist ein lizenzierter Händler, der berechtigt ist, Aktien an der TSE zu kaufen und zu verkaufen. Der zugeteilte Makler ist die für alle Transaktionen des Investors zuständige Kontaktperson. Er oder sie nimmt die Order entgegen, in der Regel per Telefon (es sei denn anderweitige Vereinbarungen wurden getroffen), und wird diese über das mit der Börse verbundene System ausführen. Um eine Kauf- oder Verkaufsorder aufzugeben, muss man seinen Makler also anrufen und die Details der Order durchgeben. Der Makler benötigt die folgenden Informationen: Kauf- oder Verkaufsorder, welche Aktie soll gekauft bzw. verkauft werden, Anzahl der Anteile, und vorzugsweise einen Kauf- bzw. Verkaufspreis.

4. **Abschluss der Transaktion.** Kauf- und Verkaufstransaktionen werden durch Bucheintrag abgeschlossen, d.h. das Eigentum an Anteilen und Geld wird elektronisch in das Aktiendepot transferiert, ohne dass Aktienzertifikate oder Geld physisch übergeben werden (die Aktienzertifikate werden bei der *Central Securities Depository of Iran Inc.* sicher verwahrt). Das Depot wird belastet, wenn Aktien gekauft werden, und erhält eine Gutschrift, wenn Aktien verkauft werden. Das Bucheintragssystem hat klare Vorteile gegenüber dem papierbasierten System. Es hat den Papieraufwand erheblich reduziert, den Handel vereinfacht und den Verlust oder die Fälschung von Zertifikaten eliminiert.

Derzeit werden Transaktionen an der TSE mit T+3 abgeschlossen, d.h. vier Tage nach dem Transaktionsdatum. Zahlungen (Geld bzw. Aktien) müssen daher am Handelstag dem Broker bereitgestellt werden, wobei stets die Zahlungsfrist beachtet werden sollte.

2.1.3.4   Globale Beziehungen

Die TSE war zwischen 1992 und 2010 Vollmitglied der WFE, und ist Gründungsmitglied der *Federation of Euro-Asian Stock Exchanges („FEAS")*, sowie Teilnehmer des *International Corporate Governance Network („ICGN")*. Die TSE ist zudem ein aktiver Teilnehmer des *OIC Member's Stock Exchange Forum*.

2.1.4   Antragsdokumente Foreign Investment License

Die folgenden Dokumente sind erforderlich zur Beantragung einer *Foreign Investment License*:

1. Antragsformular
2. Gründungslizenz / Vorvertrag / Vorvertrag der relevanten iranischen Organisation
3. Offizielles Schreiben des ausländischen Investors an die *Organization for Investment, Economic and Technical Assistance of Iran („OIETAI")*
4. Hintergrundinformationen des ausländischen Investors, einschließlich einer kurzen Unternehmenshistorie, Jahr der Gründung, Tätigkeitsfeld, oder (sofern der ausländische Investor eine natürliche Person ist) eine Kopie des Reisepasses und ein Lebenslauf

5. Eine Liste der Maschinen, Zubehör- und Ersatzteile, die als Teil des Kapitals des ausländischen Investors ins Land importiert werden sollen

6. Falls ein Teil der Investition des ausländischen Investors in Form von Knowhow erfolgt, ein Vertragsentwurf, der die Bedingungen des Technologietransfers beschreibt

7. Weitere nützliche Informationen

Das Hauptziel dieses Prozesses ist es, einen geeigneten und „akzeptablen" lokalen Partner zu finden. Sofern das beabsichtigte ausländische Investitionsprojekt mit einem vom *Ministry of Economic Affairs and Finance* verabschiedeten Plan vereinbar ist, wird dieses dem potenziellen ausländischen Investor lokale Partner vorstellen, die bereits einen Vorabgenehmigung für ein solches Projekt innehaben.

Eine solche ministerielle Vorabgenehmigung muss dann erneut gemeinsam durch den ausländischen und potenziellen lokalen Partner beantragt werden. Die Details des Projekts müssen dem *Ministry of Economic Affairs and Finance* in Form eines Standardfragebogens zusammen mit einer Machbarkeitsstudie vorgelegt werden. Sobald die Vorabgenehmigung erteilt wurde, sollten die Parteien mit den Vorbereitungsmaßnahmen für das Projekt beginnen, z.B. Import der Maschinen und Zubehörteile und Schaffung der nötigen Infrastruktur.

Der ausländische Investor muss zudem einen Teilnahmeantrag beim OIETAI stellen, um an der Durchführung des genehmigten Projektes teilnehmen zu dürfen.

Sodann wird der Antrag vom *Supervisory Board for Attraction and Protection of Foreign Investment* geprüft. Nach einer vorgelagerten Koordination mit anderen Ministerien soll das *Foreign Department of the Ministry of Economic Affairs and Finance* einen zusammenfassenden Bericht erstellen und dem *Supervisory Board* zur Entscheidungsfindung vorlegen. Sofern das Projekt als grundsätzlich im Interesse des Landes erachtet wird, gibt das *Supervisory Board* seine Entscheidung durch das *Ministry of Economic Affairs and Finance* bekannt und stellt ein *Investment Decree* aus. Dieses Dekret ist die formelle Genehmigung für den Investor, mit der Operation und dem Import des benötigten Kapitals zu beginnen, welche dann unter dem Schutz des Gesetzes stehen.

3.   Irans Freihandels- und Sonderwirtschaftszonen

Die Schaffung von Freihandels- und Sonderwirtschaftszonen dient der Förderung von Wohlstand, wirtschaftlicher Entwicklung und Wachstum, Investitionsförderung, aktiver Präsenz in lokalen und internationalen Märkten, Produktion von industriellen Gütern und Dienstleistungen und der Steigerung von nationalem Einkommen und Beschäftigung. Diese Zonen haben Handel und industrielle Betätigung erleichtert und Investitionen gefördert, u.a. durch erhebliche Reduzierung von Formalitäten in der Zollabwicklung, im Bank-, Finanz- und Versicherungswesen, im Arbeitsrecht, dem Zugang von Ausländern etc.

Insbesondere die Freihandelszonen, im Vergleich zu den Sonderwirtschaftszonen, haben erhebliche Vorteile, von denen der wichtigste das Bestehen einer unabhängigen Organisation – dem *High Council of Free Trade Industrial Zones* – ist, dem die Verwaltung der Zonen obliegt.

Da das Hauptziel der Zonen die Investitionsförderung ist, haben alle bestehenden Systeme, formell und informell, das Ziel, industrielle Aktivitäten zu bedienen und zu fördern.

Die Islamische Republik des Iran hat den ersten 5-Jahres-Plan zur Umstrukturierung und Erholung der Wirtschaft 1989 eingeführt, nach dem Ende des achtjährigen Irakkrieges. Das Hauptziel dieses Plans war die Transformation der während des Krieges bestehenden Planwirtschaft hin zu einer freien, auf Marktkräften basierenden Wirtschaft, sowie die Schaffung und Erhaltung von Beziehungen zur Weltwirtschaft.

Aufgrund der bestehenden Beschränkungen zur Anwendung der Marktwirtschaft und aus Sorge von Nebenwirkungen solch einer scharfen Transformation auf das soziale Wohlergehen der Gesellschaft wurde beschlossen, bestimmte Regionen als Freihandels- und Sonderwirtschaftszonen auszuweisen, in denen das Prinzip der freien Marktwirtschaft voll angewendet wird. Auf diese Weise konnten genügend Anreize geschaffen werden, um ausländische Investitionen anzuziehen.

Gemäß der rechtlichen Definition sind Freihandelszonen und Sonderwirtschaftszonen diejenigen Gebiete des iranischen Territoriums, die den Sondergesetzen und -statuten unterliegen und von den Gesetzen des übrigen Landes ausgenommen sind. Diese Zonen sind der Hoheit der Zollbehörden entzogen und genießen die freie Ein- und Ausfuhr von Waren und Handelsgütern. Einzigartige geografische Gegebenheiten, ausreichend entwickelte Infrastruktur und die Anreize für ausländische Investitionen bieten umfangreiche Möglichkeiten sowohl für lokale als auch für ausländische Investitionen in diesen Zonen.

Das iranische Parlament hat im September 1993 den *Free Zones Act* verabschiedet, durch den Kish Island, Qeshm Island und der Hafen von Chabahar zu Freihandelszonen Irans erklärt wurden. Der Ministerrat erließ später die Statuten für die Freihandelszonen. Diese Statuten enthalten sämtliche Regeln für Import, Export, Investitionen, Versicherungen, Bankwesen und Arbeitsrecht in diesen Zonen.

3.1   Industrie- und Freihandelszonen

3.1.1   Förderung von Investitionen in Industrie- und Freihandelszonen

Investitionen in den Industrie- und Freihandelszonen erhalten die folgenden Anreize und Vorteile:

1. Steuerbefreiung für 20 Jahre ab Beginn sämtlicher wirtschaftlicher Aktivitäten
2. Ausländische Investitionen bis zu 100%
3. Freie Ein- und Ausfuhr von Kapital und Gewinnen
4. Schutz und Garantien für ausländische Investitionen
5. Befreiung von Einreisevisa und erleichterte Ausstellung von Aufenthaltsgenehmigungen
6. Vereinfachte Regeln bezüglich Arbeitsrecht und Sozialversicherung
7. Transfer von Halbfertigwaren ins Inland ohne Importzölle
8. Befreiung von Einfuhrzöllen für Importe außerhalb der Zone
9. Beschäftigung von Fachkräften, unabhängig von Qualifikation und Berufsgruppe
10. Nutzung von Rohstoffen, Öl und Gas als Rohstoff und Treibstoff für alle industriellen Aktivitäten

3.1.2   Liste der Industrie- und Freihandelszonen Irans

1. Qeshm Industrie- und Freihandelszone
2. Chabahar Industrie- und Freihandelszone
3. Aras Industrie- und Freihandelszone
4. Anzali Industrie- und Freihandelszone
5. Arvand Industrie- und Freihandelszone
6. Kish Industrie- und Freihandelszone
7. Maku Industrie- und Freihandelszone

3.1.3   Regulierungen für Investitionen in Industrie- und Freihandelszonen

1. *Law on the Administration of Free Trade Industrial Zones*
2. *Law on the Establishment of Free Trade Industrial Zones in Abadan-Khorramshahr, Jolfa and Bandar Anzali*
3. *Executive Bylaw on Issuance of Visa to Foreign Nationals in the Free Trade Industrial Zones*
4. *Regulations on Entry and Residence of Foreign Nationals*
5. *Bylaw on Monetary and Banking Operation in the Free Trade Industrial Zones*
6. *Executive Guideline for the Monetary and Banking Operations in the Free Trade Industrial Zones*
7. *Regulations on the Establishment and Operation of Insurance Institutes in the Free Trade Industrial Zones*
8. *Criteria on Registration of Companies and Property Rights*
9. *Regulations on Exports, Imports and Customs in the Free Trade Industrial Zones*

10. *Regulations on the Use of Land and other National Resources in the Free Trade Industrial Zones*

11. *Permanent Permissibility of Import of Goods Produced in the Free Zones in to the Mainland (added to Article 8 of the Bylaw to the Export–Import General Regulations)*

12. *Bylaw on Special Facilities for Import of Goods Produced in Free Trade Industrial Zones into the Mainland*

13. *Bylaw on the Manner of Ingress of Raw Materials and Parts from the Free Zones (into the Mainland)*

14. *Bylaw on the Peculiarly Manufactured or Rebuilt Goods, Permissible into the Mainland*

15. *Regulations on Employment of Work Force, Insurance and Social Security*

16. *Comparison Table indicating Legal Status on Economic Activities in Iran's Free Trade Industrial Zones and Special Economic Zones*

17. *Regularities of Automobile Imports into Free Zones*

3.2   Sonderwirtschaftszonen

3.2.1   Anreize und Vorteile für Investitionen in Sonderwirtschaftszonen

Investitionen in den Sonderwirtschaftszonen erhalten die folgenden Anreize und Vorteile:

1. Der Import von Gütern aus diesen Zonen ins Kernland unterliegt den gewöhnlichen Zollbeschränkungen, während der Export von Gütern aus diesen Zonen ins Ausland keinen Zollformalitäten unterliegt.

2. Der Import von Gütern aus dem Ausland oder aus anderen Industrie- oder Freihandelszonen unterliegt minimalen Zollformalitäten und der interne Transit der importierten Güter unterliegt den normalen Regeln.

3. Logeinträge von Handelsware, die dem Gesetz und den Regulierungen der Sonderzonen unterfallen, unterliegen keinen Zollformalitäten.

4. Güter, die aus dem Ausland oder aus Industriezonen oder anderen Handelszonen importiert wurden, können ohne Formalitäten ins Ausland exportiert werden.

5. Die Leitung der Region kann Teile der Region unter qualifizierten natürlichen und juristischen Personen nach Klassifizierung und Bewertung aufteilen.

6. Die Eigentümer von Gütern, die in die Region importiert wurden, können alle oder Teile ihrer Waren zeitweise ins Land einführen nachdem die Zollabwicklung erfolgt ist.

7. Sofern die Verarbeitung importierter Güter die Zollklassifizierung der Güter verändert, wird der kommerzielle Mehrwert der Güter mit dem Mehrwert von Rohmaterialien und Ersatzteilen des Landes gleichgesetzt.

8. Importeure von Gütern können alle oder Teile ihrer Produkte gegen einen von der Bezirksverwaltung ausgestellten Warenlagerbeleg auf andere übertragen, wodurch der Besitzer des Beleges Eigentümer der Güter wird.

9. Die Bezirksverwaltung ist berechtigt, im Einvernehmen mit den Zollbehörden Herkunftsnachweise für Güter von Antragstellern aus der Region auszustellen.

10. Sämtliche in die Region eingeführte Güter, die für die Produktion oder Leistungserbringung benötigt werden, sind von den gewöhnlichen Import-Export-Bestimmungen befreit. Der Export von Gütern in den Rest des Landes unterliegt den gewöhnlichen Import-Export-Bestimmungen.

11. Gemäß Klausel 25 Absatz d) des *Law of the Second Economic, Social and Cultural Development Plan of the Islamic Republic of Iran* gelten weder Beschränkungen in Bezug auf das Verhältnis der in der Zone produzierten und der aus anderen Ländern importierten Güter, noch in Bezug auf den geschaffenen Mehrwert oder den Anteil von inländischen Teilen oder Materialien am Gesamtpreis. Zudem ist es nicht notwendig, einen *Letter of Credit* zu beantragen.

12. In den Sonderwirtschaftszonen produzierte Güter, Rohmaterialien und ins Land importierte Einzelteile unterliegen nicht der Preisbindung für ungenutzte Ressourcen und zugeordnete Währung.

3.2.2   Liste der Sonderwirtschaftszonen Irans

1. Salafchegan Sonderwirtschaftszone
2. Shiraz Sonderwirtschaftszone
3. Assaluye Sonderwirtschaftszone
4. Arge Jadid Sonderwirtschaftszone
5. Payam Airport Sonderwirtschaftszone
6. Persian Gulf Sonderwirtschaftszone
7. Lorestan Sonderwirtschaftszone
8. Amirabad Port Sonderwirtschaftszone
9. Bushehr Port Sonderwirtschaftszone
10. Shahid Rajaee Port Sonderwirtschaftszone
11. Sarakhs Sonderwirtschaftszone
12. Sirjan Sonderwirtschaftszone
13. Yazd Sonderwirtschaftszone
14. Bushehr Sonderwirtschaftszone

3.2.3   Regulierungen für Investitionen in Sonderwirtschaftszonen

− *The Law on the Establishment and Management of Special Economic Zones of the Islamic Republic of Iran*

4.   Gesellschaftsgründung im Iran

4.1   Gründung einer lokalen Gesellschaft

4.1.1   Joint Stock Company

4.1.1.1   Allgemeines

Die *Joint Stock Company* wird vom Gesetz definiert als Gesellschaft, deren Kapital in Gesellschaftsanteile aufgeteilt ist und deren Gesellschafter beschränkt auf den Nennwert der von ihnen gehaltenen Anteile haften. Die *Joint Stock Company* kann entweder eine Publikumsgesellschaft *(Sherkat Sahami Am)* oder eine Privatgesellschaft *(Sherkat Sahami Khass)* sein. Der wesentliche Unterschied zwischen den beiden Gesellschaftsformen ist, dass die Publikumsgesellschaft ihre Anteile und Schuldscheine der Öffentlichkeit anbieten darf, während die Privatgesellschaft dies nicht darf.

Die Gesellschafter einer *Joint Stock Company* sind gemäß dem Verhältnis der gehaltenen Anteile an Eigentum, Gewinn und Verlust, sowie der Verteilung des Gesellschaftsvermögens im Falle der Liquidation beteiligt. Wie bereits oben erwähnt, haften die Gesellschafter nur bis zum Nennwert ihrer Anteile, sodass sie (sofern keine betrügerischen oder ähnlichen Handlungen vorliegen) nicht für darüber hinausgehende Verbindlichkeiten der Gesellschaft in Anspruch genommen werden können. Die Gesellschaft hat eine eigene Rechtspersönlichkeit und kann unter ihrem Namen klagen und verklagt werden. Die Gesellschafter besitzen die üblichen Gesellschafterrechte, wie z.B. das Recht an Gesellschafterversammlungen teilzunehmen, Finanzberichte zu erhalten, das *Board of Directors* zu wählen und zu ersetzen, und über die wesentlichen Entscheidungen der Gesellschaft abzustimmen.

4.1.1.2   Anzahl der Gesellschafter

Laut Gesetz muss eine *Joint Stock Company* mindestens drei Gesellschafter haben.

4.1.1.3   Nationalität der Gesellschafter

Es gibt keine Beschränkungen in Bezug auf die Nationalität von Personen, die eine *Joint Stock Company* gründen dürfen. Im Allgemeinen fordert die iranische Regierung allerdings, dass iranische Gesellschafter beteiligt sind, sofern es um Bereiche geht, die für die nationalen Entwicklungsprogramme von Bedeutung sind.

4.1.1.4   Gesellschaftsanteile

Eine *Joint Stock Company* kann sowohl gewöhnliche als auch Vorzugsanteile ausgeben, entweder als Namensanteile oder als Inhaberanteile. Das Gesetz trifft zwar keine Aussage darüber, welche Privilegien an Vorzugsaktien gebunden sein können; es ist aber allgemein anerkannt, dass beispielsweise höhere Dividenden- und Stimmrechte sowie Bevorzugung bei der Verteilung der Liquidationsmasse vergeben werden können. Der wesentliche

Unterschied zwischen Namens- und Inhaberanteilen liegt in der Übertragungsart sowie in der steuerlichen Behandlung.

4.1.1.5 Management

Das Management einer *Joint Stock Company* obliegt dem *Board of Directors*, welches mindestens einmal alle zwei Jahre durch kumulative Wahl der Gesellschafter gewählt werden muss.

4.1.1.6 Auflösung und Liquidation

Die Grundzüge der Auflösung und Liquidation einer *Joint Stock Company* sind im Gesetz festgelegt und Gesellschaften können in ihrer Satzung bestimmte Vorschriften festlegen, solange sie nicht dem Gesetz widersprechen. Da die Vorschriften des Gesetzes eher allgemeiner Natur sind, empfiehlt es sich bei der Satzungserstellung, konkrete Verfahrensweisen zur Auflösung und Liquidation zu bestimmen.

4.1.1.7 Andere Gesellschaftsformen im Iran

Neben der *Joint Stock Company* sieht das iranische Gesellschaftsrecht die folgenden Gesellschaftsformen vor:

1. Gesellschaft mit beschränkter Haftung *(Sherkat ba Masouliyat Mahdoud)*
2. Allgemeine Partnerschaft *(Sherkat Tazamoni)*
3. Haftungsbeschränkte Partnerschaft *(Sherkat Mokhtalet Gheyr Sahami)*
4. Kommanditpartnerschaft *(Sherkat Mokhtalet Sahami)*
5. Partnerschaft mit anteiliger Haftung *(Sherkat Nesbi)*
6. Produktions- und Konsumkooperative *(Sherkat Ta'avoni Towlid va Masraf)*

Die Gesellschaft mit beschränkter Haftung und die *Joint Stock Company* bieten den Gesellschaftern eine auf den Wert ihrer jeweiligen Beteiligung begrenzte Haftung. Der wesentliche Unterschied ist, dass bei der Gesellschaft mit beschränkter Haftung das Kapital nicht in Anteile aufgeteilt wird und die Teilhaber ihre Beteiligung nur mit Zustimmung von Teilhabern, die 3/4 des Gesamtkapitals repräsentieren, übertragen dürfen. Bei der Kommanditpartnerschaft gibt es sowohl Partner mit beschränkter als auch mit unbeschränkter Haftung.

4.1.2 Kapital

4.1.2.1 Gesellschaftskapital

Das Mindestkapital bei Gründung beträgt 1.000.000 IRR (ca. 30 EUR) für die private *Joint Stock Company* und 5.000.000 IRR (ca. 150 EUR) für die öffentliche *Joint Stock Company*. Die Gesellschaftsanteile können entweder in bar oder als Sachleistung erfolgen. Falls Zahlung durch Sachleistung erfolgt, muss der Wert der Sachleistung von einem offiziellen Gutachter des Justizministeriums bestätigt werden. Bei Zahlung in bar müssen lediglich 35% bei Gründung eingezahlt werden und der Rest innerhalb von 5 Jahren nach Aufforderung durch das *Board of Directors* oder die übrigen Gesellschafter. Bei Zahlung durch Sachleistung muss die gesamte Sachleistung zum Gründungszeitpunkt übertragen werden. Das

Gesellschaftskapital kann jederzeit erhöht werden durch Gesellschafterbeschluss mit einer Zwei-Drittel-Mehrheit im Rahmen einer außerordentlichen Gesellschafterversammlung. Die Herabsetzung des registrierten Kapitals kann ebenso erfolgen und die Gesellschaft ist verpflichtet, dies zu tun, sofern die Hälfte des Gesellschaftsvermögens verloren ist.

4.1.2.2   Anteilszeichnung

Obwohl nur 35% des Gesellschaftskapitals bei Gründung eingezahlt werden müssen, müssen 100% der Anteile gezeichnet werden. Nichtsdestotrotz besteht die Möglichkeit, „autorisiertes, ungezeichnetes Kapital" zu haben, was beispielsweise die Möglichkeit von Optionsplänen für Mitarbeiter eröffnet. In der Regel erfordert dies das Abhalten einer außerordentlichen Gesellschafterversammlung, in der die Gesellschafter beschließen, die Erhöhung in vom *Board of Directors* zu bestimmender Höhe und Zeitpunkt durchzuführen.

4.1.2.3   Nennwert

Den Anteilen einer *Joint Stock Company* muss ein Nennwert (Nominalwert) zugeordnet sein. Für die Publikumsgesellschaft schreibt das Gesetz einen maximalen Nennwert von 10.000 IRR (ca. 0,30 EUR) pro Anteil vor. Für die Privatgesellschaft bestehen keine Ober- oder Untergrenzen. Der Nennwert muss allerdings, sowohl bei der Publikumsgesellschaft als auch bei der Privatgesellschaft, für alle Anteile gleich sein, was offensichtlich sowohl für gewöhnliche als auch für Vorzugsanteile gilt. Zudem muss ein Aufruf zur Einzahlung von unbezahlten Anteilen stets gleichberechtigt erfolgen. Sofern gestückelte Anteile ausgegeben werden, muss der Nennwert jedes gestückelten Anteils ebenfalls gleich sein.

4.1.2.4   Anteilszertifikate

Das Gesetz sieht genaue Regeln für Form und Inhalt von Anteilszertifikaten vor. Sie müssen einheitlich und gedruckt sein, eine Seriennummer aufweisen, und von mindestens zwei berechtigten Personen unterschrieben sein. Jedes Zertifikat muss die folgenden Informationen enthalten:

1. Name und Rechtsform der Gesellschaft und Registrierungsnummer
2. Registriertes und einbezahltes Kapital
3. Art der Anteile
4. Nennwert und einbezahlter Anteil, sowohl in Zahlen als auch in Worten
5. Anzahl der vom Zertifikat repräsentierten Anteile

4.1.2.5   Provisorische Anteilszertifikate

Laut Gesetz muss die Gesellschaft den Gesellschaftern, sofern keine Anteilszertifikate ausgegeben wurden, provisorische Zertifikate ausstellen, die die Anzahl der Anteile und den einbezahlten Anteil angeben. Das Gesetz besagt zudem, dass die Ausgabe von Inhaberanteilen erst erfolgen darf, wenn die jeweiligen Anteile komplett einbezahlt sind. Namensanteile hingegen müssen bereits vor Einbezahlung des vollen Anteils ausgegeben werden und die Vorschriften für die Übertragung von Namensaktien kommen zur Anwendung.

4.1.2.6 Anteilsübertragung
Inhaberanteile können durch physische Übergabe übertragen werden, während die Übertragung von Namensanteilen erst mit Eintragung in das Gesellschafterverzeichnis der Gesellschaft wirksam wird. Bezüglich der Übertragung von Namensaktien können Beschränkungen in die Gesellschaftssatzung aufgenommen werden.

4.1.2.7 Rücklagen
Eine gesetzlich vorgeschriebene Rücklage ist zu bilden durch Hinterlegung von jährlich 5% des Gewinns einer *Joint Stock Company* bis die Rücklage 10% des registrierten Kapitals erreicht hat. Gewinn ist insoweit definiert als Jahreseinkommen abzüglich Ausgaben, Abschreibung und Beiträge zu anderen Rücklagen.

4.1.2.8 Dividenden
Dividenden müssen von den Gesellschaftern in einer Gesellschafterversammlung autorisiert werden und müssen aus dem „zu verteilenden Gewinn" erfolgen. Dieser ist definiert als Jahresgewinn (i) abzüglich Verluste aus vorherigen Jahren, (ii) abzüglich anderer optionaler Reserven, (iii) zuzüglich nicht ausgeschütteter und zu verteilender Gewinne aus vorherigen Jahren.

4.1.2.9 Vorzugsrechte
Gesellschafter haben Vorzugsrechte bei der Zeichnung neu ausgegebener Anteile. Dieses Recht kann allerdings durch eine Zwei-Drittel-Mehrheit im Rahmen einer außerordentlichen Gesellschafterversammlung aufgehoben werden.

4.1.3 Gründung
4.1.3.1 Satzung
Die Gründungsurkunde einer *Joint Stock Company*, die sog. *Articles of Association*, entspricht in etwa der Satzung und den Statuten in anderen Ländern gegründeter Unternehmen. Die Gründungsgesellschafter müssen die *Articles of Association* genehmigen und ihre Unterschriften anbringen bevor die Gesellschaftsgründung registriert werden kann.

4.1.3.2 Einzahlung der gezeichneten Anteile
Die zu zeichnenden Gesellschaftsanteile müssen vor Gründung in ein von der Gesellschaft eröffnetes Bankkonto eingezahlt werden.[2] Ein Beleg der Bank ist eines der zur Registrierung der Gesellschaft beim *Companies Registration Office* einzureichenden Dokumente.

---

[2] Nach der Bestätigung des Firmennamens wird vom *Companies Registration Office* ein Schreiben zur Eröffnung eines Bankkontos ausgestellt.

4.1.3.3   Gründungsversammlung

Eine Versammlung der Gründungsgesellschafter ist laut Gesetz erforderlich bei der Publikumsgesellschaft, nicht jedoch bei der Privatgesellschaft. Auch für die Privatgesellschaft empfiehlt es sich jedoch, eine solche Versammlung abzuhalten, um alle zur Gesellschaftsgründung notwendigen Maßnahmen abzuwickeln. Hierbei müssen die Gründungsgesellschafter die folgenden Schritte unternehmen:

1. Genehmigung und Unterzeichnung der *Articles of Association*
2. Bestätigung, dass die erforderliche Zeichnung und Einzahlung der Anteile erfolgt ist
3. Ernennung der Direktoren und Inspektoren
4. Erhalt der Zustimmung der Direktoren und Inspektoren
5. Bestimmung einer allgemein zugänglichen Zeitung für die Publikation der Mitteilungen der Gesellschaft

4.1.3.4   Erste Versammlung des *Board of Directors*

Bevor eine *Joint Stock Company* ihre Geschäfte aufnehmen darf, muss eine Versammlung des *Board of Directors* abgehalten werden, um die folgenden Schritte zu unternehmen:

1. Wahl eines Vorsitzenden und Vizevorsitzenden
2. Ernennung des *Managing Directors* und Bestimmung seiner Pflichten
3. Genehmigung der Form der Anteilszertifikate und Bestimmung der mit deren Unterzeichnung beauftragten Gesellschaftsorgane
4. Bestimmung der Zeichnungsbefugnisse der Gesellschaftsorgane
5. Zudem empfiehlt es sich, in der ersten Versammlung des *Board of Directors* die Bank(en) zu bestimmen, bei der/denen das Gesellschaftsvermögen hinterlegt werden soll

4.1.3.5   Registrierung
4.1.3.5.1   Private Joint Stock Company

Zur Gründung einer Privatgesellschaft sind die folgenden Unterlagen beim *Companies Registration Office* einzureichen:

1. Entwurf der von allen Gesellschaftern unterschriebenen *Articles of Association*
2. Bestätigung, dass die Anteile gezeichnet wurden, sowie Bankbescheinigung, dass die erforderlichen Beträge eingezahlt wurden
3. Ein von allen Gesellschaftern unterschriebenes Dokument, mit dem die Wahl der Direktoren und Inspektoren bestätigt wird
4. Unterschriebene Zustimmung der Direktoren und Inspektoren
5. Schreiben, mit dem die allgemein zugängliche Zeitung bestimmt wird, in der die Bekanntmachungen der Gesellschaft veröffentlicht werden sollen
6. Deklaration (in der vom *Companies Registration Office* bereitgestellten Form)

4.1.3.5.2   Public Joint Stock Company

Eine Publikumsgesellschaft wird gegründet durch die Einreichung der in der Gründungsversammlung beschlossenen *Articles of Association* beim *Companies Registration Office*
zusammen mit einem Protokoll, aus dem die Wahl der Direktoren und Inspektoren und
deren Zustimmung hervorgeht. Die Gründungsgesellschafter, die mindestens 20% des
Gesellschaftskapitals zeichnen müssen, beginnen den Gründungsprozess durch die Einreichung des Entwurfs der *Articles of Association*, den Entwurf eines Prospektes sowie einer
Deklaration mit dem folgenden Inhalt beim *Companies Registration Office*:

1. Name der Gesellschaft
2. Identität und Wohnsitz der Gründungsgesellschafter
3. Gesellschaftszweck
4. Kapitalisierung, inkl. gesonderter Ausweisung von Bar- und Sacheinlagen
5. Anzahl der Namens- und Inhaberaktien und deren Nennwert, sowie die Anzahl
   der Vorzugsaktien und Beschreibung der mit ihnen verliehenen Rechte
6. Bar- und Sacheinlagen der Gründungsgesellschafter
7. Firmensitz
8. Dauer

Wenn das *Companies Registration Office* mit den von den Gründungsgesellschaftern
eingereichten Unterlagen zufrieden ist, erlaubt es die Veröffentlichung des Prospekts, welcher Informationen und Anweisungen enthalten muss, wie und wo Investoren die Gesellschaftsanteile zeichnen können. Sobald das gesamte Kapital der Gesellschaft gezeichnet
und mindestens 35% einbezahlt wurde, müssen die Gründungsgesellschafter die Anteile
den zeichnenden Gesellschaftern zuteilen und die Gründungsversammlung einberufen.
Bei dieser Versammlung sollen die zeichnenden Gesellschafter die *Articles of Association*
prüfen, die ersten Direktoren und Inspektoren ernennen, sowie eine Zeitung zur Publikation der Bekanntmachungen der Gesellschaft bestimmen. Sobald die zeichnenden Gesellschafter die *Articles of Association* genehmigt haben, müssen diese zusammen mit einem
Protokoll der Versammlung beim *Companies Registration Office* eingereicht werden.

4.1.3.6   Publikation

Die Gesellschaftsgründung muss sowohl in der Regierungsgazette als auch in der von den
Gründungsgesellschaftern bestimmten Zeitung veröffentlicht werden. Die Kosten der Veröffentlichung trägt die Gesellschaft und die Veröffentlichung soll die folgenden Informationen enthalten:

1. Name und Art
2. Zweck
3. Sitz des Hauptbüros
4. Dauer und Datum der Gründung
5. Nationalität
6. Gesellschaftskapital, Nennwert und Art der Anteile
7. Einbezahlter Anteil des Gesellschaftskapital sowie Nummer des/der Bankbeleg(e),
   der/die die Einzahlung bestätigen

8. Identität der Gründungsgesellschafter und der von ihnen gehaltenen Anteile
9. Name der ersten Mitglieder des *Board of Directors* und des *Managing Directors*
10. Zeichnungsbefugnis des *Managing Directors*
11. Personen, die zur Vertretung der Gesellschaft befugt sind
12. Zeitung, in der die Bekanntmachungen der Gesellschaft veröffentlicht werden sollen
13. Name des ersten Inspektors und alternativen Inspektors
14. Vorgehensweise zur Liquidierung

4.1.3.7 Beginn der rechtlichen Existenz

Obwohl die Registrierungs- und Veröffentlichungsbestimmungen zur Gesellschaftsgründung eingehalten werden müssen, beginnt die rechtliche Existenz der Gesellschaft bereits am Tag, an dem die Direktoren und Inspektoren ihre Positionen schriftlich anerkennen.

4.1.3.8 Kosten

Die folgenden Kosten und Gebühren entstehen im Zusammenhang mit der Gesellschaftsgründung:

1. Registrierungsgebühr, abhängig vom Gesellschaftskapital und an das *Companies Registration Office* zu entrichten
2. Gebühr zur Veröffentlichung in der Regierungsgazette zum einschlägigen Tarif
3. Kosten für die Veröffentlichung in einer allgemein zugänglichen Zeitung
4. Stempelsteuer auf Anteilszertifikate

4.1.3.9 Haftung der Gründungsgesellschafter

Die Gründungsgesellschafter sind laut Gesetz für sämtliche Handlungen im Zusammenhang mit der Gesellschaftgründung verantwortlich.

4.1.4 Board of Directors

4.1.4.1 Anzahl

Eine Publikumsgesellschaft muss mindestens fünf Direktoren haben, während für die Privatgesellschaft keine Mindestanzahl besteht. Allerdings schreibt das Gesetz sowohl für die Publikums- als auch für die Privatgesellschaft ein *Board of Directors* vor, das mindestens aus einem Vorsitzenden und einem Vizevorsitzenden bestehen muss.

4.1.4.2 Ernennung und Abberufung

Die Direktoren müssen aus dem Kreise der Gesellschafter[3] mindestens zweimal pro Jahr gewählt werden. Die Wahl muss durch Kumulativwahl im Rahmen einer Gesellschafterversammlung erfolgen. Jeder Direktor kann von den Gesellschaftern abberufen werden. Direktoren können auch wiedergewählt werden. Auch juristische Personen können Direktoren sein.

---

[3] Alle Direktoren (außer dem CEO) müssen auch Gesellschafter sein.

4.1.4.3   Amtszeit

Die Amtszeit der Direktoren muss in den *Articles of Association* geregelt sein, darf aber nicht länger als zwei Jahre sein. Sofern die Amtszeit allerdings endet, ohne dass bereits Nachfolger bestimmt sind, bleiben die bestehenden Direktoren bis zur Ernennung der neuen Direktoren für die Leitung der Geschäfte der Gesellschaft verantwortlich.

4.1.4.4   Sicherheitsanteile

Die Direktoren müssen die in den *Articles of Association* bestimmte Anzahl an Gesellschaftsanteilen halten, wobei diese Anzahl nicht unter der für ein Wahlrecht bei Gesellschafterversammlungen erforderlichen Anzahl liegen darf. Jeder Direktor muss die notwendige Anzahl an Gesellschaftsanteilen während seiner Amtszeit treuhänderisch von der Gesellschaft verwalten lassen, um eventuelle durch die Handlungen der Direktoren entstehende Schäden der Gesellschaft zu kompensieren. Hierbei muss es sich um Namensaktien handeln. Ein Verstoß gegen diese Vorschrift führt laut Gesetz dazu, dass der jeweilige Direktor als zurückgetreten angesehen wird.

4.1.4.5   Vertretungsbefugnis

Per Gesetz haben die Direktoren alle zur Leitung der Gesellschaft erforderlichen Befugnisse im Rahmen des in den *Articles of Association* festgelegten Gesellschaftszwecks. Das *Board of Directors* darf jedoch keine den Gesellschaftern vorbehaltenen Befugnisse ausüben. Zudem können Beschränkungen der Vertretungsbefugnis in den *Articles of Association* beschlossen werden, welche jedoch nur zwischen den Direktoren und Gesellschaftern wirksam sind, nicht jedoch dritten Personen entgegengehalten werden können.

4.1.4.6   Haftung

Die Direktoren sind der Gesellschaft, den Gesellschaftern sowie Dritten gegenüber zur Einhaltung der Regeln des Fair Play verpflichtet und bei Verstößen ersatzpflichtig. Zudem sind sie, sowohl allein als auch gesamtschuldnerisch, für bestimmte Handlungen und Unterlassungen strafrechtlich verantwortlich.

4.1.4.7   Versammlungen

Das *Board of Directors* handelt in Versammlungen, bei denen mindestens die Hälfte der Direktoren anwesend ist. Die Art und Weise zur Einberufung von Versammlungen, inklusive eventueller Benachrichtigungsfristen, sollte in den *Articles of Association* festgelegt sein. In jedem Falle sind der Vorsitzende sowie Direktoren, die mindestens ein Drittel des *Board of Directors* repräsentieren, berechtigt, Versammlungen einzuberufen. Beschlüsse werden mit Zustimmung der Mehrheit der anwesenden Direktoren gefasst, sofern in den *Articles of Association* keine höhere Grenze bestimmt ist.

Ein Protokoll jeder Versammlung muss aufbewahrt und von der Mehrzahl der teilnehmenden Direktoren unterzeichnet werden. Das Protokoll muss die anwesenden und abwesenden Direktoren aufführen, sowie eine Zusammenfassung der Beratungen und Beschlüsse und das Datum der Versammlung.

4.1.4.8   Handeln ohne Versammlung
Handlungen des *Board of Directors* außerhalb einer Versammlung sind durch schriftliche Zustimmung aller Direktoren wirksam.

4.1.4.9   Vertreter
Seit der Reformierung des *Commercial Code* aus dem Jahre 1969 enthält dieser zwar keine Vorschriften für die Vertretung von Direktoren mehr, jedoch ist diese in der Praxis allgemein anerkannt. Vor seiner Änderung sah der *Commercial Code* vor, dass eine Vertretung zwar möglich sei, der jeweilige Direktor jedoch für die Handlungen seines Vertreters verantwortlich bleibt.

4.1.4.10   Ersatzdirektoren
Ersatzdirektoren sind möglich aber nicht zwingend vorgeschrieben.

4.1.4.11   Managing Director
Laut Gesetz muss das *Board of Directors* mindestens eine Person als *Managing Director* bestimmen, der das tägliche Geschäft der Gesellschaft leitet. Diese Person kann, muss aber nicht Mitglied des *Board of Directors* sein, darf aber nicht zugleich die Position des Vorsitzenden des *Board of Directors* innehaben, es sei denn, die Gesellschafter haben dem mit einer Dreiviertelmehrheit zugestimmt. Die Vertretungsbefugnis des *Managing Director* sollte im Zeitpunkt seiner Ernennung vom *Board of Directors* festgelegt werden, und der *Managing Director* gilt sodann als rechtlicher Vertreter der Gesellschaft mit der Befugnis, im Namen der Gesellschaft zu zeichnen.

4.1.4.12 Aufwandsersatz
Direktoren dürfen von der Gesellschaft grundsätzlich nicht bezahlt werden, außer angemessener Aufwandsentschädigungen für die Teilnahme an Versammlungen und falls die Gesellschafter einen „Bonus" aus Gesellschaftsgewinnen beschließen. Dieser Bonus ist bei der Privatgesellschaft auf 10% der Dividenden beschränkt, bei der Publikumsgesellschaft auf 5%. Direktoren können allerdings als Angestellte der Gesellschaft fungieren und als solche Gehälter beziehen.

4.1.4.13 Geschäfte mit der Gesellschaft
Weder Direktoren noch der *Managing Director* dürfen Geschäfte mit der Gesellschaft abschließen, es sei denn, solche Geschäfte wurden vom *Board of Directors* ohne Beteiligung des betroffenen Direktors genehmigt und sowohl den Inspektoren als auch den Gesellschafter gemeldet. Selbst wenn diese Voraussetzungen vorliegen, können die Direktoren, die solchen Geschäften zugestimmt haben, für entstehende Verluste haftbar gemacht werden. Laut Gesetz sind Darlehen und Garantien, die die Gesellschaft den Direktoren gibt, nichtig, außer es handelt sich bei dem Direktor um eine juristische Person.

4.1.4.14 Wettbewerb zur Gesellschaft

Wenn ein Direktor oder der *Managing Director* Geschäfte abschließt, die einen konkurrierenden Wettbewerb zur Gesellschaft darstellen, und die Gesellschaft hierdurch Schaden erleidet, ist der Direktor zum Ersatz des Schadens verpflichtet.

4.1.5 Gesellschaftsversammlungen

4.1.5.1 Arten

Gesellschafterversammlungen werden Generalversammlungen genannt und das Gesetz sieht drei Arten vor: Die erste ist die Gründungsversammlung, welche nur für die Publikumsgesellschaft zwingend vorgeschrieben ist. Die zweite ist die (Jahres-)Hauptversammlung, die einmal im Jahr abgehalten wird, und die dritte ist die außerordentliche Versammlung, die bei Bedarf abgehalten wird. Darüber hinaus gibt es zwei weitere Arten von Versammlungen, an denen die Gesellschafter beteiligt sind. Zum einen die sog. „Sonderversammlung", die einberufen werden muss, wenn die Rechte der Inhaber von Vorzugsaktien geändert werden sollen, um diesen Gesellschaftern die Möglichkeit zu geben, über die beabsichtigten Änderungen abzustimmen. Zum anderen die sog. „außerordentliche Sitzung der Hauptversammlung", die vom *Board of Directors*, den Inspektoren oder von Gesellschaftern, die mindestens 20% der Gesellschaftsanteile halten, einberufen werden kann, um Geschäfte zu beschließen, die außerhalb des gewöhnlichen Datums der Hauptversammlung erforderlich sind.

4.1.5.2 Zuständigkeit der Hauptversammlung

Die Hauptversammlung ist zuständig für sämtliche Geschäfte der Gesellschaft, sofern diese nicht ausdrücklich der Gründungsversammlung oder der außerordentlichen Versammlung zugewiesen sind. Die Hauptversammlung ist insbesondere für die folgenden Angelegenheiten zuständig:

1. Prüfung und Genehmigung der Bilanz und Gewinn-und-Verlust-Rechnung und anderer Finanzberichte
2. Prüfung und Genehmigung des Jahresberichts der Direktoren
3. Prüfung und Genehmigung des Jahresberichts der Inspektoren
4. Wahl von Direktoren (sofern deren Amtszeit abgelaufen ist)
5. Wahl von Inspektor(en) und Ersatzinspektor(en)
6. Bestimmung der Zeitung, in der die Bekanntmachungen der Gesellschaft veröffentlicht werden

4.1.5.3 Zuständigkeit der außerordentlichen Versammlung

Die außerordentliche Versammlung ist zuständig für Änderungen der *Articles of Association* oder des Gesellschaftskapitals, sowie für die Auflösung der Gesellschaft.

4.1.5.4 Direktorat

Die Leitung von Generalversammlungen obliegt laut Gesetz dem Direktorat, welches aus einem Vorsitzenden, einem Sekretär und zwei Beobachtern besteht. Soweit die *Articles of*

Association nichts anderes vorschreiben, ist der Vorsitzende der Vorsitzende des *Board of Directors.* Der Sekretär muss kein Gesellschafter sein, die Beobachter hingegen schon.

4.1.5.5 Einladung

Schriftliche Einladungen zu Generalversammlungen müssen den Gesellschaftern mindestens zehn und höchstens 40 Tage im Voraus bekanntgegeben und in der Bekanntmachungszeitung veröffentlicht werden. Die Einladung muss den Gegenstand, sowie Datum, Uhrzeit und Ort der Versammlung enthalten. Ein Verzicht auf das Einladungserfordernis ist möglich, wenn alle Gesellschafter der Versammlung beiwohnen.

4.1.5.6 Quorum

Das Quorum für Haupt- und außerordentliche Versammlung beträgt mehr als 50% der stimmberechtigten Stimmen.

4.1.5.7 Protokoll

Der Sekretär muss ein schriftliches Protokoll jeder Versammlung erstellen, das die Beratungen und Beschlüsse der Versammlung widergibt. Die Protokolle müssen vom Direktorat unterzeichnet und eine Kopie hiervon am Hauptsitz der Gesellschaft aufbewahrt werden.

4.1.5.8 Einreichung und Registrierung von Protokollen

Wann immer eine Generalversammlung einen Beschluss bezüglich einer der folgenden Angelegenheiten trifft, muss eine Kopie des Protokolls beim *Companies Registration Office* zwecks Registrierung im dortigen Registerbuch eingereicht werden:
1. Wahl von Direktoren und Inspektoren
2. Genehmigung der Bilanz
3. Erhöhung oder Herabsetzung des Kapitals, sowie jegliche Änderungen der *Articles of Association*
4. Abwicklung der Gesellschaft und Vorgehensweise zur Liquidation

4.1.5.9 Veröffentlichung der Protokolle

Zusätzlich zu den oben genannten Registrierungserfordernissen müssen die folgenden von der Generalversammlung beschlossenen Angelegenheiten in der Regierungsgazette und der Bekanntmachungszeitung veröffentlicht werden:
1. Wahl von Direktoren und Inspektoren
2. Erhöhung oder Herabsetzung des Kapitals, sowie jegliche Änderungen der *Articles of Association*
3. Abwicklung der Gesellschaft und Namen und Einzelheiten der Liquidatoren
4. Name und Vertretungsbefugnis des *Managing Director*
5. Bestimmung der Zeitung, in der alle Bekanntmachungen der Gesellschaft veröffentlicht werden

4.1.5.10 Vertagung

Eine Generalversammlung kann durch das Direktorat mit Zustimmung der Versammlung für bis zu zwei Wochen vertagt werden. In diesem Falle ist keine neue Einladung erforderlich und das Quorum für die vertagte Sitzung ist dasselbe wie für die ursprüngliche Sitzung.

4.1.5.11 Einberufungsrecht von Minderheitsgesellschaftern

Minderheitsgesellschafter, die insgesamt mindestens ein Fünftel der Gesellschaftsanteile halten, können das *Board of Directors* und die Inspektoren jederzeit zur Einberufung einer Generalversammlung auffordern. Kommen das *Board of Directors* und die Inspektoren dieser Aufforderung nicht nach, können die Gesellschafter selbst die Versammlung einberufen.

4.1.6   Sonstiges

4.1.6.1   Inspektoren

Das Gesetz schreibt die jährliche Wahl eines Inspektors und eines Ersatzinspektors durch die Gesellschafter im Rahmen der Hauptversammlung vor. Die Wahl von mehr als jeweils einem Inspektor und Ersatzinspektor ist optional. Die Aufgabe des Inspektors ist es in der Regel, die Interessen von Gesellschaftern und Dritten zu überwachen; bei Verstößen kann er strafrechtlich belangt werden. Bestimmte Personengruppen, wie z.B. Vorbestrafte, die Direktoren und deren Angehörige, sowie Personen, die geschäftliche Beziehungen mit der Gesellschaft unterhalten, sind von der Ausübung dieses Amtes ausgeschlossen. Der Inspektor ist u.a. dazu verpflichtet, der jährlichen Hauptversammlung einen Bericht vorzulegen.

4.1.6.2   Buchführung

Sowohl die private als auch die öffentliche *Joint Stock Company* sind verpflichtet, eine handelsrechtliche Buchführung in persischer Sprache zu führen. Die Bücher dienen als Grundlage für die Steuerermittlung und falls sie nicht unter strikter Einhaltung der rechtlichen Voraussetzungen geführt werden, kann das Finanzamt eine eigene Einschätzung vornehmen, um die Steuerschuld der Gesellschaft zu ermitteln.

4.1.6.3   Gesellschaftsname

Laut Gesetz muss der Name jeder privaten *Joint Stock Company* die Worte „*Private Joint Stock Company (Sherkat Sahami Khass)*" enthalten und in auffälliger Weise auf dem Briefpapier, Bekanntmachungen und Mitteilungen der Gesellschaft erscheinen. In der Praxis fordert das *Companies Registration Office* die Nutzung von iranischen Namen und ein neuer Gesellschaftsname wird abgelehnt, wenn er dem einer bestehenden Gesellschaft zu sehr ähnelt.

4.1.7 Unterschiede zwischen privater und öffentlicher Joint Stock Company

	Private Joint Stock Company	Public Joint Stock Company
Mindestkapital	IRR 1,000,000 ca. EUR 30	IRR 5,000,000 ca. EUR 150
Maximaler Nennwert	-	IRR 10,000 ca. EUR 0,30
zu zeichnende Anteile	20%	100%
einzuzahlendes Kapital	35%	35% der Geldeinlagen 100% der Sacheinlagen
Voraussetzungen für Kapitalerhöhung	Gesellschafterbeschluss	Prospekt
Mindestanzahl von Direktoren	2	5
maximaler Bonus für Direktoren	10% der Dividenden	5% der Dividenden
Gesetz schreibt Gründungsversammlung vor	Nein	Ja
Jahresabschluss von zertifiziertem Abschlussprüfer zu bestätigen	Nein	Ja

4.1.8 Checkliste zum Inhalt der Articles of Association

Die *Articles of Association* sollten in der Regel die folgenden Informationen enthalten:

1. Name der Gesellschaft
2. Gesellschaftsform
3. Dauer der Gesellschaft
4. Gesellschaftszweck
5. Hauptsitz und Sitz von Zweigniederlassungen (sofern vorhanden)
6. Gesellschaftskapital, inkl. Aufteilung zwischen Geld- und Sacheinlagen
7. Anzahl der Namens- und Inhaberaktien und deren Nennwert, sowie Anzahl eventueller Vorzugsanteile und der mit diesen verbundenen Rechte
8. Höhe des einbezahlten Kapitals
9. Name(n) der zur Unterzeichnung der Anteilszertifikate berechtigten Person(en)
10. Art des Aufrufs und Frist zur Einzahlung der Gesellschaftsanteile
11. Art und Weise zur Übertragung von Namensaktien
12. Art und Weise der Umschreibung von Namens- in Inhaberaktien und umgekehrt
13. Voraussetzungen und Art und Weise für Kapitalerhöhung und -herabsetzung
14. Einladungsfrist und Art und Weise für die Abhaltung von Gesellschafterversammlungen
15. Bestimmungen bzgl. des Quorums und der Leitung von Gesellschafterversammlungen
16. Bestimmungen bzgl. Ablauf von Gesellschafterversammlungen und der für die Beschlussfassung benötigten Stimmenmehrheit

17. Anzahl der Direktoren, Art und Weise ihrer Wahl und der ihrer Nachfolger, Amtsdauer
18. Bestimmungen über Aufgaben und Befugnisse des *Board of Directors*
19. Einladungsfrist und -form zur Einberufung von Direktorenversammlungen
20. Bestimmungen bzgl. des Quorums für Direktorenversammlungen
21. Art und Weise der Wahl des Vorsitzenden und Vizevorsitzenden, Amtsdauer
22. Bestimmungen bzgl. Ablauf von Direktorenversammlungen und der für die Beschlussfassung benötigten Stimmenmehrheit
23. Anzahl der von den Direktoren bei der Gesellschaft zu hinterlegenden Sicherheitsanteile
24. Anzahl, Art und Weise der Wahl und Amtsdauer der Inspektoren
25. Anzahl und Amtsdauer des/der *Managing Directors*
26. Beginn und Ende des Steuerjahres, Frist zur Erstellung von Bilanz und Gewinn-und-Verlust-Rechnung und deren Vorlage an die Inspektoren und die Hauptversammlung
27. Art und Weise der freiwilligen Auflösung der Gesellschaft und Vorgehen zur Liquidierung
28. Art und Weise zur Änderung der *Articles of Association*

4.2   Zweigniederlassungen und Repräsentationsbüros

Eine ausländische Gesellschaft kann im Iran Zweigniederlassungen oder Repräsentations-
büros eröffnen. Das *Law Permitting Registration of Branches and Representative Offices of
Foreign Companies in Iran* wurde am 11. November 1997 verabschiedet. Dessen einziger
Artikel besagt:

„*Ausländische Gesellschaften mit eigener Rechtspersönlichkeit in ihrem Heimatland
können, sofern entsprechende gegenseitige zwischenstaatliche Verträge mit Iran bestehen,
Zweigniederlassungen und Repräsentationsbüros im Iran gründen, um von der Regierung
der Islamischen Republik Irans genehmigte Geschäfte im Einklang mit den Gesetzen Irans
durchzuführen.*“

4.2.1   Berechtigte Gesellschaften

Der Ministerrat hat am 2. Mai 1999 die *Executive By-Laws of the Law Permitting Registration
of Branches and Representative Offices of Foreign Companies under No.019776T/M/78-930*
verabschiedet. Gemäß Art. 1 dieser *By-Laws* können Gesellschaften, die in ihrem Heimatland gegründet wurden und eine eigene Rechtspersönlichkeit haben, auf Grundlage der
einschlägigen Gesetze im Iran Zweigniederlassungen und Repräsentationsbüros eröffnen
um die nachfolgenden Aktivitäten auszuüben.

4.2.2 Unterschiede zwischen Repräsentationsbüro, Verbindungsbüro und Zweigniederlassung ausländischer Gesellschaften im Iran

Sofern die Niederlassung der ausländischen Gesellschaft Arbeiten für die Hauptniederlassung der Gesellschaft ausführen soll, beispielsweise im Rahmen eines Vertrages zwischen dem ausländischen Mutterhaus und einem Kunden im Iran, soll die Niederlassung als Zweigniederlassung (*Branch Office*) registriert werden.

Sofern die Niederlassung das Mutterhaus gegenüber Kunden vertreten soll, Produkte des Mutterhauses im Iran verkauft, Kundendienst erbringt, sowie Verträge zwischen dem Mutterhaus und den Kunden im Iran verhandelt und solche Verträge abschließt etc., so soll die Niederlassung als Repräsentationsbüro eingerichtet werden.

Sofern die Niederlassung des Mutterhauses lediglich Marktforschung für das Mutterhaus betreiben und Geschäftsmöglichkeiten für die Gesellschaft ans Mutterhaus berichten soll um dem Mutterhaus so zu ermöglichen, Angebote direkt an Kunden im Iran zu machen, die Niederlassung also kein eigenes Einkommen generiert und sämtliche Ausgaben vom Mutterhaus getragen werden, so soll die Niederlassung als Verbindungsbüro (sog. *Liaison Office*) eingerichtet werden.

4.2.3 Zulässige Geschäftsfelder

4.2.3.1 Kundendienst

Sofern ausländische Gesellschaften Waren oder Dienstleistungen an iranische Kunden liefern, können diese Gesellschaften die Registrierung einer Zweigniederlassung oder eines Repräsentationsbüros zur Erbringung von Kundendienst (Garantie und Gewährleistung) im Iran beantragen.

4.2.3.2 Leistungserbringung

Ausländische Gesellschaften, die Verträge mit iranischen Kunden (natürliche Personen oder juristische Personen des öffentlichen und privaten Sektors) abgeschlossen haben, müssen ggf. eine Zweigniederlassung oder ein Repräsentationsbüro im Iran registrieren.

4.2.3.3 Erforschung von Investitionen im Iran

Es ist zunächst festzuhalten, dass ausländischen Gesellschaften, die im Iran investieren möchten, die folgenden beiden Möglichkeiten zur Verfügung stehen:

1. Investieren im Rahmen des FIPPA durch Genehmigung der *Organization for Investment and Economic and Technical Assistance* und Einreichung der erforderlichen Unterlagen und einzelfallabhängiger Genehmigung durch den Ministerrat
2. Eingehen eines Joint Ventures mit iranischen natürlichen oder juristischen Personen durch die Gründung einer gemeinsamen Gesellschaft oder durch Investition in eine bereits bestehende Gesellschaft

Ausländische Gesellschaften können Zweigniederlassungen oder Repräsentationsbüros gründen, um Due Diligence Prüfungen vorzunehmen und die Grundlage für Investitionen in einer der beiden oben genannten Formen zu schaffen.

4.2.3.4   Zusammenarbeit für Projekte in Drittländern

Für Fälle, in denen iranische Ingenieursbüros industrielle, technische, Entwicklungs- oder sonstige Aktivitäten in Drittländern ausführen und hierfür entsprechende Verträge mit Gesellschaften aus einem anderen Land abgeschlossen werden sollen, kann die ausländische Gesellschaft eine Zweigniederlassung oder ein Repräsentationsbüro im Iran gründen, indem sie die erforderlichen Unterlagen einreicht. Zudem kann eine ausländische Gesellschaft, die Ingenieursleistungen in einem Drittland erbringen soll und dies im Rahmen eines Joint Ventures mit einem iranischen Ingenieursbüro tun möchte, eine Zweigniederlassung oder ein Repräsentationsbüro im Iran eröffnen.

4.2.3.5   Export und Technologietransfer

Die folgenden ausländischen Gesellschaften, die zu Exportförderung und Technologietransfer beitragen, können eine Zweigniederlassung oder ein Repräsentationsbüro im Iran eröffnen:

1. Ausländische Gesellschaften, die im Bereich des Exports von iranischen Nicht-Öl-Produkten, einschließlich industriellen und landwirtschaftlichen Produkten und Handwerken, tätig sind und zu dessen Entwicklung und Förderung beitragen
2. Ausländische Gesellschaften, die Knowhow bezüglich der Produktion diverser Produkte an Iraner vermitteln
3. Ausländische Gesellschaften, die Technologie in Bezug auf industrielle Produkte besitzen und beabsichtigen, diese an Iraner zu vermitteln durch die Errichtung von Fabriken und Anlagen

4.2.3.6   Genehmigungspflichtige Aktivitäten

Ausländische Gesellschaften, die einen Vertrag mit einer staatlichen Stelle zur Leistungserbringung in diversen Bereichen abgeschlossen haben, die der Genehmigung einer Regierungsbehörde bedürfen, können eine Zweigniederlassung oder ein Repräsentationsbüro im Iran eröffnen.

In vielen anderen Fällen ist die Genehmigung der zuständigen Behörde erforderlich. Beispielsweise erfordert die Leistungserbringung im Bereich des Transportwesens zur See, Land (Straße und Schiene) und Luft die Genehmigung der *Organization for Transportation and Terminals*. Aktivitäten im Bankenwesen erfordern die Genehmigung der Islamischen Zentralbank.

4.2.4   Zweigniederlassung einer ausländischen Gesellschaft

Gemäß der Definition des Art. 2 der Verwaltungsvorschrift zum *Law Permitting Registration of Branches and Representative Offices of Foreign Companies in Iran* ist eine Zweigniederlassung einer ausländischen Gesellschaft der lokale (iranische) Teil der Gesellschaft, der Geschäfte und Funktionen im Iran für das Mutterhaus direkt durch einen oder mehrere Repräsentanten ausführt.

4.2.5 Erforderliche Dokumente für die Registrierung von Zweigniederlassungen ausländischer Gesellschaften

Ausländische Gesellschaften, die eine Zweigniederlassung im Iran eröffnen möchten, müssen die folgenden Unterlagen beim *Companies Registration Office* in Teheran einreichen:

1. Schriftlicher Antrag der Gesellschaft
2. Beglaubigte Kopien der Satzung, der Gründungsurkunde, sowie der letzten gesellschaftsrechtlichen Änderungen, die bei der zuständigen Stelle registriert wurden
3. Letzter geprüfter Jahresabschluss der Gesellschaft
4. Machbarkeitsstudie mit folgendem Inhalt:
   – Informationen bezüglich der Aktivitäten der Gesellschaft
   – Beschreibung der Gründe und der Notwendigkeit für eine Registrierung der Gesellschaft im Iran
   – Beschreibung der Zeichnungsbefugnisse und Firmensitz der Zweigniederlassung im Iran
   – Schätzung der nötigen Anzahl an iranischen und ausländischen Angestellten
   – Art und Weise der Finanzierung (in Rial und in ausländischer Währung) des Betriebs der Zweigniederlassung
5. Bestätigungsschreiben einer Regierungsstelle, sofern die Zweigniederlassung zum Zwecke der Erfüllung eines Vertrages mit einer Regierungsstelle eröffnet wird
6. Registrierungsbogen (Formular, das von der ausländischen Gesellschaft ausgefüllt und unterschrieben werden muss)
7. Registrierungszertifikat (Formular, das von der ausländischen Gesellschaft ausgefüllt und unterschrieben werden muss)
8. Schreiben, mit dem die ausländische Gesellschaft ihre(n) Vertreter im Iran bevollmächtigt
9. Schreiben, mit dem die ausländische Gesellschaft bestätigt, die iranische Zweigniederlassung abzuwickeln und zu schließen, sofern die von den iranischen Behörden gewährte Genehmigung widerrufen oder aufgehoben wird. In diesem Falle muss die Zweigniederlassung durch einen zu bestimmenden Liquidator innerhalb einer vom *Companies Registration Office* bestimmten Frist abgewickelt und geschlossen werden.

Sämtliche Unterlagen der ausländischen Gesellschaft müssen von der jeweiligen Behörde (z.B. Handelsregister) beglaubigt, vom Auswärtigen Amt des jeweiligen Landes bestätigt und sodann von der iranischen Botschaft in dem jeweiligen Land legalisiert werden. Anschließend müssen die Unterlagen von einem offiziellen Übersetzer ins Persische übersetzt und notariell beglaubigt werden. Die Übersetzungen sind dann zusammen mit den Originalen beim *Companies Registration Office* einzureichen, um die Registrierung der Zweigniederlassung vorzunehmen.

4.2.6 Verantwortlichkeit der ausländischen Gesellschaft für die Zweigniederlassung

Die Zweigniederlassung tätigt Geschäfte im Iran für das Mutterhaus, welches daher für sämtliche Handlungen der Zweigniederlassung verantwortlich ist.

4.2.7 Agenten (lokal)

Ein „Agent" der ausländischen Gesellschaft ist eine natürliche oder juristische Person, die auf der Grundlage eines Agenturvertrages Aufgaben und Funktionen der Gesellschaft im Iran übernimmt.

4.2.8 Erforderliche Dokumente für die Registrierung von Repräsentationsbüros ausländischer Gesellschaften

1. Sofern eine natürliche Person als Repräsentant der ausländischen Gesellschaft agieren soll, müssen die folgenden Unterlagen ins Persische übersetzt und beim *Companies Registration Office* eingereicht werden:

    a) Beglaubigte Kopie des Agenturvertrages mit der ausländischen Gesellschaft

    b) Kopie des Personalausweises *(shenas'nameh)*, bzw. des Reisepasses falls der Agent nicht Iraner ist

    c) Anschrift des Agenten und Anschrift seines Büros

    d) Beschreibung der bisherigen Aktivitäten des Agenten im Rahmen des Agenturvertrages

    e) Beglaubigte Kopien der Satzung, der Gründungsurkunde, sowie der letzten gesellschaftsrechtlichen Änderungen, die bei der zuständigen Stelle registriert wurden

    f) Beschreibung der Aktivitäten der ausländischen Gesellschaft und Angabe der Gründe für die Notwendigkeit eines Agenten

    g) Letzter geprüfter Jahresabschluss der Gesellschaft

    h) Bestätigungsschreiben einer Regierungsstelle, sofern das Repräsentationsbüro zum Zwecke der Erfüllung eines Vertrages mit einer Regierungsstelle eröffnet wird

    i) Registrierungsbogen (Formular, das von der ausländischen Gesellschaft ausgefüllt und unterschrieben werden muss)

    j) Registrierungszertifikat (Formular, das von der ausländischen Gesellschaft ausgefüllt und unterschrieben werden muss)

    k) Schreiben, mit dem die ausländische Gesellschaft ihre(n) Vertreter im Iran bevollmächtigt

    Sämtliche Unterlagen der ausländischen Gesellschaft müssen von der jeweiligen Behörde (z.B. Handelsregister) beglaubigt, vom Auswärtigen Amt des jeweiligen Landes bestätigt und sodann von der iranischen Botschaft in dem jeweiligen Land legalisiert werden. Anschließend müssen die Unterlagen von einem offiziellen Übersetzer ins Persische übersetzt und notariell beglaubigt werden. Die Übersetzungen sind dann zusammen mit den Originalen beim *Companies Registration Office* einzureichen, um die Registrierung des Repräsentationsbüros vorzunehmen.

2. Sofern eine juristische Person als Repräsentant der ausländischen Gesellschaft agieren soll, müssen die folgenden Unterlagen ins Persische übersetzt und beim *Companies Registration Office* eingereicht werden:

    a) Beglaubigte Kopie des Agenturvertrages mit der ausländischen Gesellschaft
    b) Beglaubigte Kopien der Satzung, der Gründungsurkunde, sowie der letzten gesellschaftsrechtlichen Änderungen der vertretenden Gesellschaft, die bei der zuständigen Stelle registriert wurden
    c) Historie der Aktivitäten der vertretenden Gesellschaft in Bezug auf die für das Repräsentationsbüro vorzunehmenden Geschäfte
    d) Satzung, die Gründungsurkunde, sowie die letzten gesellschaftsrechtlichen Änderungen der zu vertretenden Gesellschaft, die bei der zuständigen Stelle registriert wurden
    e) Historie der Aktivitäten der zu vertretenden Gesellschaft und Angabe der Gründe für die Notwendigkeit eines Agenten
    f) Letzter geprüfter Jahresabschluss der zu vertretenden Gesellschaft
    g) Bestätigungsschreiben einer Regierungsstelle, sofern das Repräsentationsbüro zum Zwecke der Erfüllung eines Vertrages mit einer Regierungsstelle eröffnet wird
    h) Registrierungsbogen (Formular, das von der ausländischen Gesellschaft ausgefüllt und unterschrieben werden muss)
    i) Registrierungszertifikat (Formular, das von der ausländischen Gesellschaft ausgefüllt und unterschrieben werden muss)

Sämtliche Unterlagen der ausländischen Gesellschaft müssen von der jeweiligen Behörde (z.B. Handelsregister) beglaubigt, vom Auswärtigen Amt des jeweiligen Landes bestätigt und sodann von der iranischen Botschaft in dem jeweiligen Land legalisiert werden. Anschließend müssen die Unterlagen von einem offiziellen Übersetzer ins Persische übersetzt und notariell beglaubigt werden. Die Übersetzungen sind dann zusammen mit den Originalen beim *Companies Registration Office* einzureichen, um die Registrierung des Repräsentationsbüros vorzunehmen.

4.2.9   Verantwortlichkeit von Zweigniederlassungen und Vertreter ausländischer Gesellschaften

Die Vertreter ausländischer Gesellschaften sollen für die im Namen der Gesellschaft im Iran ausgeführten Handlungen verantwortlich sein.

1. Auflösung und Liquidation der Zweigniederlassung im Falle eines Widerrufs der Lizenz, die es der ausländischen Gesellschaft erlaubt, im Iran Geschäfte zu tätigen
2. Einreichung eines Jahresberichts bezüglich der Aktivitäten und des geprüften Jahresabschlusses des ausländischen Mutterhauses an die zuständige iranische Behörde
3. Einreichung des Aktivitätsberichts der Zweigniederlassung oder des Repräsentationsbüros zusammen mit dem geprüften Jahresabschluss innerhalb von vier Monaten nach Schluss des Rechnungsjahres an die zuständige iranische Behörde

4. Leitung der täglichen Geschäfte der Zweigniederlassung oder des Repräsentationsbüros durch eine oder mehrere im Iran wohnende natürliche Person(en)

4.2.10 Steuern

Vertretungen von ausländischen Unternehmen, die für die Muttergesellschaft Marktinformationen sammeln und Werbung machen und hierfür von der Muttergesellschaft entlohnt werden, jedoch keine selbständigen Aktivitäten ausführen, unterliegen nicht der Einkommensteuer, wie Hinweis 3 zu Art. 107 des *Direct Taxation Law* verdeutlicht:

„Zweigniederlassungen und Repräsentationsbüros ausländischer Gesellschaften und Banken im Iran, die für die Muttergesellschaft Marktinformationen sammeln und Werbung machen, ohne das Recht, selbständige Geschäfte abzuschließen, und hierfür von der Muttergesellschaft zur Deckung der Ausgaben und finanziellen Anforderungen kompensiert werden, sollen nicht der Einkommensteuer unterfallen."

5. Überblick über das Iranische Steuerrecht

5.1 Bemessungsgrundlage und Steuersätze

Das iranische Steuersystem ist in zwei Hauptkategorien von direkten und indirekten Steuern unterteilt. Laut einer Studie der *Organization for Investment, Economic and Technical Assistance of Iran („OIETAI")* beträgt der Anteil der direkten Steuern an den gesamten Steuereinnahmen derzeit beinahe 68%. Die beiden wesentlichen Arten von direkten Steuern sind die Einkommen- und die Grundsteuer, wobei jede Art wiederum in Unterkategorien unterteilt ist. Indirekte Steuern beinhalten die Importsteuer und die Mehrwertsteuer (*Value Added Tax, VAT*). Importsteuern werden derzeit vom iranischen Zoll eingetrieben und stehen somit nicht unter der Jurisdiktion der *Iranian National Tax Administration („INTA")*. Tabellen 1 bis 4 zeigen einen Überblick über verschiedene Steuerarten des iranischen Steuersystems:

Tabelle 5.1: Einkommensteuern

Steuergrundlage	zu versteuerndes Einkommen	steuerpflichtige Personen	Steuersatz
Immobilien-einkommen	Einkünfte von Personen aus dem Verkauf von Rechten an Immobilien im Iran, abzgl. Freibeträge: Gesamtmiete abzgl. 25% der Ausgaben, Abschreibung und Verpflichtungen des Eigentümers in Bezug auf die Immobilie	Eigentümer, die ihre Immobilien an andere Personen vermietet haben	15–35%
Arbeitseinkommen	Gehälter, Löhne und alle anderen Einkünfte von natürlichen Personen für die Erbringung von Arbeitsleistung. Zahlungen für Arbeiten, die außerhalb Irans ausgeführt werden, sind ebenfalls steuerpflichtig, sofern der Zahlende im Iran ansässig ist.	Natürliche Person	10% für Angestellte im öffentlichen Dienst; 15–35% für andere
Gewerbesteuer	Nicht-inkorporierte Geschäftsaktivitäten (Summe der Waren- und Dienstleistungsverkäufe) abzgl. Freibeträge laut DBA	Natürliche Person	15–35%

| Körperschaftsteuer | Gesamterlös von Gesellschaften, sowie Erlös aus gewinnerzielender Tätigkeit anderer juristischer Personen, aus Quellen innerhalb und außerhalb Irans, abzgl. Kosten aus nicht-befreiten Quellen und abzgl. der vorgeschriebenen Freibeträge | Juristische Person | 25% |
| Schenkungsteuer | Einkünfte durch Schenkung etc. | Natürliche oder juristische Person | 15–35% |

Tabelle 5.2:   Grundsteuer

Steuergrundlage	zu versteuerndes Einkommen	steuerpflichtige Personen	Steuersatz
Steuer auf Transfer von Immobilien	Der finale Transfer von Immobilien und Goodwill ist zum Transferdatum steuerpflichtig.	Natürliche oder juristische Person	5% & 2%
Steuer auf Transfer von Gesellschaftsanteilen	Nennwert der übertragenen Anteile	*Joint Stock Companies* und andere Gesellschaften	0,5% & 4%
Erbschaftsteuer	Jegliches vom Verstorbenen erhaltenes Vermögen	Natürliche Person	5–65%
Stempelsteuer	Von Banken gedruckte Schecks (200 IRR (ca. 0,01 EUR) pro Blatt), Wechsel, Schuldschein (0,3%), sowie andere Dokumente und Vertragspapiere mit bestimmten Beträgen	Natürliche oder juristische Person	gemäß Art. 44 – 51 des *Direct Taxation Law*

Tabelle 5.3:   Importsteuer

Steuergrundlage	zu versteuerndes Einkommen	steuerpflichtige Personen	Steuersatz
Importsteuern werden derzeit vom iranischen Zoll eingetrieben.			

Tabelle 5.4:   Mehrwertsteuer („VAT")

Steuergrundlage	zu versteuerndes Einkommen	steuerpflichtige Personen	Steuersatz
Mehrwertsteuer	Mehrwert aus dem Verkauf von Waren und Dienstleistungen und deren Import, außer 17 in Art. 12 des *VAT Act („VATA")* aufgeführte (mehrwertsteuerfreie) Posten	Natürliche oder juristische Person	derzeit 9%

5.2 Besteuerung ausländischer Investoren im Iran

Alle ausländischen Investoren, die im Iran Geschäfte betreiben oder Einkommen aus iranischen Quellen beziehen, sind im Iran steuerpflichtig. Je nach Art der vom ausländischen Investor ausgeübten Aktivität kommen unterschiedliche Steuern und Freibeträge zur Anwendung, einschließlich Gewinnsteuer, Einkommensteuer, Grundsteuer, etc.

5.2.1 Direkte Steuern

Alle nicht-iranischen natürlichen und juristischen Personen sind steuerpflichtig in Bezug auf im Iran erzielte Einkünfte, sowie auf Einkünfte aus der Gewährung von Lizenzen und anderen Rechten, technischer und Bildungsunterstützung und aus Filmverträgen innerhalb Irans.

Ausländische Investoren genießen dieselben Privilegien wie iranische Investoren, d.h. ausländische und iranische Investoren zahlen die gleichen Steuern. Auch Steuerbefreiungen und -vergünstigungen werden gleichberechtigt an inländische und ausländische Investoren gewährt. Da ausländische Investitionen in der Regel im Rahmen von juristischen Personen erfolgen, beschränken wir uns nachfolgend auf die Regelungen der Körperschaftsteuer.

5.2.2 Körperschaftsteuer

5.2.2.1 Allgemeine Hinweise

Ausländische juristische Personen, die ihren Sitz im Ausland haben, werden pauschal mit 25% besteuert auf ihr gesamtes im Iran erzieltes Einkommen durch Investitionen oder andere Aktivitäten, entweder direkt oder indirekt durch Agenten. Es fallen keine weiteren Steuern an auf Dividenden oder Partnerschaftserlöse, die das Unternehmen von der investierten Gesellschaft erhält.

Unternehmen müssen spätestens vier Monate nach dem Ende des Steuerjahres (21. März bis 20. März des Folgejahres) eine Steuererklärung (Bilanz und Gewinn-und-Verlust-Rechnung) zusammen mit der Gesellschafter- und Partnerliste, deren Anteilen und Adressen bei dem für die Aktivität des Unternehmens zuständigen Finanzamt einreichen, selbst während des Befreiungszeitraums.

5.2.2.2 Befreiungen

Das *Direct Taxation Law* und andere einschlägige Gesetze sehen bestimmte Befreiungen für Unternehmen vor, wie aus Tabelle 5 ersichtlich:

Tabelle 5.5:   Wesentliche Steuerbefreiungen

Aktivität	Höhe der Steuerbefreiung	Befreiungszeitraum	Befreiungsart
Landwirtschaft	100%	unbefristet	dauerhafte Befreiung
Industrie und Bergbau	80%	4 Jahre	Steuerbefreiung
Industrie und Bergbau in wenig entwickelten Gebieten	100%	20 Jahre	Steuerbefreiung
Tourismus	50%	unbefristet	Steuergutschrift
Export von Dienstleistungen und Nicht-Öl-Produkten	100%	während der Laufzeit des *5th Development Plan* (bis Ende 2016)	Steuerbefreiung
Kunsthandwerk	100%	unbefristet	dauerhafte Befreiung
Bildungs- und Sportdienstleistungen	100%	unbefristet	dauerhafte Befreiung
Kulturelle Aktivitäten	100%	unbefristet	dauerhafte Befreiung
Gehalt in wenig entwickelten Gebieten	50%	unbefristet	Steuergutschrift
Sämtliche wirtschaftliche Betätigung in Free Zones	100%	20 Jahre	Steuerbefreiung
Erlöse privater und kooperativer Gesellschaften, die für die Entwicklung, Rekonstruktion und Renovierung von bestehenden industriellen und Bergbauanlagen genutzt werden	50%	unbefristet	Steuergutschrift

5.2.2.3   Abzüge

Die im Rahmen der Ermittlung des steuerpflichtigen Einkommens abzugsfähigen Ausgaben sind im *Direct Taxation Law* geregelt. Diese Ausgaben müssen angemessen dokumentiert sein und in Zusammenhang mit in dem jeweiligen Jahr erzieltem Einkommen stehen. Es bestehen die folgenden Kategorien abzugsfähiger Ausgaben:

1. Kosten für Waren und Rohmaterialien
2. Personalkosten
3. Miete für Geschäftsräume
4. Ausgaben für die Instandhaltung von Geschäftsräumen im eigenen Eigentum
5. Geringfügige Ausgaben im Zusammenhang mit gemieteten Geschäftsräumen
6. Kosten für Treibstoff, Strom, Licht, Wasser und Kommunikation
7. Miete für Maschinen und Zubehör

8. Reparaturkosten für Maschinen und Zubehör
9. Geschäftsversicherung
10. Schadensersatz, der für aus der Betriebsführung resultierende Schäden gezahlt wurde
11. Reserven gegen zweifelhafte Ansprüche
12. Lizenzgebühren
13. Ausgaben für Forschung, Entwicklung und Schulung
14. Ausgaben für Kultur, Sport und Wohlfahrt der Arbeitnehmer, die an das *Ministry of Labour and Social Affairs* gezahlt wurden
15. Ausgaben für den Kauf von Büchern und anderen kulturellen oder künstlerischen Gütern für Angestellte und deren Angehörige
16. Verluste von juristischen Personen
17. Beförderungsausgaben
18. Ausgaben für Beförderung und Unterhaltung von Angestellten
19. Lagerhaltungskosten
20. Gebühren, die im Zusammenhang mit erbrachten Dienstleistungen stehen
21. Zinsen und Gebühren, die für den Geschäftsbetrieb gezahlt wurden
22. Verluste für die Erforschung potenzieller Minen
23. Mitgliedsgebühren im Zusammenhang mit dem Geschäftsbetrieb
24. Forderungsausfall, sofern nachgewiesen
25. Währungsverluste, die anhand anerkannter Buchhaltungsprinzipien ermittelt wurden
26. Normaler Produktionsabfall
27. Reserve im Zusammenhang mit akzeptablen Kosten während der Begutachtungsphase

Andere, hier nicht aufgeführte Ausgaben, die aber mit der Einkommenserzielung des Unternehmens zusammenhängen, können als abzugsfähige Ausgaben anerkannt werden, wenn sie von der INTA vorgeschlagen und vom *Ministry of Economic Affairs and Finance* anerkannt werden.

5.2.2.4   Verluste

Verluste, die Steuerzahler im Bereich Handel oder anderen Aktivitäten erleiden, werden von den Steuerbehörden anerkannt und können vorgetragen und mit zukünftigen Gewinnen verrechnet werden für einen Zeitraum von drei Jahren.

5.2.2.5   Quellensteuern

Zuvor mussten 5% jeder vertraglichen Zahlung vom Zahlenden einbehalten und ans Finanzamt abgeführt werden. Solche einbehaltenen Steuern stellten eine Vorauszahlung der endgültig anfallenden Steuer dar. Diese Art der Quellensteuer wurde jedoch durch die Neufassung des *Direct Taxation Law* abgeschafft.

Zahlende von Gehältern müssen allerdings bei der Auszahlung oder Weiterberechnung von Gehältern die entsprechenden Steuern einbehalten und innerhalb von 30 Tagen zusammen mit einer Liste der Namen und Adressen der Zahlungsempfänger und der Zahlbeträge an das lokale Finanzamt übermitteln.

5.2.2.6 Abschreibung

Die Abschreibung von Betriebsvermögen ist im Rahmen der Ermittlung des zu versteuernden Einkommens möglich. Die Abschreibungsraten reichen von 5% bis 100% und die Abschreibungsdauer reicht von 2 bis 15 Jahren.

5.2.3 Mehrwertsteuer

Die iranische Mehrwertsteuer (*Value Added Tax, VAT*) fällt auf den Verkauf sämtlicher Waren und Dienstleistungen und deren Import an, außer auf 17 in Art. 12 des *VAT Act* („*VATA*") aufgeführte mehrwertsteuerbefreite Posten. Der VATA beinhaltet allerdings nicht den Export von Waren und Dienstleistungen durch offizielle Zollwege. Die für den Export von Waren und Dienstleistungen gezahlte Steuer erfolgt daher durch die Einreichung der Zollpapiere.

Die Mehrwertsteuer beträgt derzeit 9% (geringfügig erhöhter Satz für zwei besondere Güter, namentlich Zigaretten und Flugzeugtreibstoff). Um die Abhängigkeit des Landes von Öleinnahmen zu reduzieren, bestimmt das *Law on the Fifth Five-Year Development Plan* eine jährliche 1-prozentige Steigerung auf 9% bis zum Ende des Plans, also bis 2016.

Wirtschaftliche Aktivitäten in Freihandels- und Industriezonen sind von der Mehrwertsteuer befreit.

5.2.4 Abkommen zur Vermeidung der Doppelbesteuerung

Um die Kooperation zwischen iranischen und ausländischen Personen sowie Handels- und Wirtschaftsbeziehungen mit ausländischen Staaten zu fördern, hat die Regierung der Islamischen Republik Irans mit den folgenden Ländern beiderseitige Abkommen zur Vermeidung der Doppelbesteuerung abgeschlossen:

Tabelle 5.6:   Liste der anwendbaren Abkommen zur Vermeidung der Doppelbesteuerung Irans

Algerien	Jordanien	Pakistan	Südkorea
Armenien	Kasachstan	Polen	Syrien
Aserbaidschan	Katar	Rumänien	Tadschikistan
Bahrain	Kirgistan	Russland	Türkei
Bulgarien	Kroatien	Schweiz	Tunesien
China	Kuwait	Serbien	Turkmenistan
Deutschland	Libanon	Spanien	Ukraine
Frankreich	Malaysia	Sri Lanka	Usbekistan
Georgien	Österreich	Sudan	Venezuela
Indonesien	Oman	Südafrika	Weißrussland

5.2.5 Wirtschaftsprüfung

Das System der Wirtschaftsprüfung von Gesellschaften im Iran stimmt mit internationalen Wirtschaftsprüfungskriterien überein. Zudem werden Systeme wie GAAP von den Steuerbehörden anerkannt und ausländische Gesellschaften unterliegen keinen Beschränkungen, ihre eigenen Systeme zu verwenden. Nach Registrierung einer Gesellschaft im Iran wird der Gesellschaft ein Inspektor der lokalen Steuerbehörde als Verbindungsbeamter zugeteilt und es empfiehlt sich, diesem einen Bericht des Wirtschaftsprüfungssystems der Gesellschaft als Referenz zuzusenden.

5.2.6 Prüfung der Steuererklärung durch unabhängige Wirtschaftsprüfer

Buchhalter von Gesellschaften können Vorbereitungen zur Erstellung der Steuererklärung und deren Einreichung treffen. Art. 272 des *Direct Taxation Law* besagt:

„Im Falle einer Wirtschaftsprüfung durch zertifizierte Buchhalter sollen deren Ansicht und Meinungen vom Finanzamt akzeptiert werden. Das von ihnen vorgelegte steuerpflichtige Einkommen soll als Grundlage der Steuerermittlung im Vorfeld der Wirtschaftsprüfung dienen.“

Gemäß Art. 272 des *Direct Taxation Law* soll der Jahresabschluss daher entweder von der Steuerbehörde oder von zertifizierten Buchhaltern begutachtet werden; sodann sollen die nötigen Schritte zur Ermittlung des steuerpflichtigen Einkommens und der fälligen Steuern unternommen werden.

6.   Arbeitsrecht: Beschäftigung von Ausländern im Iran

Ausländern ist es verboten, ohne Arbeitserlaubnis im Iran zu arbeiten (selbst wenn sie ihr Gehalt außerhalb Irans erhalten).

Die Arbeitserlaubnis für die Beschäftigung von Ausländern wird auf Antrag des iranischen Arbeitgebers vom *Department General for Employment of Foreign Nationals* (auch *Department for Employment of Expatriates* genannt) des *Ministry of Cooperatives, Labour and Social Welfare* erteilt. In Provinzhauptstädten wird sie von der *Foreign Citizens Division* des *Department General of Cooperatives, Labour and Social Welfare* erteilt.

Der iranische Arbeitgeber ist verpflichtet, vor dem Abschluss von Verträgen, die zur Beschäftigung von Ausländern im Iran führen könnten, die Genehmigung des *Department General for Employment of Foreign Nationals* einzuholen. Die Vorschriften zur Erlangung von Arbeitserlaubnissen für Ausländer sind im iranischen Arbeitsgesetz von 1990 (Art. 120 bis 129 und Verwaltungsvorschrift Art. 129) geregelt (der allgemeine Ablauf zur Zulassung von Arbeitskräften für ausländische Investitionen ist im folgenden Abschnitt dargelegt).

Aufgrund der hohen Anzahl an gebildeten Arbeitssuchenden im Land und dem Ziel, deren Arbeitslosigkeit zu senken, hat das *Technical Board for Employment of Foreign Nationals* für die Ausstellung von Arbeitserlaubnissen strenge Vorschriften (geregelt in Art. 121 des Arbeitsgesetzes) erlassen. Allerdings sieht der *Foreign Investment Promotion and Protection Act* („FIPPA") aus dem Jahre 2002 vielversprechende Vorschriften für die Ausstellung von Arbeitserlaubnissen für ausländische Investoren, Manager und Experten in Bezug auf die Investition im Rahmen des FIPPA vor.

6.1   Zulassung von Arbeitskräften für ausländische Investitionen gemäß der Vorschriften des FIPPA

Gemäß Art. 35 der Verwaltungsvorschrift zum FIPPA gilt das Folgende:

„Die zuständigen Verwaltungsbehörden, einschließlich des Ministry of Foreign Affairs, des Ministry of Interior, des Ministry of Labour and Social Affairs [seit 2011 und dem Zusammenschluss der Ministerien, das Ministry of Cooperatives, Labour and Social Welfare] und des Disciplinary Forces of the Islamic Republic of Iran (die Polizei), sollen Visa, Aufenthaltsgenehmigungen und Arbeitserlaubnisse ausstellen für ausländische Investoren, Direktoren, Experten und deren unmittelbare Familienangehörige in Bezug auf die vom FIPPA umfassten Investitionen, auf Anfrage der OIETAI zur Bestätigung des Investitionsstatus, in der folgenden Art und Weise:

Das Ministry of Foreign Affairs muss nach Erhalt der Anfrage der OIETAI die Missionen der Islamischen Republik Irans im Ausland ermächtigen, Visa mit einfacher oder mehrfacher Einreise (für drei Jahre) mit dreimonatiger Aufenthaltserlaubnis je Einreise für die betroffenen Personen auszustellen, je nach Art des beantragten Visums.

Die oben genannten Personen, die Visa für Investitionen erhalten haben, können nach der Einreise eine dreijährige Aufenthaltsgenehmigung von der Iranischen Polizei erhalten, nachdem die formale Bestätigung der Investitionen durch die OIETAI vorgelegt wurde. Das Ministry of Labour and Social Affairs soll solchen Personen im Anschluss an die Ausstellung der Aufenthaltsgenehmigung eine Arbeitserlaubnis ausstellen."

Der Erhalt der oben beschriebenen dreijährigen Aufenthaltsgenehmigung befreit die ausländischen Investoren vom Erfordernis, Ein- und Ausreisevisa für die Ein- und Ausreise zu beantragen.

6.2   Erhalt von Arbeitserlaubnissen außerhalb des FIPPA

Sofern ein iranischer Arbeitgeber Bedarf an der technischen Expertise ausländischer Fachkräfte hat, werden auf seinen Antrag hin ein Arbeitsvisum und eine Arbeitserlaubnis für den Ausländer gewährt. Laut der gesetzlichen Vorschriften kann ein Ausländer die Arbeitserlaubnis nicht selbst beantragen, es sei denn er gründet eine eigene Gesellschaft.

Vor Abschluss eines Vertrages mit dem ausländischen Experten soll der iranische Arbeitgeber eine Anfrage beim *Department General for Employment of Foreign Nationals* stellen und die notwendigen Unterlagen einreichen. Die Unterlagen werden dann ans *Technical Board for Employment of Foreign Nationals* weitergeleitet, dessen Zustimmung oder Ablehnung dem Arbeitgeber durch die zuständigen Beamten mitgeteilt wird.

Die Ausstellung, Verlängerung und Erneuerung der Arbeitserlaubnisse für Ausländer erfolgte in der Vergangenheit durch das *Department General for Employment of Foreign Nationals* in Teheran. Um Antragstellern entgegenzukommen, wurden diese Angelegenheiten zum Teil den *Departments General of Cooperatives, Labour and Social Welfare* in den Provinzen übertragen. Arbeitgeber und Ausländer können die Beantragung, Verlängerung und Erneuerung daher nun bei den Provinzämtern durchführen.

6.3   Gültigkeitsdauer von Arbeitserlaubnissen

Die Arbeitserlaubnisse für Ausländer werden für einen Zeitraum von einem Jahr ausgestellt, verlängert oder erneuert.

6.4   Verlängerung von Arbeitserlaubnissen

Sofern der iranische Arbeitgeber die Expertise der ausländischen Fachkräfte bei Ablauf der Arbeitserlaubnis weiterhin benötigt, kann eine Verlängerung der Arbeitserlaubnis beantragt werden. Der Antrag ist an das *Technical Board for Employment* zu richten und bei Genehmigung wird die Arbeitserlaubnis um ein Jahr verlängert.

6.5   Erneuerung von Arbeitserlaubnissen

Sofern der Arbeitsvertrag eines Ausländers aufgehoben oder nichtig ist, muss die Arbeitserlaubnis beim Wechsel des Arbeitgebers erneuert werden. Die Erneuerung der Arbeitserlaubnis „beim Wechsel des Arbeitgebers oder der Art der Arbeit" wird von der zuständigen Abteilung des *Ministry of Cooperatives, Labour and Social Welfare* nach Genehmigung
des *Technical Board for Employment of Foreign Nationals* durchgeführt.

6.6   Strafe für die Beschäftigung von Ausländern ohne
            Arbeitserlaubnis

Arbeitgeber, die Ausländer ohne oder mit abgelaufener Arbeitserlaubnis oder in einem
anderen als dem in der Arbeitserlaubnis ausgewiesenen Bereich beschäftigen oder das
Ministry of Cooperatives, Labour and Social Welfare nicht über die Beendigung eines
Arbeitsverhältnisses informieren, können mit Geld- und Freiheitsstrafen bestraft werden.

6.7   Gebühren

Derzeit kostet die Ausstellung und Erneuerung von Arbeitserlaubnissen für Ausländer
1.400.000 IRR (ca. 40 EUR) und die Verlängerung kostet 1.000.000 IRR (ca. 30 EUR). Ausländer bestimmter Staaten sind von diesen Gebühren ausgenommen, sofern ihr Heimatland ein entsprechendes gegenseitiges Abkommen mit Iran hat.

6.8   Vorteile für ausländische Investoren bei der Beschäftigung von
            Arbeitskräften

Gemäß Art. 80 des *Law on the Fifth Five-Year Development Plan* können Investoren
bestimmte Vergünstigungen und Reduzierungen von Versicherungsbeiträgen in Anspruch
nehmen, wenn sie vom *Ministry of Cooperatives, Labour and Social Welfare* vermittelte
Arbeitskräfte einstellen und ihr Betrieb neu gegründet ist oder sie im letzten Jahr keine
Verringerung der Belegschaft vorgenommen haben.

7.   Recht des geistigen Eigentums im Iran

7.1   Trademarks

In den folgenden Fällen ist ein Trademark nicht registrierungsfähig:

1. Wenn das Trademark nicht geeignet ist, die Waren oder Dienstleistungen eines Unternehmens von denen eines anderen Unternehmens zu unterscheiden
2. Wenn es gegen die Gebote der Scharia, des Ordre Public oder der Moral verstößt
3. Wenn es wahrscheinlich ist, dass es die Öffentlichkeit oder Handelszentren irreführt, insbesondere in Bezug auf die geografische Herkunft der Waren oder Dienstleistungen oder ihrer Natur oder Charakteristika
4. Wenn es identisch mit einem Wappenzeichen, einer Flagge oder einem anderen Emblem, einem Namen oder einer Abkürzung oder die Initialen eines Namens von, oder ein offizielles Zeichen oder Kennzeichen eines Staates, einer zwischen-staatlichen Organisation unter einer internationalen Konvention ist oder eine Imitation derselben oder Elemente derselben enthält, es sei denn es ist von der jeweiligen zuständigen Behörde des Staates oder der Organisation genehmigt
5. Wenn es identisch oder zum Verwechseln ähnlich ist mit oder eine Übersetzung darstellt von einer Marke oder einem Handelsnamen, der im Iran wohlbekannt ist für identische oder ähnliche Waren oder Dienstleistungen eines anderen Unternehmens
6. Wenn eine identische oder ähnliche Marke bereits registriert oder wohlbekannt ist für ähnliche Dienstleistungen, sofern eine übliche Verbindung zwischen der Benutzung der Marke und dem Eigentümer der wohlbekannten Marke besteht und die Registrierung wahrscheinlich die Interessen des Eigentümers der wohlbe-kannten Marke schädigt
7. Wenn es identisch ist mit einer im Namen eines anderen Inhabers registrierten Marke, die früher beantragt oder mit einem Prioritätsrecht belegt ist in Bezug auf die gleichen Waren und Dienstleistungen oder für Waren und Dienstleistungen, die wegen Verbindung oder Ähnlichkeit wahrscheinlich zu Verwirrung oder Ver-wechslung führen

7.1.2   Erforderliche Dokumente für die Registrierung eines Trademark

Die erforderlichen Dokumente für die Registrierung eines Trademark sind für natürliche und juristische Personen dieselben. Der einzige Unterschied besteht in der Registrierungs-gebühr. Die Trademarkregistrierung erfordert eine Erklärung gegenüber der Registerbe-hörde mit dem folgenden Inhalt:

1. Die Registrierungserklärung soll in zweifacher Kopie und in einem besonderen Formular (E-1) erfolgen in persischer Sprache und vom Antragsteller oder Vertre-ter mit Datum unterzeichnet werden.
2. Sofern Nachweise oder andere zugehörige Dokumente in einer anderen als der persischen Sprache verfasst sind, so sind zwingend die Originaldokumente

zusammen mit einer inoffiziellen Übersetzung einzureichen. Sofern erforderlich, kann die Registerbehörde eine offizielle Übersetzung verlangen, während sie den Antrag bearbeitet.

3. Der Antrag soll die folgenden Punkte enthalten:
   a) Name, Landeskennnummer, Adresse und Postleitzahl und Nationalität des Antragstellers. Sofern der Antragsteller eine juristische Person ist, müssen zudem die Art der Aktivität, der Sitz, Registrierungsort und -nummer, Nationalität, Hauptsitz und, sofern erforderlich, andere Identifikationsnummern angegeben werden.
   b) Name, Landeskennnummer, Adresse und Postleitzahl des gesetzlichen Vertreters des Antragsteller, sofern vorhanden
   c) Name, Wohnsitz und Postleitzahl der Person(en) im Iran, die zur Entgegennahme von Mitteilungen befugt ist/sind, sofern der Antragstellers nicht im Iran ansässig ist
   d) Anbringen eines Musters der Marke an der vorgesehen Stelle
   e) Beschreibung und Erläuterung der Komponenten der Marke und Erläuterung von Buchstaben oder Zeichen, sofern die Marke Sonderbuchstaben oder -zeichen beinhaltet
   f) Angabe der Waren und Dienstleistungen, für die die Marke benutzt wird unter Angabe der beantragten Klasse(n) gemäß internationaler Klassifizierung
   g) Angabe, ob Prioritätsrecht beantragt wird
   h) Geschäftsfeld des Markeninhabers
   i) Angabe, ob Kollektivmarke beantragt wird
   j) Sofern die Marke nicht-persische Schrift enthält, Transkription und Übersetzung
   k) Angabe der Farbe, sofern die Marke eine spezifische Farbe hat
   l) Angabe, ob Marke dreidimensional registriert werden soll
   m) Angabe von Anhängen

   Hinweis 1: Sofern die Erklärung und begleitenden Dokumente von einer juristischen Person eingereicht werden, sollen sie von einem autorisierten Vertreter unterschrieben werden.
   Hinweis 2: Im Falle von mehreren Antragstellern soll eine Person als Bevollmächtigter unter Angabe des Wohnsitzes benannt werden, um die Registerbehörde zu kontaktieren und andere Formalitäten abzuwickeln, außer für die Entgegennahme des Trademarkzertifikats.
   Hinweis 3: Name und Adresse eines ausländischen Antragstellers sollen neben persischer auch in lateinischer Schrift angegeben werden und sollen ebenso registriert und veröffentlicht werden.
   Hinweis 4: Bei der Registrierung und Veröffentlichung der Marke untersucht die Registerbehörde die Klassifizierung der Waren und Dienstleistungen auf der Grundlage internationaler Klassifizierung. Sofern die Marke Bilder enthält, muss die Registerbehörde deren Klassifizierung zwingend untersuchen.

4. Für die Registrierung jeder Marke soll eine getrennte Erklärung abgegeben werden. Eine gemeinsame Erklärung ist zulässig für die Registrierung einer Marke für Waren und Dienstleistungen in einer oder mehrerer Klassen.

5. Wird gleichzeitig die Registrierung mehrerer Marken beantragt, soll im Einklang mit dieser Regulierung eine getrennte Erklärung für jede Marke abgegeben werden. Falls die Antragstellung durch einen Vertreter erfolgt, sollen die originalen Vertretungsunterlagen einer der Erklärungen beigefügt werden und einfache Kopien bei den anderen Erklärungen.

6. Die folgenden Dokumente sollen der Erklärung beigefügt werden:
   a) Original der Vertretungsurkunde, sofern der Antrag durch einen Vertreter erfolgt
   b) Präsentation von 10 Mustern der Marke in grafischer Darstellung, die der der Erklärung beigefügten Marke entspricht und eine maximale Größe von 10 x 10 cm hat. Wenn die Präsentation der Marke nicht grafisch ist, wird die Marke in derselben Größe und im Ermessen der Registerbehörde vorgelegt.
   c) Sofern die Marke dreidimensional ist, ist es erforderlich, die Marke als grafisches Muster oder zweidimensionales Bild auf Papier in der Weise zu präsentieren, dass es aus sechs verschiedenen Winkeln gezeigt werden kann, sowie ein Muster, das die dreidimensionale Form zeigt.
   d) Sofern ein Prioritätsrecht beantragt wird, sollen die entsprechenden Unterlagen zeitgleich mit Antragstellung eingereicht werden oder innerhalb von 15 Tagen danach.
   e) Vorlage von Dokumenten, die die Geschäftsaktivität in der entsprechenden Branche darstellen, im Ermessen der Registerbehörde
   f) Dokumente zur Identifizierung des Antragstellers
   g) Beleg über Zahlung der Registergebühren

7. Die Trademarkregistrierung erfolgt in den folgenden Schritten:
   a) Sammeln erforderlicher Informationen
   b) Ausfüllen des Antragsformulars (Erklärung)
   c) Prüfung des Antrags und der Begleitdokumente: In dieser Phase werden Angestellte der Registerbehörde die Erklärung und Anhänge prüfen und eine der folgenden Entscheidungen treffen:
      (i) Sofern sie einen Fehler in den Unterlagen finden, wird ein Korrekturhinweis ausgestellt und der Antragsteller hat den Fehler innerhalb der gesetzten Frist zu beheben.
      (ii) Sofern der Antrag abgelehnt wird, wird ein Ablehnungsbescheid ausgestellt.
      (iii) Annahme des Antrags
   d) Veröffentlichung des Antrags: Wenn der Antrag angenommen wird, fordert die Registerbehörde den Antragsteller zur Veröffentlichung des Antrags in der offiziellen Gazette auf.
   e) Beantragung der Registrierungsnummer: Einen Monat, nachdem der Antrag veröffentlicht wurde, kann der Antragsteller die Registrierungsnummer beantragen, indem er der Registerbehörde ein Foto des in der offiziellen Gazette veröffentlichten

Antrags vorlegt und die Registergebühr bezahlt. Die offizielle Registrierung des Trademark muss ebenfalls veröffentlicht werden.

f) Beantragung des Registrierungszertifikats: Einen Monat nach der offiziellen Registrierung des Trademark kann der Antragsteller das Registrierungszertifikat beantragen.

7.1.3   Irans Mitgliedschaft in internationalen Trademark-Konventionen

7.1.3.1   Pariser Konvention zum Schutz geistigen Eigentums (1883)

Iran ist seit 1998 Mitglied der Pariser Konvention zum Schutz geistigen Eigentums.

7.1.3.2   Madrid Abkommen (1891) und Protokoll zum Madrid Abkommen (1989) bezüglich der internationalen Registrierung von Marken

Am 25. September 2003 ist Iran dem Madrid Abkommen sowie dem Madrid Protokoll zur internationalen Registrierung von Marken der *World Intellectual Property Organization* („WIPO") beigetreten. Das Madrid Abkommen und das Madrid Protokoll traten im Iran am 25. Dezember 2003 in Kraft.

7.2   Patente

Art. 1 des *Patents, Industrial Designs and Trademarks Registration Act (2008)* besagt:
  „*Eine Erfindung ist das Ergebnis der Gedanken eines oder mehrerer Individuen, das ein bestimmtes Produkt oder einen Prozess zum ersten Mal hervorbringt und eine Lösung für ein bestimmtes Problem schafft in einem bestimmten Bereich der Spezialisierung, Technik, Technologie, Industrie o.ä.*"

Ein Patent ist im Wesentlichen das von der Regierung verliehene ausschließliche Recht einer Person zur Herstellung, Nutzung und Verkauf ihrer neuen und nützlichen Entdeckung, Design, Prozess, Maschine, Herstellung, oder anderer Zusammensetzung, oder jegliche neue und nützliche Verbesserung derselben.

Die Beantragung eines Patents ist nicht zwingend. Die Erlangung eines Patents gibt dem Eigentümer (Patenthalter) jedoch das Recht und die Sicherheit, andere rechtlich von der Ausnutzung der patentierten Erfindung oder Entdeckung ohne seine Zustimmung auszuschließen.

7.2.1   Arten patentierbarer Entdeckungen und Erfindungen

Gemäß Art. 2 des *Patents, Industrial Designs and Trademarks Registration Act (2008)* gilt:
  „*Eine Erfindung ist patentierbar, wenn sie eine neue Innovation beinhaltet und industriell anwendbar ist. Eine Innovation beinhaltet alles, was zuvor auf einem Gebiet nicht bekannt war und für eine Person mit gewöhnlichem Wissen auf diesem Gebiet nicht offensichtlich ist. Eine Erfindung gilt als industriell anwendbar, wenn sie in einem gegebenen Industriebereich hergestellt und genutzt werden kann. Der Begriff Industrie ist weit auszulegen und beinhaltet Handwerk, Landwirtschaft, Fischerei sowie Dienstleistungen.*"

7.2.2 Nicht-patentierbare Entdeckungen und Erfindungen

Art. 4 des *Patents, Industrial Designs and Trademarks Registration Act (2008)* regelt das Folgende:

> „Die Folgenden sollen nicht vom Patentschutz umfasst sein:

1. *Entdeckungen, wissenschaftliche Theorien, mathematische Methoden und Kunstwerke*
2. *Schemata, Regeln oder Methoden der Geschäftswelt oder zur Ausübung geistiger oder sozialer Akte*
3. *Methoden zur Behandlung oder Diagnose von menschlichen oder tierischen Krankheiten: Diese Unterkategorie beinhaltet nicht Produkte, die unter die Definition eines Patents fallen oder in den genannten Methoden genutzt werden.*
4. *Genetische Ressourcen und genetische Komponenten derselben, sowie biologische Prozesse zur Herstellung derselben*
5. *Jegliches bereits in der jeweiligen Industrie und Technik Vorhergesehene"*

7.2.3 Erforderliche Dokumente zur Registrierung einer Erfindung oder Entdeckung im Iran

Der Erfinder oder Entdecker muss einen schriftlichen Antrag beim *Tehran Office for Industrial Property* (Patentamt) stellen und, zusammen mit der erforderlichen Gebühr, eine Erklärung mit folgendem Inhalt einreichen:

1. Die Patenterklärung soll in dreifacher Ausfertigung und in einem speziellen Formular (A-1) in persischer Sprache erfolgen und vom Antragsteller oder seinem Vertreter mit Datum versehen und unterschrieben werden.
2. Sofern beigefügte Urkunden oder andere Dokumente in einer anderen als der persischen Sprache eingereicht werden, müssen die Originale zusammen mit einer inoffiziellen Übersetzung vorgelegt werden. Falls eine perfekte Übersetzung dieser Unterlagen nicht möglich ist, kann eine Zusammenfassung in persischer Sprache vorgelegt werden. Falls erforderlich, kann die Registerbehörde eine offizielle Übersetzung der Dokumente verlangen, während die Erklärung begutachtet wird. Falls die technischen und wissenschaftlichen Termini der Dokumente kein persisches Äquivalent haben, können sie in der Originalsprache widergegeben werden.
3. Der Antragsteller soll die Patenterklärung bei der Registerbehörde persönlich oder per Einschreiben oder auf Grundlage von Art. 167 dieses Gesetzes einreichen. Das Absendedatum oder das Datum der Einreichung soll als Datum der Erklärung gelten.
4. Die Patenterklärung soll die folgenden Punkte beinhalten:
   a) Name, Landeskennnummer, Adresse, Postleitzahl, Nationalität und Position des Antragsteller, und falls der Antragsteller eine juristische Person ist, soll zusätzlich der Name, Geschäftsfeld, Sitz, Registrierungsort und -nummer, Nationalität, Hauptsitz und, falls erforderlich, die Identifikationsnummer angegeben werden.
   b) Name, Landeskennnummer, Adresse und Postleitzahl des Vertreters des Antragstellers, falls vorhanden

c) Name, Wohnsitz und Postleitzahl der Person im Iran, die zur Entgegennahme von Mitteilungen für den Antragsteller befugt ist, falls der Antragsteller nicht im Iran ansässig ist

d) Name, Adresse und Position des Erfinders, falls der Antragsteller nicht selbst der Erfinder ist

e) Titel der Erfindung, der den Anspruch beschreibt und keine Worte wie »besser" etc. enthält. Der Titel sollte zwischen drei und zehn Wörter haben.

f) Datum, Ort und Nummer der Erklärung oder des ausländischen Erfindungszertifikats, sofern Prioritätsrecht beantragt wird

g) Information bezüglich der ursprünglichen Erklärung, falls die Erfindung eine Weiterentwicklung ist

h) Seitenanzahl der Beschreibung, des Anspruchs und kurze Erklärung der Erfindung und des Plans

i) Bestimmung der Erfindungsklasse auf Grundlage der internationalen Klassifizierung für Erfindungen

j) Benennung von Anhängen

k) Falls Anhänge und dazugehörige Unterlagen von einer juristischen Person eingereicht werden, sollen diese vom autorisierten Vertreter unterschrieben werden.

l) Name und Adresse des Antragstellers sollen sowohl in persischer als auch in lateinischer Schrift angegeben, registriert und veröffentlicht werden.

5. Die folgenden Unterlagen sollen der Erklärung beigefügt werden:

a) Detaillierte Beschreibung der Erfindung

b) Anspruch der Erfindung

c) Kurzbeschreibung der Erfindung

d) Design(s), falls erforderlich

e) Nachweise zur Bestätigung der Identität von Antragsteller und Erfinder

f) Schriftlicher Antrag auf Nichtnennung des Namens des Erfinders, falls dieser seinen Namen nicht nennen möchte

g) Dokumente bezüglich des Prioritätsrechts sollen zusammen mit der Einreichung der Erklärung oder innerhalb von 15 Tagen danach vorgelegt werden.

h) Beleg über Zahlung der Gebühren

i) Vertretungsurkunde, falls ein Vertreter den Antrag stellt

Hinweis 1: Falls die Erklärung bei Einreichung nicht den Anforderungen von Art. 11 entspricht, gibt die Registerbehörde dem Antragsteller eine 30-tägige Frist, die notwendigen Korrekturen vorzunehmen, und das Datum der Erklärung soll das Datum sein, an dem die erforderlichen Korrekturen eingereicht wurden. Falls die Berichtigungen nicht rechtzeitig vorgenommen werden, ist die Erklärung nichtig. Für im Ausland ansässige Personen beträgt die Frist 60 Tage.

Hinweis 2: Falls die Erklärung auf Designs Bezug nimmt, die nicht beigefügt sind, gibt die Registerbehörde dem Antragsteller eine 30-tägige Frist, diese nachzureichen. Bei Einreichung der Designs wird dann das Datum der

Einreichung als Antragdatum gewertet. Anderenfalls wird das Datum der ursprünglichen Antragstellung festgehalten und die Registerbehörde wird die Bezugnahme auf die nicht eingereichten Designs nicht beachten. Für im Ausland ansässige Personen beträgt die Frist 60 Tage.

j) Jede Seite der Beschreibung, des Anspruchs, der Kurzbeschreibung und des Erfindungsdesigns sollen vom Antragsteller oder seinem Vertreter unterschrieben werden.

k) Die Erklärung soll lediglich eine Erfindung oder eine Gruppe verbundener Erfindungen, denen eine allgemeine Erfindung zugrunde liegt, enthalten. Anderenfalls soll der Antragsteller seine Erklärung in zwei oder mehr selbständige Erklärungen aufteilen.

6. Nach Erhalt der Erklärung und der zugehörigen Anhänge wird die Registerbehörde die Unterlagen innerhalb von 6 Monaten begutachten hinsichtlich ihrer Konformität mit den Verfahrens- und inhaltlichen Vorschriften dieses Gesetzes

Hinweis 1:   Die Registerbehörde wird die betroffene private oder staatliche Stelle oder Spezialisten und Experten befragen und um ihre Meinung bitten hinsichtlich der inhaltlichen Anforderungen der Erfindung. Die Stellungnahmen sollen innerhalb von 3 Monaten abgegeben werden.

Hinweis 2:   Die Erklärung der betroffenen Stellen oder Personen ist lediglich beratend und falls keine Stellungnahme eingeht, wird die Registerbehörde trotzdem entscheiden.

Hinweis 3:   Die Bitte um Stellungnahme der betroffenen Stellen und Personen kann auf der Grundlage entsprechender Verträge erfolgen.

7. Falls nach Untersuchung der Erklärung und der Anhänge Korrekturen notwendig sind, wird die Registerbehörde den Antragsteller auffordern, die entsprechenden Korrekturen innerhalb von 30 Tagen vorzunehmen. Anderenfalls ist die Erklärung nichtig. Für im Ausland ansässige Personen beträgt diese Frist 60 Tage. Die Registerbehörde wird dem Antragsteller innerhalb von 30 Tagen Bescheid geben, ob das Patentzertifikat gewährt wird. Der Antragsteller soll die Erfindung sodann registrieren und veröffentlichen und die entsprechenden Gebühren entrichten. Falls die Gebühren nicht rechtzeitig bezahlt werden, ist die Erklärung nichtig.

8. Die Erfindung wird im Patentregister registriert gemäß der folgenden in Formular A-2 vorzulegenden Informationen:

a) Nummer und Datum der Erklärung unter Angabe von Stunde, Tag, Monat und Jahr

b) Nummer und Datum des Patents

c) Name, Adresse und Nationalität des Erfinders

d) Name, Adresse und Nationalität des Antragsteller falls dieser nicht der Erfinder ist, es sei denn, der Erfinder hat schriftlich beantragt, seinen Namen nicht im Patentzertifikat zu nennen

e) Name und Adresse des Vertreters des Erfinders, falls das Patent durch ihn beantragt wurde

    f) Titel der Erfindung

    g) Internationale Klassifizierung der Erfindung unter Angabe des wissenschaftlichen Bereichs, dem die Erfindung zuzuordnen ist

    h) Falls Prioritätsrecht beansprucht und akzeptiert wurde, Datum, Nummer und Ort der Einreichung der vorangegangenen Erklärung

    i) Schutzdauer

Hinweis 1:   Jeder Erfindung werden im Patentregister zwei Seiten zugeordnet, auf denen alle Änderungen, Korrekturen sowie teilweisen oder vollständigen Übertragungen der Erfindung festgehalten werden.

Hinweis 2:   Die genannten Eintragungen sollen vom Erfinder oder dessen Vertreter sowie vom Leiter des Patentamtes unterschreiben werden.

9. Nach der Registrierung wird diese innerhalb von 30 Tagen in der offiziellen Gazette bekanntgegeben unter Angabe der in Art. 31 dieses Gesetzes genannten Informationen. Die Bekanntmachung wird vom Leiter des Patentamtes unterzeichnet und zur Veröffentlichung an die offizielle Gazette weitergeleitet.

10. Nach der Veröffentlichung der Bekanntmachung und Einreichung von drei Kopien der Veröffentlichung bei der Registerbehörde wird das Patentzertifikat ausgestellt und dem Antragsteller oder seinem Vertreter zugestellt. Das Patentzertifikat soll mittels moderner Technologie erstellt werden und eine Kopie der Beschreibung, des Anspruchs, der Kurzbeschreibung und des Designs enthalten und geöst, gestempelt und vom Leiter des Patentamtes unterzeichnet werden. Das Patentzertifikat soll auf Grundlage des Formulars A-3 die folgenden Informationen enthalten:

    a) Nummer und Datum der Erklärung

    b) Nummer und Datum des Patents

    c) Name, Adresse und Nationalität des Erfinders

    d) Name, Adresse und Nationalität des Antragsteller falls dieser nicht der Erfinder ist, es sei denn, der Erfinder hat schriftlich beantragt, seinen Namen nicht im Patentzertifikat zu nennen

    e) Titel der Erfindung

    f) Internationale Klassifizierung der Erfindung unter Angabe des wissenschaftlichen Bereichs, dem die Erfindung zuzuordnen ist

    g) Falls Prioritätsrecht beansprucht und akzeptiert wurde, Datum, Nummer und Ort der Einreichung der vorangegangenen Erklärung

    h) Schutzdauer

11. Art. 16 des *Patents, Industrial Designs and Trademarks Registration Act (2008)* regelt das Folgende:

„Die Gültigkeitsdauer des Patentzertifikats beträgt 20 Jahre ab dem Datum der Einreichung der Erklärung. Um die Gültigkeit des Zertifikats aufrechtzuerhalten, müssen jährliche Kosten gemäß der Kostentabelle spätestens 2 Monate vor Ablauf des jeweiligen Jahres gezahlt werden. Anderenfalls ist das Patent nichtig."

7.2.4 Irans Mitgliedschaft in internationalen Patent Konventionen

7.2.4.1 Pariser Konvention zum Schutz geistigen Eigentums (1883)

Iran ist seit 1998 Mitglied der Pariser Konvention zum Schutz geistigen Eigentums. Die Mitglieder dieser Konvention gewähren den Staatsangehörigen der jeweiligen Mitgliedstaaten dieselben Patent- und Trademarkrechte wie ihren eigenen Staatsangehörigen. Das Prioritätsrecht ist einer der wesentlichen Vorteile der Pariser Konvention. Es gibt einer Person, die in einem Mitgliedstaat ein Patent beantragt hat, das Recht, innerhalb eines Jahres den Schutz des Patentes auch in den anderen Mitgliedsstaaten zu beantragen.

Diese nachfolgenden Anträge sollen so behandelt werden, als wären sie am Tag des ursprünglichen Antrags eingereicht worden. Diese Vorschrift ist ein bedeutender Vorteil für Ausländer, die ihre Patente in einer Vielzahl von Staaten, einschließlich Iran, registrieren und schützen möchten.

7.2.4.2 Patent Kooperationsabkommen (1970)

Am 4. Juli 2013 hat die Islamische Republik Iran ihre Ratifizierungsurkunde zum Patent Kooperationsabkommen hinterlegt und ist somit der 148. Mitgliedsstaat geworden. Das Abkommen trat am 4. Oktober 2013 im Iran in Kraft. Dadurch genießt jeder Antrag, der seitdem gestellt wird, auch im Iran Patentschutz.

Zudem bedeutet dies, dass Iran aufgrund seiner Bindung an Kapitel II des Abkommens automatisch zu jeder Voruntersuchung eines internationalen Antrags hinzu geladen wird. Zudem können Staatsangehörige und Ansässige der Islamischen Republik Irans internationale Anträge unter dem Abkommen stellen.

8.   Anhang

Tabelle 8.1: Wichtige iranische Webseiten

Ministry of Finance & Economy	www.mefa.gov.ir
Ministry of Industry & Mines	www.min.gov.ir
Ministry of Commerce	www.iranministryofcommerce.com
Iran Chamber of Commerce & Mines	www.iccim.org
Duties Islamic Republic	www.irica.gov.ir
Ministry of Foreign Affairs	www.mfa.gov.ir
Ministry of Oil	www.nioc.com
Ministry of Labour	www.irimlsa.ir
Organization of Managing & Planning	www.mpzog.ir
Value Added Tax Organization	www.vat.ir
Iranian Association of Certified Accountants	www.iacpa.ir
Tehran Stock Exchange Organization	www.tse.or.ir
Central Bank of Iran	www.cbi.ir
State Tax Organization	www.intamedia.ir
Iranian Privatization Organization	www.ipo.ir
Organization for Investment Economic & Technical Assistance of Iran (OIETAI)	www.investiniran.ir
Iran Foreign Investment Co.(IFIC)	www.ific.org.ir
Audit Organization	www.audit.org.ir
Electronic Visa for Iran	wvisa.mfa.gov.ir

Rechtsbelehrung

Beim Verfassen dieses Handbuch wurde mit viel Aufwand versucht, aktuelle, korrekte und klar verständliche Informationen bereitzustellen. Nichtsdestotrotz soll die Information dieses Beitrags lediglich ein allgemeiner und rechtlicher Leitfaden sein. Die Autoren sind weder verantwortlich für auf der Grundlage dieses Leitfadens vorgenommene Handlungen noch für Fehler und Unvollständigkeiten. Die Autoren möchten mit dieser Publikation keine rechtliche oder finanzielle Beratung geben. Leser sollten professionelle Beratung in Anspruch nehmen, bevor sie irgendwelche Entscheidungen treffen.

Stichwortverzeichnis

Investment in Iran

A Practical Guidebook for the post-sanction era
in German, English and Farsi

© Springer Fachmedien Wiesbaden 2017
E. Karimian, M. S. Jaberi, S. Soltani, M. Lorenz,
Investment im Iran | Investment in Iran | سرمایه‌گذاری در ایران
DOI 10.1007/978-3-658-14433-3_2

Table of Contents

List of Abbreviations

ADR	Alternative Dispute Resolution
GDP	Gross Domestic Product
BOT/BOOT	Build-Operate-Transfer / Build-Own-Operate-Transfer
CIS	Commonwealth of Independent States
DTA	Double Taxation Agreement
EPC	Engineering, Procurement and Construction
ESCWA	Economic and Social Commission for Western Asia
FEAS	Federation of Euro-Asian Stock Exchanges
FIPPA	Foreign Investment Promotion and Protection Act
GMT	Greenwich Mean Time (time zone)
ICGN	International Corporate Governance Network
INTA	Iranian National Tax Administration
IOR/EOR	Improved Oil Recovery / Enhanced Oil Recovery
IPC	Iran Petroleum Contract
IRR	Iranian Rial (currency of Iran)
JVC	Joint Venture Company
LAPFI	Law on the Attraction and Protection of Foreign Investment
MENA	Middle East and North Africa Region
OIC	Organisation of Islamic Cooperation
OIETAI	Organisation for Investment, Economic and Technical Assistance of Iran
OTC	Over-the-Counter
PPP	Purchasing Power Parity
SAARC	South Asian Association for Regional Cooperation
SSF	Single Stock Features
TSE	Tehran Stock Exchange
UNECE	United Nations Economic Commission for Europe
VAT	Value Added Tax
VATA	Value Added Tax Act of Iran
WFE	World Federation of Exchanges
WIPO	World Intellectual Property Organization

1. Introduction

1.1 Geographical Location and Population

The Islamic Republic of Iran with an area of 164,819.6 sq.km and nearly 81 million people is located in South West Asia. The country neighbors with Turkey and Iraq in the West, Afghanistan and Pakistan in the East, Armenia, Azerbaijan, Russia, Kazakhstan and Turkmenistan in the North and Kuwait, Saudi Arabia, Qatar, Bahrain, the United Arab Emirates and Oman in the South through the Persian Gulf and the Oman Sea.

Therefore, Iran is a strategic country with common borders; with states of ESCWA in the South and West, SAARC in the East and CIS as well as UNECE in the North. Iran has long been of geostrategic importance because of its central location in Eurasia and Western Asia, and its proximity to the Strait of Hormuz.

The country is regarded as one of the richest countries in hydrocarbon reserves, so that it ranks second in the world for gas reserve and its export, as well as, second for exporting crude oil. According to the reports of international institutions, like the World Bank, the Islamic Republic of Iran has a GDP of approx. US$ 425 billion and scores eighteenth with regards to purchasing power parity (PPP). The domestic market of more than 80 million inhabitants and planned large-scale government spending will further increase this share.

1.2   Economic Environment

Based on a World Bank Survey, Iran is the second largest economy in the Middle East and North Africa (MENA) region after Saudi Arabia, with an estimated GDP of US$ 425 billion in 2014. Iran's economy is characterized by a large hydrocarbon sector, small scale agriculture and services sectors, and a noticeable state presence in manufacturing and financial services. Iran ranks second in the world in natural gas reserves and fourth in proven crude oil reserves. Aggregate GDP and government revenues still depend to a large extent on oil revenues and are therefore intrinsically volatile.

Petroleum and natural gas are two of the predominant natural resources in Iran which encourage investment and trade. Iran has continued to grow to become one of the largest economies in Asia and specifically in the Middle East. The country offers endless investment opportunities to local and international investors and attracts trade due to a number of free zones located throughout the country which offer lucrative incentives. Currently, there are over 20 free zones and special economic zones in Iran which offer differing benefits throughout the region allowing investors to choose the favorable option for their needs.

1.3. Investment and Business Opportunities

At a Glance:
– The diversified economy and broad industrial base with over 40 industries directly involved in the Tehran Stock Exchange is the core market in the MENA region.
– Resource-rich economy
– Young and educated population
– Large domestic market
– The Middle East market is a prime market opportunity for Iran's non-oil exports.
– An increasingly sophisticated infrastructure and human capital base provides the foundation for an emerging knowledge-based economy.

Since 2006, the U.S. government has imposed sanctions against Iran and doing business with Iran. This has led foreign companies to withdraw from major projects (e.g. the South Pars / North Dome Gas Condensate field development) or to delay further investment and foreign finance has mostly become unavailable. Iran has turned more to its own resources preferring Iranian investors and engineering companies and to moot the establishment of a Pars Investment Fund for the sale of US$ 3.5 billion of participation bonds to fund the South Pars / North Dome developments.

As you may know, international sanctions against Iran are being gradually revoked which provides a good opportunity for many business entities to start or resume their activities in Iran. Considering this, it is highly recommended that international companies should take into account these changes and use this opportunity to make investments.

The law on foreign investment in Iran under the name of "Foreign Investment Promotion and Protection Act" (FIPPA) was ratified by the parliament in 2002. Some specific enhancements introduced by the FIPPA for foreign investment in Iran can be outlined as follows:

1. Broader fields for involvement by foreign investors including major infrastructure;
2. Broader definition given to foreign investment, covering all types of investments from FDI to different types of project financing methods including: Joint Venture, buy-back arrangements, counter trade and various BOT schemes;
3. Streamlined and fast tracked investment licensing application and approval process;
4. Creation of a one stop shop called the "Center for Foreign Investment Services" at the organization for investment; for focused and efficient support of foreign investment undertakings in Iran;
5. More flexibility and facilitated regulatory practices for better access by foreign investors for foreign exchange and capital transfer purposes;
6. Any foreign investor who registers his investment in Iran through the FIPPA has the right to export the capital and dividends according to the articles 12, 13, 14 and 15 of the FIPPA:

    Article 12: "The rate of conversion of foreign exchange applicable at the time of importation or repatriation of Foreign Capital as well as the exchange rate for all foreign exchange transfers, in case of applicability of a unified exchange rate, shall be the same rate prevailing in the country's official network; otherwise, the applicable exchange rate shall be the free market rate as acknowledged by the Central Bank of the Islamic Republic of Iran."

There are many options open to international companies seeking to establish a business in Iran. Apart from forming a trading relationship through commercial agencies, for many companies there are distinct advantages in having an on-the-spot presence. This makes it easier to research market prospects, make contacts, liaise with customers and see through the details of any transactions.

Having a presence is also important in the context of the commercial culture of the Middle East. Business owners and people in the region prefer to deal with someone they know and trust by building a personal relationship. Another regional factor that adds to the importance of having a physical presence is that the buying patterns of some countries served by Iran are unpredictable, creating a need for first-hand market intelligence and information.

1.4   Political System

Iran is a constitutional Islamic Republic, whose political system is laid out in the 1979 constitution called Qanun-e Asasi, Basic Law. Iran's makeup has several governing bodies, some of which are democratically elected and some of which operate by co-opting people based on their religious inclinations.

Its unique political system combines elements of a parliamentary democracy with a religious theocracy governed by the country's clergy, wherein the Supreme Leader wields significant influence.

The Iranian Constitution affirms the division of power into three branches, namely the Executive, the Legislative and the Judicial branches. These powers are structured within the same framework like in other countries.

Iran is a multicultural nation comprised of numerous ethnic and linguistic groups, where the majority of inhabitants are Shia'ite. The native language of Iran is Persian which is widely spoken by the local community. English is the second language of Iran.

1.5   Currency

The Iranian Rial is the currency of Iran (IRR, ﷼). The most common currency exchange is IRR to US$ and vice versa.

1.6   Business Hours / Time Zone

The working week in Iran is Saturday to Thursday with Friday being the national weekend. Ministries are closed on Thursday. Normal working hours for government offices are 8am to 2pm. Generally, banking hours are Saturday to Wednesday, 7.30am to 1.30pm. Thursday working hours are 7.30am to 12.30pm. Shops and bazaars are open 8.30am to 8.30pm, except on Friday.

The time zone is +3.5   hours GMT which allows Iran to continue to respond to international business needs throughout the world.

1.7   Iranian Public Holidays 2016

Date	Occasion
20 – 23 March	Nowruz (New Year)
31 March – 1 April	Iran National Day – End of Nowruz
21 April	Birthday of Imam Ali
5 May	Eid-e-Mab'ath
22 May	Birthday of Imam Mahdi
4 June	Khordad Uprising
27 June	Martyrdom of Imam Ali
6 July	Eid-e-Fitr
7 July	Eid-e-Fitr
30 July	Martyrdom of Imam Sadeq
12 September	Eid-e-Qorban
20 September	Eid-e-Ghadir
11 October	Tasua
12 October	Ashura
20 November	Arbaeen
28 November	Martyrdom of Imam Hasan and Muhammad (pbuh)
30 November	Martyrdom of Imam Reza
17 December	Birthday of Muhammad and Imam Sadegh (pbuh)

1.8   Country Background at a Glance

Capital	Tehran
Main language	Persian
Main religion	Shia Islam
Currency	ریال Rial (IRR)
Area	1,648,195 sq.km / 636,372 sq.mi
Population	2014 estimate: 80.8 million
International dialing code	+98

2.   Foreign Investment in Iran

After nearly 48 years, the new law on foreign investment in Iran under the name of "Foreign Investment Promotion and Protection Act" (FIPPA) was ratified by the Parliament in 2002. FIPPA replaced the "Law for the Attraction and Protection of Foreign Investment" (LAPFI) which was in effect since 1955. FIPPA's replacement of LAPFI has further enhanced the legal framework and operational environment for foreign investors in Iran.

2.1   Methods of Foreign Investment

According to article 3 of the FIPPA, methods of investment are:
1. Foreign Direct Investment (FDI) – only permitted in the private sector;
2. Foreign investment within the framework of "joint-venture", "buy-back" or "build-operate-transfer (BOT)" schemes where the return of capital and profits accrued is solely emanated from the economic performance of the project in which the investment is made, and such return of capital and profit shall not be dependent upon a guarantee by the government, state-owned companies or banks – permitted in all sectors.

2.1.1   Foreign Direct Investment (FDI)

Foreign direct investment is a kind of cross-border investment in a business enterprise by a natural person or a legal entity based in another country with the aim of achieving long-term profit. In this type of investment, control and management of the enterprise as a whole or in part will often be in the hands of the foreign investor. Based on the FIPPA, foreign direct investment can be attained in the following ways:
1. Through the use of foreign investment in a new Iranian company or by the purchase of an already-established company's shares by the foreign investor.
2. Through contractual arrangements between the parties with or without formation of a company.

Needless to say, foreign direct investment in the private sector will only be allowed in accordance with the procedures prescribed by the FIPPA. Furthermore, it can be construed from article 3 of the FIPPA and related regulations that foreign investment in economic sectors that are monopolized by the government will only be permitted where the return of capital and its profits is solely through the economic activity of the same investment project and does not rely on any guarantee by the government or government companies or banks. In fact, this article outlines the specific criteria for foreign investment in the public and private sectors of Iran's economic system. Under article 44 of the Constitution of the Islamic Republic of Iran,

"The economy of the Islamic Republic of Iran is to consist of three sectors: state, cooperative, and private, and is to be based on systematic and sound planning.

The state sector is to include all large-scale and mother industries, foreign trade, major minerals, banking, insurance, power generation, dams, and large-scale irrigation networks, *radio and television, post, telegraph and telephone services, aviation, shipping, roads, railroads and the like; all these will be publicly owned and administered by the State.*

The cooperative sector is to include cooperative companies and enterprises concerned with production and distribution, in urban and rural areas, in accordance with Islamic criteria.

The private sector consists of those activities concerned with agriculture, animal husbandry, industry, trade, and services that supplement the economic activities of the state and cooperative sectors.

Ownership in each of these three sectors is protected by the laws of the Islamic Republic, in so far as this ownership is in conformity with the other articles of this chapter, does not go beyond the bounds of Islamic law, contributes to the economic growth and progress of the country and does not harm society. The scope of each of these sectors as well as the regulations and conditions governing their operation, will be specified by law."

Based on section "A" of the general policies of Article 44 of the Constitution of the Islamic Republic of Iran,

"Investment in and management and ownership of those sectors that fall under Article 44 are permissible by non-state enterprises and public institutions, and the cooperative and private sectors as described below:

a) *Large-scale industries, mother industries (including large downstream oil and gas industries) and large mines (except oil and gas)*
b) *Foreign trade activities in the framework of trade and foreign currency policies of the country*
c) *Banking operations by non-state enterprises and public institutions, publicly-held cooperatives and joint stock companies, provided maximum shareholding of each shareholder is as determined by law*
d) *Insurance*
e) *Power supply, generation and importation of electricity for domestic consumption and export*
f) *All postal and telecommunication activities, except the main telecommunication grid, assigning of frequencies and main networks of postal exchanges, routing and management of distribution of mails and basic postal services*
g) *Roads and railways*
h) *Aviation (air transport) and shipping (marine transport)*

The optimal share of the State and non-State sectors in the economic activities covered under the preamble of Article 44 will be determined by law by taking into view the sovereignty and independence of the country, social justice and economic development and growth."

Considering the above-mentioned general policies of Article 44, which has been instructed by the Supreme Leader of Iran, the private sector can invest, manage and own economic activities specified in this instruction. As a result, foreign direct investment is allowed in these eight sectors by foreign investors.

2.1.2   Contractual Schemes

Regarding paragraph (b) of article 3 of FIPPA, foreign investment is possible in all sectors within the framework of "joint venture", "buy-back" and "build-operate-transfer (BOT)" schemes. These three schemes are briefly discussed below.

2.1.2.1   Joint Ventures

The term "Joint Venture" is frequently used in the field of foreign investment, as this contractual framework is employed by investors in many legal systems for investment. The joint venture model, as a favorable contract which decreases risks and costs of investing, has always been of interest to investors. However, the joint venture is usually subject to the laws and regulations governing the joint venture's place of operation.

Considering the laws and regulations of a host country, the subject matter of the project and its performance requirements, it is sometimes advisable to build a joint venture in the form of a company which has a separate legal personality from its members which is often called a "corporative joint venture". Alternatively, partnering without establishing a company and through concluding a contract can be a safer choice for investment, and is known as "contractual joint venture". A contractual partnership is not for the purpose of investment, but is a method by which foreign investors achieve their investment objectives as specified in their business plan.

In various legal systems, this form of investment has different names such as "joint venture", "partnership", "consortium" and sometimes "shareholders agreement". In some legal systems, these titles differ in some aspects and this is why analyzing them is beyond our brief discussion. In Iran's legal literature, the legal form of partnership is mentioned in the Civil Law (article 501-606), the Commercial Code (companies' section) and also implied in the Interest-Free Banking Regulation (article 18). Article 3 of the FIPPA also states the civil partnership as a method of investing, which can be established in the form of a joint venture.

In the corporative joint venture, partners establish a separate legal entity known as the joint venture company (JVC). Each of the partners possesses a specific percentage of the JVC's shares. In this case, partners are known as shareholders and it is the company which is responsible for the implementation of the project which is the subject of the joint venture. On the other hand, in the contractual joint venture, partners who decided not to establish a company directly implement the investment scheme based on their contract.

2.1.2.2   Iran's Petroleum Contracts

2.1.2.2.1 Buy-back Agreements

The second method of investment which is expressed in article 3 of FIPPA is "buy-back". In recent years, buy-back contracts, as a contractual investment technique, have had a prominent role in Iran's economy. This type of contract is mainly known for its use in the development of discovered oil and gas fields. In addition, buy-back contracts are also usable in other industries.

A buy-back contract is a kind of counter-trade arrangement which is also classified as a hybrid contract. It is often defined as a contract between a purchaser and a vendor in which the vendor agrees to repurchase the property from the purchaser if a certain event occurs within a specified period of time. The buy-back price is usually set out in the agreement. However, the buy-back transaction has acquired a broader meaning under Iranian law. As defined by Article 2 of the Executive Rules approved by the Council of Ministers, a buy-back transaction refers to a deal in which the supplier, wholly or partially, puts the goods and services required for the establishment, expansion, reconstruction, improvement or continued production of manufacturing enterprises of the country at the disposal of the producer.

The price of the said goods and services, after deducting the amount of down payments plus the related costs dispersed on the basis of the concluded contract, is paid to the supplier through the delivery of goods or services of the producer and/or through delivery of other industrial and mineral goods and services produced in Iran. Due to some requirements in Iran's Constitution and Petroleum Act, buy-back contracts are usually employed in the development of oil and gas fields in Iran.

Oil and gas buy-back contracts where the exploration is also under the offered scope of services will be categorized as a "Risk Service Contract" with a special payment procedure. According to this type of contract, the contractor concludes a contract with the host government and utilizes cash and non-cash items of the provided capital in order to develop oil and gas fields. Further, various costs such as contractors' remuneration are defined in such contracts and are secured by selling the produced oil and gas and through a "Long Term Crude Oil Sales Agreement" which is an annex to the buy-back contract.

2.1.2.2.2 Iran Petroleum Contract (IPC)

These days, one of the most important debates in scientific and technical circles is optimizing contractual mechanisms for upstream oil and gas projects in Iran. In February 2014, a seminar was held in Tehran and some provisions of the new oil contracts, which have been prepared by the "Oil Contracts Revision Committee", were unveiled under the title of "Iran Petroleum Contract (IPC)". This type of contract has been prepared to rectify failures and gaps in different generations of buy-back contracts and is the beginning of an evolution in Iran's petroleum contracts. In addition, Iran's Parliament has played a significant role in this evolution by passing a few important laws, especially the 2012 "Act on the Duties and Powers of the Ministry of Petroleum".

The IPC is not a new kind of petroleum contract alongside concession contracts, production sharing contracts, risk service contracts or joint venture. Instead, it is a hybrid contract which contains some features of joint venture contracts (regarding the procedure of implementing petroleum projects) and some traits of production sharing contracts (regarding the cost recovery mechanism).

Based on the IPC, in the exploration stage, contractors and the National Iranian Oil Company establish an "Oil Exploration Operations Company" in which the contractor leads the operation and performs exploration by using his own budget and by taking his own risks. The National Iranian Oil Company is a technical partner who accompanies the contractor without sharing the costs and risks of exploration. If exploration does not lead to the discovery of a commercial field, the contractor's costs incurred in the operation will not be refunded. But if a commercial field is discovered, the contractor's costs will be transferred from the exploration stage to the development stage and those costs will be recovered during the amortization period.

Following the discovery of a commercial field and assessment operation, the project will step into a new stage. In this phase, in order to implement a development project, another company is established which is usually known as "development operation company".

Like the previous stage, the contractor incurs all costs and risks of the development operation while he has the power to lead the operation. Once again, the National Iranian Oil Company is a technical partner who accompanies the contractor without sharing the costs and risks of the development operation. All direct and indirect costs of such an operation incurred by the contractor or the National Iranian Oil Company will be amortized by the allocation of a specific percentage of products to the company.

The next phase is the production operation phase and is more varied than the exploration and development phases. Therefore, either (i) the production operation may be implemented by the National Iranian Oil Company or its affiliated companies along with financial and technical support of the contractor; or (ii) the development company also takes part in the production operation; or (iii) in order to implement and manage the field production operation, a production operations company is established while the development company, which was set up in the previous stage, provides financial and technical support to the production company.

It should be noted that, based on the above-mentioned seminar's panels, the production operations company shall implement **IOR/EOR**[1] and report on them to the development company.

Finally, at the end of a payment period, which according to the conditions of each field is ranging from 15 to 20 years, the petroleum contract is terminated.

The seminar's panels did not determine any specific forms of a company for exploration and development operations; however, the production operation company will be formed as a "non-profit Joint Operating Company".

2.1.2.3 Build, Operate, Transfer Contract (BOT)

According to the FIPPA, another contractual framework for investment is the "Build, Operate, Transfer (BOT) Contract". This method of investment is often used for building infrastructures such as power plants, telecommunications, airports and highways. Nevertheless, it can also be used in recreational projects such as building cable cars. In BOT contracts, a government organization confers the concession of building and operation of

---

[1]   IOR (Improved Oil Recovery) and EOR (Enhanced Oil Recovery) means the implementation of various techniques for increasing the amount of crude oil that can be extracted from an oil field.

a specific project to a private sector contractor, and in return, the private sector contractor is responsible for financing, designing, supplying materials, building, testing and managing the project. During the operation period, the private sector contractor recovers its costs and interest of its investment by selling the project's output. At the end of the operation period, ownership of the facility is transferred to the government organization free of charge.

The BOT contract is a kind of public-private partnership in which the government or a public sector organization decides to build an infrastructure project by partnering with the private sector. Experience has proven that it is much faster and more cost-effective when governments build necessary facilities and infrastructures by partnering with the private sector. Choosing an appropriate company from the private sector (which usually is a consortium) is through a tendering process, after which the state or public sector organization signs a BOT contract with the selected company.

2.1.2.4   Investment in Iran's Construction Projects

With property values exceeding those of similar-sized countries, Iran has seen a recent boom in the real estate market. Encouraged by the country's youthful demographic trends, investors are increasingly putting their faith in real estate, which has stood the test of time as a safe, fixed asset. At the same time, contractors and consultants have spotted opportunities throughout the country in terms of catering to both tourists and local residents seeking modern and convenient new homes. Investors are also eager to invest in these projects, which will satisfy growing demand and guarantee returns for years to come.

Growth is also occurring in the country's infrastructures. Iran's government and public sectors try to build or renovate infrastructures all over the country which provides great opportunities for investors to invest in these projects by setting up public-private partnerships (BOT, BOOT, Joint Venture, etc.). Such projects offer a favorable interest rate for investors' capital. In recent years, the construction industry has been thriving due to an increase in national and international investment to the extent that it is now the largest in the Middle East region.

2.1.2.4.1 Construction Contracts

What forms of contract are used in Iran's construction industry depends on the position of employers (owners). If an employer is a private individual or a legal entity from the private sector, any sorts of contract can be applied between the employer and a contractor. Contracting parties can negotiate almost any type of project delivery mechanism such as Design-Bid-Build, Design and Build, EPC, turnkey etc. On the other hand, if the employer is a government or public organization, there is limited space for negotiations upon choosing a contract form. Government and public sector organizations in Iran are required to utilize pre-designed forms of contracts which have been issued by the government.

2.1.2.4.2 Selection of a Contractor

In the private sector of Iran, employers are able to negotiate with contractors directly so that they can find an appropriate contractor who has technical knowledge and adequate resources to implement the project. However, government institutes are required to use a tendering process in order to choose a contractor for implementing public projects. The Tender's Law of Iran which was passed in 2005 provides in its first article that:

"All three powers of the Islamic Republic of Iran shall follow the stipulations of this Law in organizing a bidding; this includes: ministries, public organizations, institutions, and companies, profitable institutes affiliated to the Government, public financial establishments and banks, public insurance companies ..."

The tendering process in the state and public organizations of Iran is not an open one, but it is subject to a pre-qualification procedure after which bidders are short listed and invited to bid for the project. Based on article 12 of the Tender's Law:

"In pre-qualification of bidders, the following shall be taken into account: (i) Guarantee on quality of services and goods; (ii) Experience and knowledge in the relevant field; (iii) Reputable record; (iv) Work permit or qualification certificates, if necessary; (v) Financial capacity of the bidder for implementation, if necessary."

2.1.2.4.3 Pricing Methods

Contracting parties in the private sector are free to take any kinds of pricing method that they wish. Depending on the conditions of a project's site and other factors, parties can choose one of the pricing methods such as lump sum, cost plus, re-measurement, time charge, estimation etc. However, in the state and the public sector, the employer determines the pricing method which is often known as a "unit price" contract. This kind of contract is based on estimated quantities of items included in the project and their unit prices. The final price of the project is dependent on the quantities needed to carry out the work.

2.1.2.4.4 Dispute Resolution

Similar to the construction industry of many other countries, most of construction contracts in Iran refer to "Alternative Dispute Resolution" (ADR) techniques to solve related disputes. Negotiation and mediation are usually applied to resolve such disputes; even so, contracting parties can agree to resort to arbitration or litigation if their dispute remains unresolved. On the other hand, where the employer is a representative of the state or public sector, a dispute resolution mechanism has already been embedded in the construction contract and it is not open to free negotiation. Although such construction contracts stipulate ADR methods in their pre-designed terms, there are notable differences between practicing ADR methods according to these contracts, and well-known procedures of performing them in other disputes. As a result, it is advisable to seek legal advice before signing construction contracts.

2.1.3   Foreign Portfolio Investment (FPI)

2.1.3.1   Iran's Stock Exchange

The Tehran Stock Exchange (TSE) was established in 1968, and is the primary equities market in Iran. In 2005, the new Capital Market Law of Iran was approved by parliament and in 2006, according to this Law, the TSE was demutualized and established as a joint stock company with over 6,000 shareholders. The TSE enjoys a reputation for having maintained an orderly market and a cost-effective trading capability since its inception. The fully computerized trading system, which was launched in 1994, has helped boost the trading capacity and efficiency of the stock market. In 2007, the TSE moved to a more powerful trading system (powered by Atos Euronext) to meet the high trading volume. TSE has been awarded the quality system certificate of ISO9001 in 2009 and it is also planning to obtain the ISO27001 certification for its IT Security Management System.

The TSE has implemented many reform measures in the past few years in order to bring it in line with international practices, and to better reflect investors' diversified needs. The TSE is set to continue making progress towards liberalization and internationalization. The TSE, with its fully automated trading systems and book entry mechanisms, is known as one of the most active exchanges in the Middle East region. At the end of March 2015, the total market capitalization of the 314 companies listed on the TSE surpassed USD 172 billion. The ratio of total market capitalization to GDP was approximately 60% in 2015. In this year, the total trading value was US$ 180 billion, representing a market turnover rate of 132.5%. The market price/earnings (P/E) ratio of the TSE was 5.4.

In order to enhance the core competitiveness of the TSE and to make faster progress towards liberalization and internationalization, the authorities have also promoted the introduction of new financial products, new financial institutions and implemented many reform measures, such as the listing of Single Stock Futures (SSF), relaxing limitations on foreign investment, streamlining foreign registration procedures, and adjusting various trading systems and mechanisms so that they are more in line with international standards.

2.1.3.2   Foreign Investments in the Tehran Stock Exchange

As with several emerging stock markets, the TSE historically set several limitations on foreign investment. With the growth of Iran's stock market and development of the economy, the stock market authorities have gradually relaxed these limitations on foreign investors. Since April 2010, the process for investment by foreign investors in the stock market has been changed from the 'permit' system to the 'repatriation' system. On 18 April 2010, upon the recommendation of the Ministry of Economic Affairs and Finance, and by virtue of paragraph 3 of article 4 of the Securities Market Law ratified in 2005, the Council of Ministers approved "The Regulations Governing the Foreign Investment in the Exchanges and OTC Markets". This has consequently simplified the application procedures for foreign investment in the TSE.

According to Article 7 of these "Regulations", the restrictions imposed on the possession of shares by non-strategic foreign investors on every exchange or over-the-counter

(OTC) markets are set forth as follows: The number of shares owned by the total foreign investors shall not exceed 20% of the total shares number of the companies listed on the exchange or on the OTC market or 20% of the shares number of any company listed on the exchange or on the OTC market. The number of shares owned by each foreign investor in any company listed on the exchange or on the OTC market shall not exceed 10% of the shares number of such companies.

Based on Article 4, foreigners/foreign entities shall have to submit the required information and documents to the *Securities Exchange Organization* along with an application based on the forms prescribed by the Organization so as to obtain a license for trading in securities on every exchange or OTC market.

2.1.3.3   Buying and Selling Stocks

The following steps should be taken when trading stocks on the TSE:

1. **Choose a stockbroker.** In choosing a broker, you should check if that broker (person or corporation) is a member in good standing at the TSE. A complete listing of the TSE member-brokers can be found in various publications or from the TSE Membership Department. It is important that you trust your broker and that you are satisfied with the services they provide. Brokerage services include market reports, advice regarding the stock selection and timing of purchases and sales, trade executions, on time delivery of important documents – such as confirmation receipts – and other trading-related activities that their clients may require.
2. **Open a brokerage account.** Once the investor has chosen his brokerage firm, a brokerage account has to be opened. This account allows the client to perform stock transactions (buy and sell shares) any time – similar to a bank account which enables you to deposit, transfer and withdraw money. Opening a brokerage account is relatively easy to accomplish and takes no longer than opening a bank account. A specimen signature card needs to be filled out, containing: the name, address (professional and private), telephone number(s), and most importantly, the client's signature. Frequently, bank and professional references have to be submitted. Once an account has been opened, the client may buy or sell immediately according to the trading instructions between the investor and broker. Trading instructions can vary depending on the investor's objective – whether it is short-term or long-term, minimum or maximum value of trades (trading limit), etc. All transactions are handled confidentially and the broker will not reveal to any person the details of any purchases or sales done for his client.
3. **Place your order with your broker.** After opening the account, a trader will be assigned to the investor. A trader is a licensed salesman who is authorized to buy and sell securities at the TSE. The assigned trader will be your contact person for all transactions. He/she will receive your order, most likely by telephone (unless arrangements are made), and will execute the order through the trading terminal connected to the main system of the Exchange. Thus, when placing an order to buy or sell, you have to call your trader and give the details of your order. The trader needs to know the following specifications:

buy or sell order, which stock to buy or sell, the number of shares to buy or sell, and preferably also the bid price (when buying) or asked price (when selling).

4. **Settle your transaction.** Buying and selling transactions are settled by book-entry. This means the ownership of shares and cash is transferred electronically to the brokerage account, without the stock certificates and cash being handed over physically. (Instead, stock certificates are simply immobilized and kept in a safe place – Central Securities Depository of Iran, Inc.) The account is credited when buying shares, and debited in the case of selling shares. The book-entry system is clearly an advantage over the paper-based system. It has dramatically reduced paper work, facilitated the trading and eliminated the loss or forgery of shares.

Currently, the TSE settles trades on T+3, i.e., four days after the transaction date. Therefore, payments and/or securities must be delivered to your broker on trading day. Be sure to always verify the settlement deadline with your broker for future transactions.

2.1.3.4   Global Relationship

TSE had been a full member of WFE (between 1992 to 2010) and also is a member and one of the founders of the Federation of Euro-Asian Stock Exchanges (FEAS) (since 1995) and also a subscriber of the International Corporate Governance Network (ICGN). The TSE is also an active participant of OIC Members' Stock Exchange Forum.

2.1.4   Required Documents for the Issuance of a Foreign Investment License

The following documents are required to apply for a Foreign Investment License:

1. Application Form
2. Establishment License / Primary Agreement / Preliminary agreement of the pertinent Iranian organization
3. Official letter of the foreign investor to be submitted to the Organization for Investment, Economic and Technical Assistance of Iran (OIETAl)
4. The foreign investor's background including a brief history of the company, the year of establishment, area of activities, or (in case the foreign investor is a natural person) a photocopy of their passport and resume
5. A list of machinery, equipment and parts which may be imported into the country as a part of the foreign investor's capital (if available)
6. In the case where a part of the foreign investor's share is in the form of technical know-how, a draft of the contract outlining the conditions of the transfer of technology.
7. Any further useful information.

The primary objective in this process is to find a suitable and "acceptable" local partner. If the contemplated foreign investment project complies with the plan already sanctioned, the Ministry of Economic Affairs and Finance may introduce, to the potentially interested foreign investor, the local partners already holding an "agreement in principle" for taking part in such a project.

A ministerial "agreement in principle" must be applied for again jointly by both the foreign and the local potential investors. Details of the project are to be submitted to the Ministry of Economic Affairs and Finance as per a standard questionnaire, together with a feasibility study. Once the agreement, in principle, is issued, the parties should take the preliminary steps along with implementation of the project, such as importation of the machinery, equipment and setting up the required infrastructure.

An "application for participation" is required to be filed by the foreign investor with the OIETAI to the effect of participation in implementation of the sanctioned project.

Then, the process is followed by a review of the application by the Supervisory Board for Attraction and Protection of Foreign Investment. The Foreign Department of the Ministry of Economic Affairs and Finance, upon preliminary coordination with the Ministries concerned, shall prepare a comprehensive report for submission to the Supervisory Board to adopt the decision. If the project is deemed to be in the country's overall interest, the Supervisory Board conveys its favored decision through the Ministry of Economic Affairs and Finance for approval and issues an Investment Decree. The Decree, once issued, is the formal permission for the investor to begin operation and to import the necessary capital which will be protected under the law.

3.   Iran's Special Economic & Free Trade Zones

The philosophy for the establishment of Free Zones and Special Economic Zones is, as it has been mentioned in respective laws, to provide prosperity, economic development and growth, promotion of investment, active presence in local and international markets, production of industrial goods and services, increase in national income and increase in employment. Such zones have facilitated trade and industrial activities and they have promoted investment benefiting from great reduction in formalities such as: customs, banking and financial systems, insurance and labour laws, foreigner entrance etc.

Free Zones, in comparison to Special Economic Zones, have significant advantages, the most important of which is having an independent organization, the High Council of Free Trade Industrial Zones, which acts as administrator of the zones.

Since the investment promotion has been the main target of the zones, consequently all the existing systems, formal and informal, have the intention to serve and promote industrial activities.

The Islamic Republic of Iran began to implement the first five-year economic plan aimed at the reconstruction and economic recovery in 1989, after the end of the eight-year Iraqi imposed war. The main objective of this plan was to transform the managed economy of the war to an open economy based on market forces and establish and maintain relations with the world economy.

Due to the existing limitation for the application of the market economy and concern for the side effects of such a sharp transformation on the social wellbeing of the society, it was decided to assign some locations and establish free or special economic zones in order to completely apply the principle of a free market economy. This way, enough incentives could be introduced so as to attract foreign investment.

According to the legally accepted definition, the free trade zones and special economic zones are those parts of the Iranian territory that are managed according to the special laws and bylaws and are excluded from the laws of the governing motherland. These zones are excluded from the domain of the customs authorities and enjoy the full freedom of the in- and outflow of goods and commodities. Unique geographical locations, sufficiently developed infrastructure and the foreign investment incentives have provided ample opportunity for internal as well as foreign investment in these zones.

The Iranian Parliament approved the Free Zones Act in September 1993. According to this act, Kish Island, Qeshm Island and the Port of Chabahar were declared as the Free Zones of Iran. The council of ministers later adapted the bylaws of the free zones. These bylaws have defined and set out all regulations pertaining to import, export, investment, insurance, banking, labour and employment in these zones.

3.1   Free Trade Industrial Zones

3.1.1   Incentives and Advantages for Investment in Free Trade Industrial Zones

The following incentives and advantages are granted to investments in the Free Trade Industrial Zones:

1. Tax exemption for 20 years from the date of operation for all economic activities
2. Foreign investment in any amount
3. Freedom of entry and exit of capital and profits
4. Protection and guarantees for foreign investments
5. Abolition of entry visas and easier issue of residence permits for foreigners
6. Facilitated regulation on labour relations, employment and social security
7. Transfer of partly manufactured goods to the mainland without paying customs duties
8. Elimination of customs duties on imports from outside to the region
9. Employing trained and skilled manpower in all different skill levels and professions
10. Utilization of raw materials, oil and gas as feedstock and fuel for all industrial activities.

3.1.2   List of Free Trade Industrial Zones of Iran

1. Qeshm Free Trade Industrial Zone
2. Chabahar Free Trade Industrial Zone
3. Aras Free Trade Industrial Zone
4. Anzali Free Trade Industrial Zone
5. Arvand Free Trade Industrial Zone
6. Kish Free Trade Industrial Zone
7. Maku Free Trade Industrial Zone

3.1.3   Regulations on Investment in Free Trade Industrial Zones

1. Law on the Administration of Free Trade Industrial Zones
2. Law on the Establishment of Free Trade Industrial Zones in Abadan-Khorramshahr, Jolfa and Bandar Anzali
3. Executive Bylaw on Issuance of Visa to Foreign Nationals in the Free Trade Industrial Zones
4. Regulations on Entry and Residence of Foreign Nationals
5. Bylaw on Monetary and Banking Operation in the Free Trade Industrial Zones
6. Executive Guideline for the Monetary and Banking Operations in the Free Trade Industrial Zones
7. Regulations on the Establishment and Operation of Insurance Institutes in the Free Trade Industrial Zones
8. Criteria on Registration of Companies and Property Rights
9. Regulations on Exports, Imports and Customs in the Free Trade Industrial Zones
10. Regulations on the Use of Land and other National Resources in the Free Trade Industrial Zones

11. Permanent Permissibility of Import of Goods Produced in the Free Zones into the Mainland (added to Article 8 of the Bylaw to the Export–Import General Regulations)
12. Bylaw on Special Facilities for Import of Goods Produced in Free Trade Industrial Zones into the Mainland
13. Bylaw on the Manner of Ingress of Raw Materials and Parts from the Free Zones (into the Mainland)
14. Bylaw on the Peculiarly Manufactured or Rebuilt Goods Permissible into the Mainland
15. Regulations on Employment of Work Force, Insurance and Social Security
16. Comparison Table indicating Legal Status on Economic Activities in Iran's Free Trade Industrial Zones and Special Economic Zones
17. Regularities of Automobile Imports into Free Zones

3.2 Special Economic Zones

3.2.1 Incentives and Advantages for Investment in Special Economic Zones

The following incentives and advantages are granted to investments in the Free Trade Industrial Zones:

1. Import of goods from the above mentioned zones into the mainland for domestic consumption will be subordinate to export and import regulations, and export of goods from these areas into other countries will be carried out without any formalities.
2. Import of goods from abroad or other free trade zones or industrial areas will be carried out with minimal customs formalities and internal transit of imported goods will be performed in accordance with the relevant regulations.
3. Log entry of merchandise subject to the laws and regulations of special zones will be done without any customs formalities.
4. Goods imported from outside or industrial areas or other commercial zones can be exported without any formalities.
5. Management of the region is allowed to assign parts of the region to qualified natural or legal persons after classification and valuation.
6. Owners of goods imported to the region can send all or part of their goods for temporary entry into the country after following customs clearance regulations.
7. If the processing of imported goods results in a change of the tariff of goods, the rate of commercial benefit of the goods would be calculated equal to the commercial benefit of raw materials and spare parts of the country.
8. Importers of goods are permitted to hand over, to others, part or all of their products against warehouse receipt, which will be issued by the district administration. In this case the breakdown warehouse receipt holder would be the owner of the goods.
9. The management of each district is authorized to issue certificates of origin for goods per applicant with the approval of the customs authorities.

10. All the goods imported to the region required for production or services are exempted from the general import-export laws. Exports of goods to other parts of the country will be subject to export and import regulations.
11. Based on paragraph (d) of clause (25) of the Law of the Second Economic, Social and Cultural Development Plan of the Islamic Republic of Iran, the ratio of goods produced in the zone and imported to the country (the proportion of total value added and domestic parts and materials used in the total price of the commodity production) is allowed without any limitation. In addition, it is not required to order and open letter of credit.
12. Goods manufactured in special economic zones, as well as raw materials and CKD parts, which are imported into the country, are not subject to price regulation due to un-utilized resources and/or allocated currency.

3.2.2   List of Special Economic Zones of Iran
1.   Salafchegan Special Economic Zone
2.   Shiraz Special Economic Zone
3.   Assaluye Special Economic Zone
4.   Arge Jadid Special Economic Zone
5.   Payam Airport Special Economic Zone
6.   Persian Gulf Special Economic Zone
7.   Lorestan Special Economic Zone
8.   Amirabad Port Special Economic Zone
9.   Bushehr Port Special Economic Zone
10. Shahid Rajaee Port Special Economic Zone
11. Sarakhs Special Economic Zone
12. Sirjan Special Economic Zone
13. Yazd Special Economic Zone
14. Bushehr Special Economic Zone

3.2.3   Regulations on Investment in Special Economic Zones
The Law on the Establishment and Management of Special Economic Zones in the Islamic Republic of Iran

4. Establishing a Legal Presence in Iran

4.1 Incorporating a Local Entity

4.1.1 Joint Stock Company

4.1.1.1 General

The Joint Stock Company is defined, by law, as a company whose capital is divided into shares and the liability of the shareholders is limited to the par value of their shares. The Joint Stock Company may be either a public company (Sherkat Sahami Am) or a private company (Sherkat Sahami Khass). The main difference between the two is that the public company may offer its shares and debt securities to the public while the private company may not.

The shareholders of a joint stock company participate in the ownership, profit and losses, and distribution of assets in liquidation in proportion to the shares held. As indicated above, the liability of each shareholder is limited to the par value of his shares and in the absence of fraud or other deceptive practices, there should be no recourse to shareholders for the liabilities of the company. The company has a separate juridical personality, by law, and can sue or be sued in its own name. The shareholders possess the usual shareholder rights including, in general, the right to attend shareholders meetings, receive financial reports, elect and replace the board of directors, and vote on major decisions of the company.

4.1.1.2 Number of Shareholders

The law specifies that a joint stock company must have a minimum of three shareholders.

4.1.1.3 Nationality of Shareholders

There are no legal restrictions with respect to the nationality of persons who may form joint stock companies. As a matter of policy, however, the Iranian Government generally requires Iranian shareholder participation in fields of activity deemed important to the nation's development programs.

4.1.1.4 Shares

A joint stock company may issue both ordinary and preferred shares in either bearer or registered form. While the law does not specifically state what privileges may be accorded to preferred shares, it is understood that priorities as to dividends and distribution of assets in liquidation, and multiple voting powers will be honored under the law. The principal differences between registered and bearer shares relate to the manner of transfer and tax implications.

4.1.1.5   Management

Management of a joint stock company is the responsibility of the board of directors which must be elected by the cumulative voting of the shareholders at least once every two years.

4.1.1.6   Dissolution and Liquidation

General provisions governing the dissolution and liquidation of a joint stock company are provided in the law and companies are authorized to specify in their Articles of Association any particular provisions they may desire so long as they are not inconsistent with the law. Since the provisions of the law on this subject are general in nature, it is advisable, when drafting Articles of Association, to include procedures for dissolution and liquidation.

4.1.1.7   Other Forms of Business Association in Iran

In addition to the Joint Stock Company, the Iranian Commercial Code provides for the following types of business association:

1. Limited liability company (Sherkat ba Masouliyat Mahdoud)
2. General partnership (Sherkat Tazamoni)
3. Limited partnership (Sherkat Mokhtalet Gheyr Sahami)
4. Mixed joint stock partnership (Sherkat Mokhtalet Sahami)
5. Proportional liability partnership (Sherkat Nesbi)
6. Production and consumption cooperative (Sherkat Ta'avoni Towlid va Masraf)

Of these entities, the limited liability company and the joint stock company provide for a limitation of shareholders' liability to the value of their shares. The principal difference between the two is that with the limited liability company, the capital may not be divided into shares and the participants may not transfer their interests therein without the approval of a majority of the participants representing three-fourth (3/4) of the company capital. In the case of the mixed joint stock partnership, the law provides for both shareholders and unlimited liability partners.

4.1.2   Capital

4.1.2.1   Share Capital

A minimum capital, at time of formation, of IRR 1,000,000 is required for the private Joint Stock Company, and of IRR 5,000,000 for the public Joint Stock Company. Payment for shares may be either in cash or in kind. If payment is made in kind, the value of the property involved must be appraised by an official appraiser of the Ministry of Justice. In the case of payments in cash, only 35% needs to be paid in at the time of formation and the remainder within five years upon the call of the board of directors or shareholders. In the case of payments in kind, the full amount of the property must be transferred to the company at the time of formation. The share capital may be increased at any time by a two-thirds (2/3) vote taken at an extraordinary general meeting of the shareholders. Decrease in the capital may also be effected at any time by a two-thirds (2/3) vote taken at an extraordinary general meeting and there is a legal requirement for the reduction of registered capital whenever half of the company's capital is lost.

4.1.2.2 Subscriptions

Although only 35% of the company's capital needs to be paid in at the time of formation, 100% of the capital must be subscribed. Notwithstanding the 100% subscription requirement, a procedure has been developed in practice for "authorized but un-issued stock", enabling the use of such desirable arrangements as employee stock purchase plans. In general, the procedure involves the holding of an extraordinary general meeting at which the shareholders approve to implement the increase in such amounts and at such times as the board may determine.

4.1.2.3 Par Value

A par value, or nominal value, is required to be assigned to the shares of a joint stock company. For the public Joint Stock Company, the law prescribes a maximum par value of IRR 10,000 per share. There is no minimum or maximum par value fixed for the shares of a private Joint Stock Company. There is a requirement applicable to both the public and private Joint Stock Company that all shares must be of equal par value. Where both ordinary and preferred shares are issued, all must have the same par value. There is also a related requirement that all calls of the unpaid portion of shares must be made without any discrimination. If provision for the issue of fractional shares is made, the par value of each fraction must also be equal.

4.1.2.4 Share Certificates

Specific requirements as to the form and content of share certificates are provided in the law. They must be uniform, printed, and bear a serial number and be signed by at least two authorized persons. Each certificate must contain the following information:

1. Name, style and number of the company under which it is registered at the Companies Registration Office
2. Registered share capital and paid-up portion
3. Type of shares
4. Par value of the shares and paid-up portion both in words and figures
5. Number of shares represented by the certificate

4.1.2.5 Provisional Share Certificates

The law provides that when share certificates have not been issued, the company must issue provisional certificates to the shareholders indicating the number of shares and the amount paid up. The law also provides that until the full par value is paid on bearer shares, the issuance of bearer certificates is prohibited; however, registered certificates may be issued to the subscribers of such shares before the full par value has been paid and in this case the provisions of law regarding the transfer of registered shares will be applicable to such shares.

4.1.2.6   Transfer of Shares

Bearer shares may be transferred by physical delivery while the transfer of registered shares is not complete until the transfer is recorded in the share register of the company. In the case of registered shares, restrictions on transfer may be written into the Articles of Association.

4.1.2.7   Reserves

A legal reserve is to be funded by transfer of 5% of the net profit of a joint stock company each year until the fund reaches 10% of the registered capital. Net profit is defined as income derived during the year less the expenses, depreciation and any transfers to other reserves.

4.1.2.8   Dividends

Dividends must be authorized by the shareholders at a general meeting and may be made only out of "distributed profit" which is defined as the net profit earned during the year (i) less losses incurred during preceding years, (ii) less other optional reserves, (iii) plus distributed profit of the preceding years not previously distributed.

4.1.2.9   Preemptive Rights

Shareholders have the preemptive right to subscribe to new shares. This right may be rescinded, however, by a two third (2/3) vote taken at an extraordinary general meeting.

4.1.3   Formation

4.1.3.1   Articles of Association

The constitutional document of a joint stock company is called the Articles of Association which is roughly equivalent to a combination of the charter and by-laws of a corporation formed in other countries. The subscribing shareholders or founders must approve the Articles of Association and affix their signatures thereto before the company formation may be registered.

4.1.3.2   Payment of Subscriptions

Subscriptions, in the required amount, must be paid into a bank account opened in the name of the company before the company may be formed.[2] A receipt from the bank is required as one of the documents to be filed with the Companies Registration Office when the company is registered.

4.1.3.3   Founders Meeting

A meeting of the subscribing shareholders or founders is required by law for the public company but not for the private company. Even with the private company, however, it is

---

[2]   After the company's name has been confirmed, the Companies Registration Office issues a letter to open a bank account under the company's name.

advisable to hold such a meeting as it remains the simplest means for accomplishing all of the actions required in connection with the company formation. All of the founding shareholders must:

1. Approve and sign the Articles of Association
2. Confirm the required subscriptions and that payments thereon have been made
3. Elect directors and inspectors
4. Receive acceptances of directors and inspectors
5. Designate a general circulation newspaper for publication of the company's legal notices.

4.1.3.4   First Meeting of the Board of Directors

Before a joint stock company may begin doing business, the Board of Directors must hold a meeting to:

1. Elect a Chairman and a Vice Chairman
2. Appoint the Managing Director and specify his duties
3. Approve the form of share certificates and designate the company officers to sign them
4. Designate the officers authorized to sign on behalf of the company
5. In addition, it is advisable in the first meeting of the Board of Directors to designate the bank or banks to serve as depository of the company funds.

4.1.3.5   Registration

4.1.3.5.1 Private Joint Stock Company

In forming a private company, the following documents are required to be filed with the Companies Registration Office:

1. Draft Articles of Association signed by all shareholders
2. Statement that the shares have been subscribed together with a bank certification that the required amounts have been paid in
3. A document signed by all shareholders evidencing the election of directors and inspectors
4. Signed acceptances of the directors and inspectors
5. Statement designating the general circulation newspaper in which the legal notices of the company will be published
6. A declaration (on a form furnished by the Companies Registration Office)

4.1.3.5.2 Public Joint Stock Company

A public company is formed when its Articles of Association have been approved by the shareholders at the founders (or statutory) meeting and filed with the Companies Registration Office together with a minute showing the election of directors and inspectors and their signed acceptances of their positions. The public company's promoters, who must subscribe to at least 20% of the company's capital, begin the process of formation by submitting to the Companies Registration Office (in Tehran Draft Articles), a draft prospectus and a declaration which must state:

1. Name of the company
2. Identity and domicile of promoters
3. Objectives of the company
4. Capitalization, including separate identification of stock paid in kind and in cash
5. Number of registered and bearer shares together with their par value and the number of preferred shares together with a description of the rights of preferred shareholders
6. Contributions, cash and kind, of the promoters
7. Principal office, and
8. Duration of the company

When the Companies Registration Office is satisfied with the information furnished by the promoters, it will permit publication of the prospectus which must include information and instructions regarding how and where interested investors may subscribe for shares of the company's stock. When the total capital of the company has been subscribed and at least 35% has been paid in, the promoters are required to allot the shares to the subscribing shareholders and then call a founders (or statutory) meeting. At this meeting, the subscribing shareholders are to review the Articles of Association, elect the first directors and inspectors and designate a newspaper for publication of the company's legal notices. Upon approval of the Articles by the subscribing shareholders, the Articles must be submitted to the Companies Registration Office together with the minutes of the meeting.

4.1.3.6   Publication

A notice of the company formation is required to be published both in the Official Gazette and the general circulation newspaper designated by the founding shareholders. Publication of this notice is paid for by the company and usually contains the following information:

1. Name and style
2. Objects
3. Location of the head office
4. Duration and date of formation
5. Nationality
6. Share capital, par value of shares and type of shares
7. Paid-up portion of the share capital and number of bank receipt or receipts evidencing the payments
8. Identity of founders and number of shares held by them
9. Names of first board members and managing director
10. Managing director's authorities
11. Persons authorized to sign on behalf of the company
12. General circulation newspaper in which legal notices will be published
13. Names of the first statutory inspector and alternate inspector
14. Manner of liquidation

4.1.3.7 Commencement of Legal Existence

Although the registration and publication requirements must be met to complete the formation process, the legal existence of the company commences on the date the directors and inspectors accept their positions in writing.

4.1.3.8 Costs

The following charges and fees will be incurred in connection with the formation of the Company:

1. Registration fee based on the capitalization of the company payable to the Companies Registration Office
2. Charges for publication in the Official Gazette of the notice of registration payable to the Official Gazette at current rate
3. Charges for publication in a general circulation newspaper at current rate
4. Stamp taxes on share certificates

4.1.3.9 Liability of Promoters

The law provides that the promoters of the company are jointly liable for all acts and functions which they perform in connection with the formation of the company.

4.1.4 Board of Directors

4.1.4.1 Number

Although the law prescribes that a public joint stock company must have a minimum of five directors, there is no minimum prescribed for private joint stock companies. However, since the board of a private company, as well as that of a public company, is required to elect a Chairman and a Vice Chairman, and a board is required by law, the board of a private company must consist of at least two directors.

4.1.4.2 Election and Removal

Directors must be elected from among[3] the shareholders at least once every two years. It is mandatory that the election be by cumulative voting and that it take place at an ordinary general meeting. Any one or more of the directors are subject to removal by the shareholders. Directors are also eligible for re-election. Legal entities may be elected as directors.

4.1.4.3 Duration of Office

The term of office for directors must be fixed in the Articles of Association but may not be for more than two years. However, if the term expires before successor directors are elected, the existing directors continue to be responsible for the affairs and management of the company until the new directors are elected.

---

[3] All directors (except the CEO) must also be shareholders of the company.

4.1.4.4   Security Shares
Directors are required to possess the number of shares specified by the Articles of Association and this may not be less than the number required for voting at general meetings. Each director must place the required number of shares in the custody of the company for the duration of his term of office to serve as security against losses which may result to the company through violation of duties by the directors. These shares must be registered shares. The law provides that failure to comply with the requirements will result in the offending director being considered to have resigned from his office.

4.1.4.5   Authority
The law specifically provides the board with all necessary authorities for the management of the company within the limits of the company's objectives as stated in the Articles of Association. However, the board may not exercise any power which has been expressly reserved to the shareholders acting in general meetings. Limitations on the board's authority, which will be valid as between the directors and shareholders but not in respect of third parties, may be written into the Articles of Association.

4.1.4.6   Liability
Directors are not only subject to the ordinary rules of fair play in respect of the company, its shareholders, and third parties dealing with the company, and thus liable for any violations of these rules, but they are also, individually and jointly, subject to criminal prosecution for specified acts and omissions.

4.1.4.7   Meetings
The board is expected to act in meetings at which a quorum of a majority of the directors is present. The manner of calling board meetings including any notice requirement should be specified in the Articles of Association. In any event, the law provides the board chairman and any group of directors constituting one-third of the board with authority to call meetings. Resolutions will be adopted when passed by the favorable votes of a majority of the directors present at the meeting, unless a higher vote requirement is specified in the Articles of Association.

Minutes for each meeting must be kept and signed by a majority of the directors who have attended the meeting. The minutes must show the names of the directors who have attended and who were absent, a summary of the deliberations and actions taken, and the date of the meeting.

4.1.4.8   Actions without Meeting
Actions of the board are valid without a meeting if approved in writing by all of the directors.

4.1.4.9 Proxies

Although there is no specific authority in the 1969 amendments to the Commercial Code for directors' proxies, such have been recognized in practice. The Code, prior to the amendments, provides for proxies, with a caveat, that the director remains responsible for his proxy's acts.

4.1.4.10 Alternate Directors

Alternate directors are authorized but are not mandatory.

4.1.4.11 Managing Director

The law requires that at least one person be appointed by the board as the managing director to manage the daily operations of the company. This person may or may not be a member of the board but he may not also hold the position of chairman of the board unless the shareholders meet and approve the arrangement by a three-fourth (3/4) vote. The scope of the managing director's authority should be specified by the board at the time of his appointment and he is then considered to be the company's legal representative with the authority to sign on behalf of the company.

4.1.4.12 Compensation

Directors, as such, may not be paid by the company except reasonable fees for attending meetings, and a "bonus" voted by the shareholders out of company profits. For a private company, this bonus is limited to 10% of dividends and for a public company, 5% of dividends. Directors may serve as officers or employees of the company and be compensated for such capacities.

4.1.4.13 Doing Business with the Company

A director (and the managing director) may not enter into an enforceable business transaction with the company unless the transaction is approved by the board without the interested director participating in the vote, and the matter is reported both to the company inspectors and the shareholders. Even where this is done, if losses result to the company from the transaction, the directors who approved may be held liable. The law specifically provides that loans and guarantees by the company to directors are void except where the director is a legal entity.

4.1.4.14 Competing with the Company

If any director (or the managing director) concludes transactions in competition with the company, and the company suffers a loss of profits as a result, the director will be liable to indemnify the company for the loss.

4.1.5   Shareholders Meetings

4.1.5.1   Types

Shareholders meetings are called general meetings and the law provides for three types. The first is the statutory or founders meeting which is mandatory only for a public company. The second is the ordinary (annual) meeting which must be held once a year and the third is an extraordinary meeting which is held on demand. In addition, there are two other types of meetings involving the shareholders. One is a "special meeting" which must be called whenever the rights of holders of preferred shares are to be altered so as to enable these shareholders to vote on the intended alteration. The other is called an "extraordinary session of the ordinary general meeting" and may be called by the board of directors, inspectors, or holders of 20 percent of the company's shares whenever action is required on a matter within the competence of the ordinary meeting at times other than when the ordinary meeting is scheduled to be held.

4.1.5.2   Competence of Ordinary Meeting

The ordinary meeting is competent to deal with all of the affairs of the company except those which are expressly within the competence of the statutory and extraordinary meetings. It is expressly required to take action on the following matters:
1. Review and approval of the balance sheet and profit and loss account and other financial reports
2. Review and approval of the directors annual report
3. Review and approval of the inspectors annual report
4. Election of directors (if their term has expired)
5. Election of inspector(s) and alternate inspector(s)
6. Designation of the general circulation newspaper in which the company's legal notices will appear

4.1.5.3   Competence of Extraordinary Meeting

The extraordinary meeting is competent to deal with any changes in the Articles of Association or the share capital, and dissolution of the company.

4.1.5.4   Directorate

The law provides for management of general meetings by a directorate composed of a chairman, a secretary, and two observers. Unless the Articles of Association provide otherwise, the chairman will be the chairman of the board of directors. The secretary need not be a shareholder but the observers must be.

4.1.5.5   Notice

Written notice for general meetings must be given to the shareholders not less than 10 days and not more than forty days prior to the date of the meeting and such notice must be published in the general circulation newspaper designated for the company's legal notices.

The notice must state the agenda and the date, hour, and place of the meeting. Waiver of these requirements is authorized whenever all of the shareholders attend the meeting.

4.1.5.6   Quorum
The quorum requirement for both the ordinary and extraordinary meetings is more than 50 percent of the shares entitled to vote.

4.1.5.7   Minutes
Written minutes of all general meetings are required to be made by the secretary of the meeting as a record of the deliberations and actions taken. The minutes must be signed by the directorate and a copy thereof must be kept at the principal office of the company.

4.1.5.8   Filing and Registration of Minutes
Whenever a general meeting takes action on any of the following matters, a copy of the relevant resolution must be filed with the Companies Registration Office for registration in a register (book) maintained by that office:
1. Election of directors or inspectors
2. Approval of the balance sheet
3. Decrease or increase in the capital and any change in the Articles of Association
4. Winding up of the company and the manner of liquidation

4.1.5.9   Publication of Minutes
In addition to the filing and registration requirements mentioned above, notice of action taken by a general meeting (or by the board) on the following matters is required to be published in the general circulation newspaper designated by the shareholders and in the Official Gazette:
1. Election of directors or inspectors
2. Decrease or increase in the capital and any change in the Articles of Association
3. Winding up of the company and name and particulars of the liquidators
4. Name and power of the Managing Director
5. Designation of the newspaper in which all the legal notices of the company will be published

4.1.5.10   Adjournment
A general meeting may be adjourned for a period of up to two weeks by the directorate with the approval of the meeting. In such a case, no new notice is required and the quorum requirement for the adjourned session will be the same as for the original session.

4.1.5.11   Minority Shareholders Calls
Minority shareholders owning in the aggregate one-fifth (1/5) of the company's shares are entitled to request the board and the inspectors to call a general meeting at any time. If the

board and the inspectors fail to call the requested meeting, then the shareholders, them-
selves, are entitled to call a meeting.

4.1.6   Miscellaneous

4.1.6.1   Statutory Inspectors (Auditors)

The law requires the election, by the shareholders, of a statutory inspector and alternate
inspector once a year at the ordinary general meeting. The election of more than one
inspector and alternate inspector is optional. In general, the function of the inspector is
to serve as a watchdog over shareholders' and third parties' interests and he may be pros-
ecuted criminally for violation of his duties. Certain categories of persons such as crimi-
nals, the directors and their relatives, and persons doing business with the company are
disqualified from serving in this post. In addition, the inspector is required to submit a
report to the ordinary general meeting each year.

4.1.6.2   Books of Account

Both the public and private joint stock companies are required to maintain the journal,
ledger, inventory and copy book of merchants in the Persian language. These books serve
as the basis for determining the company's tax liability and failure to keep them strictly in
accordance with the legal requirements may result in the tax authorities making their own
determination of what the company's tax liability should be.

4.1.6.3   Company Name

The law requires that the words, "Private Joint Stock Company (Sherkat Sahami Khass)"
appear with the name of a private company and that these words be displayed in a con-
spicuous way on all letterheads, publications and notices of the company. As a matter of
practice, the Companies Registration Office requires the use of Iranian names and will
refuse to register a new company name that is too similar to the name of a company already
registered.

4.1.7   Some of the Differences between Public and Private Joint Stock Companies

	Private Joint Stock Company	Public Joint Stock Company
Minimum Capital	IRR 1,000,000	IRR 5,000,000
Maximum Nominal Share Value	-	IRR 10,000
Minimum Share Subscription	20%	100%
Minimum Paid-up Capital	35%	35% of cash capital 100% of non-cash capital
Requirements for Capital Increase	shareholders resolution	prospectus
Minimum Number of Directors	2	5
Maximum Bonus for Directors	10% of dividends	5% of dividends
Statutory Meeting Required by Law	No	Yes
Annual Financial Reports Must be Certified by Officially Recognized Accountants	No	Yes

4.1.8   Checklist for Articles of Association

Generally, the Articles of Association should include the following information:

1. Name of the company
2. Style of the company
3. Duration of the company
4. Objectives of the company expressed and defined
5. Location of the head office and branch offices, if any
6. Details of the share capital of the company specifying the amount paid in cash and the amount paid in kind, separately
7. Number of bearer shares and of registered shares and the par value thereof as well as the number of preferred shares, if any, particulars and the privileges attached thereto
8. Details of the amount of the shares which is paid up
9. Name(s) of authorized officer(s) who will sign the share certificates
10. Manner of call of the par value of shares and the period over which the balance should be paid
11. Manner of transfer of registered shares
12. Manner of conversion of registered shares into bearer shares and vice versa
13. Manner and conditions of increasing or decreasing the capital of the company
14. Period and manner of calling general meetings
15. Regulations governing the quorum for general meetings and the manner of running such meetings
16. Manner of transacting business and the number of votes required to give validity to the actions taken by general meetings
17. Number of directors, the manner of their election, their term of office, the manner of election of the successors of such directors who die or resign or become incapacitated or have been removed from their office or otherwise deprived of their office by any legal impediment
18. Details of the scope of the functions and authorities of the board of directors
19. Time for and the manner of calling the meetings of the board of directors
20. Regulations governing the quorum for the meetings of board of directors
21. The manner of the election of the chairman and vice chairman of the board and their term of office
22. Manner of transacting business and the number of votes required to give validity to the actions taken by the board of directors
23. Number of directors' security shares to be deposited with the company
24. Whether the company shall have one or several legal inspectors and the manner of their election and their terms of office
25. Whether the company shall have one or several managing directors and their terms of office
26. Date of commencement and end of the fiscal year of the company, the time limit for preparing the balance sheet and profit and loss account and the submission thereof to the legal inspectors and to the annual general meeting

27. Manner of voluntary winding up of the company and the proceedings for liquidating its affairs
28. Manner of making alterations to the Articles of Association.

4.2 Branches and Representative Offices of Foreign Companies

A foreign company may establish branches or representative offices in Iran. The Law Permitting Registration of Branches and Representative Offices of Foreign Companies in Iran was approved on 11 November 1997:

Sole Article:
"The foreign companies considered as being legal in their own countries of origin may, on provision of reciprocal treatment by their governments in respect of Iranian companies, set up branches and representative offices in Iran to carry out the businesses authorized by the government of the Islamic Republic of Iran in due compliance with the Laws of Iran."

4.2.1 Authorized Companies
The Council of Ministers approved the Executive By-Laws of the Law Permitting Registration of Branches and Representative Offices of Foreign Companies under No.019776T/M/78-930 on 2 May 1999. According to Article 1 of these By-Laws, the companies that are considered as legal companies in their countries of origin, i.e. have been formed on the basis of the laws and regulations of those countries and are legal entities, may set up their branches or representative offices in Iran, on the basis of the applicable laws and regulations, in order to carry out the businesses mentioned hereafter.

4.2.2 Differences between a Representative Office, Liaison Office and Branch of a Foreign Company in Iran
In case the office of the foreign company shall become engaged in carrying out the works undertaken by the head office of the company, such as executing the works under a contract concluded by and between the head office of the company outside Iran and a client in Iran, the registered office shall be known as a Branch Office.

In situations where the office shall represent its head office and sell the products of its head office in Iran or carry out after-sales services and negotiation of the terms of agreements to be concluded by and between the company and its clients in Iran, conclude agreements with those clients, etc., the office shall be known as a Representative Office.

In situations where the office of a company shall be solely engaged in conducting market research activity (on behalf of its head office) and shall report about available business opportunities for the company to its head office in order that the relevant proposals (Performa Invoices) be made directly by the head office to the clients in Iran and therefore the office shall not be in a position to generate any income of its own in Iran and its expenses shall be covered by transfer of funds by the head office from outside Iran, then the office shall be called a Liaison Office.

4.2.3   Permitted Activities

4.2.3.1   Supply of After-Sales Services

In cases where foreign companies supply goods or services to Iranian subjects, said companies may apply for registration of their branches or representative offices in Iran for the supply of after-sales (guarantee and warranty) services in Iran.

4.2.3.2   Carrying out Executive Works

Foreign companies, being parties to contracts concluded with Iranian subjects (Iranian natural persons and legal entities of private and public sectors), may require that their branches or representative offices be registered in Iran.

4.2.3.3   Investigating Investments in Iran

It must be first noted that those foreign companies wishing to make an investment in Iran may take any one of the following two actions:

1. Investing within the framework of the FIPPA with authorization granted by the Organization for Investment and Economic and Technical Assistance and approval by the Council of Ministers, which shall be granted on a case-by-case basis after submitting the required documents.
2. Entering into joint ventures directly with Iranian natural persons and legal entities by creating a joint venture company or by making an investment in an already existing joint venture company.

Foreign companies may set up branches or representative offices in order to conduct due diligences and prepare grounds for investment by using any one of the above two methods.

4.2.3.4   Cooperation for Projects in a Third Country

In cases where Iranian technical and engineering companies have been designated to carry out industrial, technical, development, and other activities in a third country and for such purpose, agreements shall be concluded by and between the Iranian company and companies from other countries. The foreign company, being party to such agreements, may set up a branch or representative office of its company in Iran by submitting the required documents. Also, in the case where a foreign company, designated to carry out a technical or engineering work in a third country, wishes to carry out such work, through a joint venture with an Iranian technical and engineering company, it may set up its branch or representative office in Iran.

4.2.3.5   Export and Technology Transfer

The following foreign companies contributing to export increases and technology transfers may register a branch or representative office of their company in Iran:

1. Foreign companies operating in the field of and contributing to development and increase of exports of Iranian non-oil products, including industrial and agricultural products and handicrafts
2. Foreign companies transferring know-how on production of various products to Iranian nationals
3. Foreign companies possessing the technology in respect of industrial products that intend to transfer the technology for the production of the said products to Iranian nationals by setting up factories and plants

4.2.3.6   Activities that require a Permission

Foreign companies that have entered into a contract with a government body to supply services in various fields that require a permission to be issued by a government organization may register a branch or representative office of their companies in Iran.

Foreign companies operating in many other fields shall require permission from the pertinent organizations to carry out business in Iran. E.g. offering services in the fields of transportation at sea, on land (road and rail) and by air all require permission from the Organization for Transportation and Terminals. Also, operation in the field of banking requires permission from the Central Bank of the Islamic Republic of Iran.

4.2.4   Branch Office of a Foreign Company

According to Article 2 of the Executive By-Laws of the Law Permitting Registration of Branches and Representative Offices of Foreign Companies in Iran, a branch of a foreign company is a local (Iranian) wing of the original company that carries out the business and functions of the head office of the company in Iran directly through one or more principal representative(s).

4.2.5   Required Documents for the Registration of Branch Offices of Foreign Companies

Foreign companies intending to set up a branch office of their companies in Iran must submit the following documents to the Companies Registration Office in Tehran:
1. Request in writing to be submitted by the company
2. Certified photocopies of the articles of association, notice of incorporation, and the last changes in the company registered with the authorities concerned
3. The last confirmed financial report of the company
4. A feasibility study containing the following information:
   - Information concerning activities of the company
   - A description of the reasons and the needs for registration of the company in Iran
   - A description of the type and scope of authorities and the place of operation and business of the branch office of the company in Iran
   - An estimate of the required local and expatriate work force
   - The manner of procurement of the funds in Rials and in foreign currencies required for running the affairs of the branch office

5. A letter of introduction from a government entity in case the branch has been set up for implementation of an agreement between the foreign company and that government entity

6. Statement of Registration (a form to be filled in and signed by the foreign company)

7. Certificate of Registration (a form to be filled in and signed by the foreign company)

8. Letter of Authorization given by the foreign company to its principal representative(s) in Iran

9. A Letter of Undertaking whereby the foreign company undertakes to wind up and close down its branch office in Iran in case the activity permit given to the branch office by Iranian authorities shall be revoked and canceled. The branch office in such a case must be closed down by designating a liquidator who shall wind up and liquidate the branch office within a period to be specified by the Companies Registration Office.

All documents prepared by the foreign company for the above purpose must be certified by the authorities concerned (such as local registries), followed by confirmation by the Foreign Ministry of that country and then confirmed by the Iranian embassy of said country. The above said documents must thereafter be translated into Persian by official translators and certified by the Judiciary and the translations and original documents must then be submitted to the Companies Registration Office for registration of the branch office of the company.

4.2.6 Responsibilities of a Foreign Company in Respect of its Branch Office

A branch office is deemed to be carrying out business in Iran on behalf of the head office of the company. Therefore, the head office of the company shall be responsible for all activities performed by the branch office.

4.2.7 Agents (local)

"Agent" of a foreign company means a natural person or a legal entity that, on the basis of an agency agreement, carries out some of the activities and functions of the principal company in Iran.

4.2.8 Required Documents for the Registration of Representative Offices of Foreign Companies

1. In cases where a natural person shall act as the representative of a foreign company, the Persian translation of the following documents and evidences must be submitted to the Companies Registration Office:

    a) Certified photocopy of the Agency Agreement concluded with the foreign company

    b) Photocopy of the Identification Booklet (shenas'nameh), or of the passport, if the agent is not an Iranian national

    c) The address of the place of residence of the agent and the address of the office of the agent

d)   Presentation of the past record of activities of the agent in respect of the works to be carried out under the agency agreement

e)   A certified photocopy of the articles of association of the principal foreign company, together with the notice of registration and the last changes of the company registered with the competent authorities.

f)   A report on the activities of the principal foreign company and a description of the reasons for the necessity of obtaining agency

g)   The last audited fiscal report of the principal foreign company

h)   A letter of introduction by the ministry concerned (in case the contract has been concluded with a government entity)

i)   Statement of Registration of foreign company

j)   Certificate of Registration of foreign company

k)   A letter of authorization of the principal representative(s) of the foreign company

2. In cases where a legal entity acts as the representative of a foreign company, it must submit the Persian translation and the original copies of the following documents to the Companies Registration Office:

a)   A certified photocopy of the agency agreement concluded with the foreign company

b)   A certified photocopy of the articles of association of the principal foreign company, together with the notice of registration and the last changes of the representative company registered with the competent authorities.

c)   The records and history of activities of the legal entity applying for registration as representative in respect of the works undertaken under the agency agreement

d)   The articles of association of the foreign principal company, its notice of incorporation and its last changes registered with the authorities concerned

e)   A report on the activities of the principal foreign company and a description of the reasons for the necessity to obtain the agency of that company

f)   The last audited financial report of the foreign principal company

g)   Submit a letter of introduction of the ministry concerned (in case the contract has been concluded with a government entity)

h)   Statement of Registration of the foreign company

i)   Certificate of Registration of the foreign company

In both cases, all documents of the principal company that are drawn up in foreign countries must be certified by the authorities concerned (such as the Companies Registry), confirmed by the Foreign Ministry in those countries and certified by Iranian embassy. The above said documents shall be translated in to Persian by official translators and certified by judicial authorities. The translations and the original documents shall then be submitted to the Companies Registration Office for registration of the representative office

4.2.9 Responsibilities of Branch Office and Agent(s) of Foreign Companies

The Agent(s) of a foreign company shall be responsible for the activities in Iran carried out in the name of the principal company.

1. Winding up and liquidation of the branch office in case of revocation of the permission granted to the foreign company to operate in Iran.
2. Submission of the annual report on the activities of the head office comprising of fiscal statements audited by independent auditors in the company's country of origin, to the authority concerned in Iran.
3. Submission of the activity report of the branch or representative office in Iran together with the audited fiscal statements within four (4) months after expiry of the fiscal year, to the authority concerned in Iran.
4. Management and running the affairs of the branch or representative office by one or more natural person(s) domiciled in Iran.

4.2.10 Tax Applicable to the Agencies & Branches of Foreign Companies in Iran

Representatives and branches of foreign companies in Iran, that are working for the parent company, to gather economical information and data as well as marketing, without the right to carry out transactions, and receive money from the parent company to compensate for their expenses, shall not be subject to income tax. Note 3 of Article 107 of the Direct Taxation Law illustrates this more clearly:

Note 3: "The branches and representative offices of foreign companies and banks in Iran which shall proceed to render activities for marketing and gathering of economic data and information in Iran for the holding company, without having the right to enter into a transaction in Iran, and which shall collect amounts from the holding company in order to meet the expenses and its financial requirements, shall not be liable to income tax."

5.   Taxation: A Review of the Iranian Tax System

5.1   Tax Bases and Rates

The Iranian tax system is divided into two general categories of direct and indirect taxes. Based on a survey of the Organization for Investment, Economic and Technical Assistance of Iran ("OIETAI"), the share of direct taxes from the total tax revenues is currently almost 68%.

There are two major types of direct taxes, including income taxes and property taxes. Each category of direct taxes, in turn, is divided into sub-parts. Indirect taxes include taxes on imports and Value Added Tax (VAT). Taxes on imports are currently collected by the Iranian Customs Organization and are not within the jurisdiction of the Iranian National Tax Administration (INTA). Tables 1 to 4 briefly show various types of taxes in the Iranian taxation system:

Table 5.1:   Income Taxes

Tax Base	Taxable Income	Taxable Persons	Tax Rates
Real Estate Income Tax	Income of persons derived from transfer of rights in immovable properties situated in Iran, less the exemptions: total rent, less a deduction of 25% for expenses, depreciations, and commitments of the owner in regard to the property.	Owners who have rented their immovable properties to others	15–35%
Employment Income Tax	Salaries, wages or any other remuneration received by individuals in respect of their employment services. Payments for works conducted out of Iran, shall be subject to the tax, provided that the payer is an Iranian resident.	Individuals	10% for public sector employees and the others 10–35%
Individual Business Income Tax	Unincorporated business activities (aggregate sale of goods and services) less the exemptions provided in the DTA	Individuals	15–35%
Corporate Income Tax	Aggregate profits of companies, and the profits from the profit-making activities of other legal persons, derived from sources in Iran or abroad, less the losses from non-exempt sources and minus the provisioned exemptions	Legal persons	25%
Tax on Incidental Income	Income earned ex gratia or through favoritism or as an award	Individuals or legal persons	15–35%

Table 5.2:   Property Taxes

Tax Base	Taxable Income	Taxable Persons	Tax Rates
Tax on Transfer of Real Properties	Final transfer of real estates & goodwill shall be subject to taxation at the date of transfer.	Individuals or legal persons	5% & 2%
Tax on Transfer of Shares	Nominal value of transferred shares	Joint Stock Companies and other companies	0.5% & 4%
Inheritance Tax	Any estate left from the deceased individual	Individuals	5–65%
Stamp Duties	Each sheet of cheques printed by banks (IRR 200), bill of exchange, promissory notes (0.3%), and other documents and negotiable papers with specified amounts	Individuals or legal persons.	As provisioned in Articles 44-51of the Direct Taxation Law

Table 5.3: Import Tax

Tax Base	Taxable Income	Taxable Persons	Tax Rates

Taxes on Imports: Currently collectible by the Iranian Customs Organization.

Table 5.4:   VAT

Tax Base	Taxable Income	Taxable Persons	Tax Rates
Value Added	Value added resulting from the sale of all goods and services and their imports, except 17 items listed in Article 12 of the VAT Act (VATA) as the exempted ones	Individuals or legal persons	currently 9%

5.2   Taxation of Foreign Investors in Iran

All foreign investors doing business in Iran or deriving income from sources in Iran are subject to taxation in Iran. Depending on the type of activity the foreign investor is engaged in, different taxes and exemptions are applicable, including profit tax, income tax, property tax, etc.

5.2.1   Direct Taxes

All non-Iranian individuals or legal entities, for the income earned in Iran and also for the income gained through granting of license or other rights, technical and educational assistance or movie contracts in the territory of Iran, are subject to taxation.

Foreign investors in Iran enjoy the same supports and privileges that are offered to Iranian investors. This means both Iranian and foreign investors pay the same amount of taxes. Tax exemptions and discounts are also equally granted to domestic and foreign investors. Since foreign investments are usually carried out through legal entities, we will hereunder focus on rules and regulations for Corporate Income Tax.

5.2.2 Corporate Income Tax

5.2.2.1 General Issues

Foreign legal entities, residing abroad, shall be taxed at the flat rate of 25% in respect of the aggregate taxable income derived from the operation of their investment in Iran or from the activities performed by them, directly or through the agencies in Iran. The legal entities shall not be subject to any other taxes on the dividends or partnership profits they may receive from the capital recipient companies.

Legal entities are obligated, even within the exemption period, to submit declaration and profit and loss balance sheets, provided from their official statutory books, not later than four months after the tax year (March 21 each year until March 20 next year) along with the list of partners and shareholders, their shares and addresses to the tax department within the area of the activity of the legal entity. If these legal entities do not submit the documents within the stipulated time span, the tax exemption will be null and void.

5.2.2.2 Exemptions

The Direct Taxation Law and other pertinent legislations have considered certain exemptions for the legal entities as shown in table 5:

Table 5.5:   Highlights of Tax Exemptions

Activity	Level of Tax Exemption	Duration of Exemption	Incentive Type
Agriculture	100%	Perpetual	Permanent Exemption
Industry and Mining	80%	4 Years	Tax Holiday
Industry and Mining in Less-Developed Areas	100%	20 Years	Tax Holiday
Tourism	50%	Perpetual	Tax Credit
Export of Services & Non-oil Goods	100%	During 5th Development Plan (until the end of 2016)	Tax Holiday
Handicrafts	100%	Perpetual	Permanent Exemption
Educational & Sport Services	100%	Perpetual	Permanent Exemption

Cultural Activities	100%	Perpetual	Permanent Exemption
Salary in Less-Developed Areas	50%	Perpetual	Tax Credit
All Economic Activities in Free Zones	100%	20 Years	Tax Holiday
Profits of Private and Cooperative Companies used for development, reconstruction and renovation of existing industrial and mining units	50%	Perpetual	Tax Credit

5.2.2.3 Deductions

Expenses which are deductible in the assessment of taxable income are listed in the Direct Taxation Law. These expenditures must be supported to a reasonable degree by documentary evidence and must be exclusively connected with the earning of income during the year in question. The categories of deductible expenditure are as follows:

1. The cost of goods and raw materials
2. Personnel costs
3. Rental of enterprise's premises in case of being rented
4. Expenses incurred in the maintenance and upkeep of the premises owned by the enterprise
5. Minor expenses incurred in connection with the rented premises of the enterprise
6. Costs of fuel, electricity, lighting, water and communication
7. Rent of machinery and equipment
8. Cost of repair and maintenance of machineries and business equipment
9. Business insurance
10. Compensation paid for damages resulted from the business operations
11. Reserves against doubtful claims
12. Royalties, duties, rights and taxes paid
13. Research, development and training expenditure
14. Cultural, sports and welfare expenditures paid to the Ministry of Labour and Social Affairs in respect of workers
15. Expenses for purchasing of books and other cultural and art goods for employees and their dependents
16. Losses of legal persons
17. Transportation expenses
18. Expenses related to transportation and entertainment for employees
19. Warehousing costs
20. Fees paid in proportion to the services rendered
21. Interest and fees paid for the carrying out of the enterprise operation
22. Abortive exploration expenditures for deemed mines
23. Membership and subscription fees connected with the business operations

24. Bad debts, if proved
25. Currency exchange losses computed in accordance with accepted accountancy practice
26. Normal wastage of production
27. The reserve related to acceptable expenses of the assessment period

Other expenses that are not referred to above, but are related to the earning of the enterprise's income, may be accepted as deductible expenses if proposed by the INTA and with approval of the Ministry of Economic Affairs and Finance.

5.2.2.4   Losses
Losses sustained by all taxpayers, engaged in trading and other activities, are accepted by the tax authorities and can be carried forward and written off against future profits for a period of three years.

5.2.2.5   Withholding Taxes
Previously, five percent of every contract payment had to be withheld by the payer and accounted for to tax authorities. Such a withheld tax constituted an advance payment of the final tax due. However, this kind of withholding tax has been abolished in the recent revision of the Direct Taxation Law.

On the other hand, the payers of salaries are obliged, when paying or allocating the same, to compete and withhold therefrom the applicable taxes and to remit, within 30 days, the deducted amounts together with a list containing the names and addresses of recipients and the amount of payment, to the local tax assessment office.

5.2.2.6   Depreciation
Depreciation of assets is deductible in the assessment of taxable income. Depreciation rates range from 5% to 100% and the period over which assets may be depreciated ranges from 2 to 15 years.

5.2.3   Value Added Tax (VAT)
The VAT in Iran is levied on the sale of all goods and services and their imports, except 17 items listed in Article 12 of the VAT Act (VATA) as the exempted ones. The VATA, however, does not include the export of goods and services through official customs gates. Therefore, the taxes paid for the export of goods and services will be refundable by submitting the customs clearance sheets and valid documents.

Currently, the VAT rate stands at 9% (VAT rate for two special goods of cigarettes and jet fuel is relatively higher). To reduce the country's dependency on oil revenue, the Law on the Fifth Five-Year Development Plan provisioned an annual one-percent increase in the VAT rate to put it at 9% at the end of the Plan, i.e. 2016.

Economic activities in Free Trade Industrial Zones are exempted from VAT.

5.2.4   Agreements for the Avoidance of Double Taxation

To facilitate cooperation between Iranian and foreign residents and to promote trade and economic exchanges with foreign countries, the Government of the Islamic Republic of Iran has concluded mutual Agreements for the Avoidance of Double Taxation with the following countries:

Table 5.6:   List of Iran's Applicable Agreements for the Avoidance of Double Taxation

Algeria	Georgia	Pakistan	Sudan
Armenia	Germany	Poland	Switzerland
Austria	Indonesia	Qatar	Syria
Azerbaijan	Jordan	Romania	Tajikistan
Bahrain	Kazakhstan	Russia	Tunisia
Belarus	Kuwait	Serbia	Turkey
Bulgaria	Kyrgyzstan	South Africa	Turkmenistan
China	Lebanon	South Korea	Ukraine
Croatia	Malaysia	Spain	Uzbekistan
France	Oman	Sri Lanka	Venezuela

5.2.5   Standard Audit Systems

The actual audit system of companies in Iran meets all international standard audit criteria. Moreover, systems like GAAP are accepted and recognized by tax authorities and there is no restriction for foreign companies to use their own systems. After registering a company in Iran, one inspector from the local tax department will be introduced to the company as a liaison officer and it is recommended to send a report on the audit system of the company to him for further references.

5.2.6   Audit of Financial Statements by Independent Auditors

Accountants of a company can make arrangements to prepare financial statements and to prepare and submit tax declarations. Article 272 of the Direct Taxation Law states:

„In case of tax auditing by certified accountants, their view and opinion shall be considered and accepted by the Tax Department. The income subject to tax declared by them shall be the basis for computing tax prior to tax auditing."

Therefore, financial statements shall be considered by either the Tax Department or certified accountants subject to Article 272 of the Direct Taxation Law, and necessary steps shall be taken to determine income subject to tax and issuance of slip for tax determination.

6.   Labour Law: Employment of Foreign Nationals in Iran

Foreign nationals are prohibited from working in Iran unless they receive work and employment permits (even if they are supposed to receive a wage and/or salary outside the Iranian territory).

The work permit for the employment of foreign nationals in Iran is issued by the "Department General for Employment of Foreign Nationals" (also called Department for Employment of Expatriates) of the Ministry of Cooperatives, Labour and Social Welfare upon a request by Iranian employers. In provincial capitals it is issued by the Foreign Citizens Divisions of the Department General of Cooperatives, Labour and Social Welfare. (The general procedure for admission of employees of foreign investors has been brought separately in the following part.)

The Iranian employers are obligated to seek the permission of the Department General for Employment of Foreign Nationals before concluding any contract that may lead to the employment of foreign citizens in Iran. The rules and regulations for acquiring work permits for the foreign nationals are available in the Labour Law of the Islamic Republic of Iran, ratified in 1990 (articles 120 through 129 and the executive bylaw of Article 129).

Due to abundance of educated and skilled job-seekers in the country and the purpose of reducing the unemployment rate, the Technical Board for Employment of Foreign Nationals has strict rules and regulations (stipulated in Article 121 of the Labour Law) for the issuance of work permits. However, the Foreign Investment Promotion and Protection Act (FIPPA), passed in 2002, contains promising provisions for issuance of work permits for foreign investors, managers and experts in relation to investments under the FIPPA.

6.1   Admission of Employees of Foreign Investors According to FIPPA Rules and Regulations

By virtue of Article 35 of the Executive Bylaw of the FIPPA:

"The relevant executive agencies, including but not limited to, the Ministry of Foreign Affairs, the Ministry of Interior, the Ministry of Labour and Social Affairs [since 2011 and after merging of ministries, the Ministry of Cooperatives, Labour and Social Welfare] and the Disciplinary Forces of the Islamic Republic of Iran (the Police), are required to proceed with the issuance of visas, residence permits and work permits for foreign investors, directors, experts and their immediate family members in relation to the investments covered by the FIPPA, at the request of the OIETAI and confirmation of their status as investors, in the following manner:

The Ministry of Foreign Affairs is required, upon receipt of the request of the OIETAI, to communicate to the Missions of the Islamic Republic of Iran abroad, the authorization for the issuance of single entry visa, or multi-entry visa (for three years) with a three-month residence permit on each entry for relevant individuals, depending on the type of visa requested.

The above mentioned persons who have obtained entry visas for investment may, after entry into the Country, refer to the Disciplinary Forces of the Islamic Republic of Iran (the Police) so as to obtain a three-year residence permit, upon submission of the OIETAI's formal note confirming the coverage of such investments under the FIPPA. The Ministry of Labour and Social Affairs is obliged to issue work permits for such individuals after the issuance of the residence permit."

Obtaining three-year residence permits by foreign investors, as stipulated above, shall exempt them from entry and exit visas normally required for travelling to or from the Country.

6.2   Issuing Work Permit outside FIPPA Framework

In cases when Iranian employers need the technical specialty of foreign experts, the issuance of a visa with a work permit privilege, as well as the work permit for the foreign nationals, will be carried out upon request by the Iranian employer. According to pertinent rules and regulations, no foreign citizen can personally apply for employment and/or work permit in Iran, unless he/she registers an enterprise legally.

Upon inquiry from the Department General for Employment of Foreign Nationals, before concluding any contract with foreign experts, the Iranian employers should deliver the request and required documents to the Department General for verification. The documents are sent for further investigation to the Technical Board for Employment of Foreign Nationals. The approval or disapproval of the Board is thereby announced to the employer through the related experts.

In the past, the responsibility of issuance, extension and renewal of the work permits of foreign nationals used to be carried out only in Tehran (at the Department General for Employment of Foreign Nationals).

For the welfare of the applicants, the authority of these affairs, to certain degrees, has been delegated to the Departments General of Cooperatives, Labour and Social Welfare in the provinces. Therefore, employers and foreign nationals can refer to the provincial Department General for issuance, extension or renewal of their work permit.

6.3   Validity Period of Work Permits

The work permits of foreign nationals are issued, extended or renewed for a period of one year.

6.4   Extension of Work Permits

Upon expiry of the work permit, if the Iranian employer still needs the specialty of the expatriate, he can apply for the extension of the work permit of said foreign labourer or expert. The application is sent to the Technical Board for Employment and upon approval the permit is extended for a period of one year.

6.5   Renewal of Work Permits

Foreign nationals with valid work permits, whose contracts with their employer become null and void for any reason, will be subject to renewal of the work permit after changing the employer. The renewal of the work permit – upon the change of the employer or the type of work – will be carried out by the responsible divisions of the Ministry of Cooperatives, Labour and Social Welfare after the approval of the Technical Board for Employment of Foreign Nationals.

6.6   Legal Punishments for Employment of Foreign Nationals without Work Permits

Employers who hire foreign nationals, whose work permits have expired or have no work permit, or employ them in jobs other than those stipulated in their work permits, or do not notify the Ministry of Cooperatives, Labour and Social Welfare about cases where the employment agreement between them and foreign nationals is terminated, shall be sentenced to prison terms or cash fines.

6.7   Fees

At present, the issuance and renewal of work permits for foreign nationals costs IRR 1,400,000 and the extension of permits costs IRR 1,000,000. Expatriates of some countries will be exempted from such charges upon mutual agreement with their respective countries granting similar privileges.

6.8   Unique Advantage for Foreign Investors Employing Labour Force in Iran

Foreign investors, employing those introduced by the affiliated units of the Ministry of Cooperatives, Labour and Social Welfare, will enjoy growing discounts or exemption from paying part of the insurance duties in the case where their units are newly established, or when no reduction in their employment rate the year before occurred (part of Article 80 of the Law on the Fifth Five-Year Development Plan).

7.   Iranian Intellectual Property Law

7.1   Trade Mark

In accordance with Article 30 of the Iran Patents, Industrial Designs and Trademarks Registration Act (2008):

1. Mark means any visible sign capable of distinguishing the goods or services of legal entities or of natural persons.
2. Collective Mark means any visible sign designated as such in the application for registration and capable of distinguishing the origin or any other characteristics, including the quality of goods or services of natural persons or of legal entities which use the sign under the control of the registered owner of the Collective Mark;
3. Trade Name means the name or designation identifying and distinguishing a natural person or a legal entity.

The exclusive right to use a Mark shall belong to the person who registers his Mark in accordance with the provisions of this Act.

7.1.1   Non-Registrable Marks under the Law of Iran

A Mark is not registrable in the following cases:

1. If it is not capable of distinguishing the goods or services of one enterprise from those belonging to another enterprise.
2. If it is contrary to Rules of Sharia, public order or morality.
3. If it is likely to mislead the public or trade centers, in particular, with regard to the geographical origin of the goods or services concerned or their nature or characteristics.
4. If it is identical with, or is an imitation of or contains an element, an armorial bearing, flag or other emblem, a name or abbreviation or initials of the name of, or official sign or hallmark adopted by, any State, intergovernmental organization created under an international convention, unless authorized by the competent authority of that State or organization.
5. If it is identical with, or confusingly similar to, or constitutes a translation of, a mark or trade name which is well known in Iran for identical or similar goods or services of another enterprise.
6. If an identical or similar mark has been registered or become well-known for services that are not similar, provided that customarily there is a connection between the use of the mark and the owner of the well-known mark and that its registration is likely to damage interests of the owner of the well-known mark.
7. If it is identical with a mark registered in the name of a different proprietor with an earlier filing date or a priority right in respect of the same goods or services or for goods and services that, due to connection or resemblance, is likely to deceive or cause confusion.

7.1.2   Documents Required for the Registration of a Trade Mark in Iran

Required documents to register a trade mark in Iran are the same for an entity and an individual. The only difference is in the registration fee. Trade Mark registration requires submission of a declaration to the Registration Authority as follows:

1. Mark registration declarations shall be drawn up in two copies and in a special form (E-1) and in Persian language and signed by the applicant or his legal representative, after mentioning the date.
2. In case where deeds attached to the declaration and other related documents are drawn up in another language but Persian language, it is obligatory to submit the original documents with their unofficial translation. If necessary, the registration authority may request for official translation of said documents while studying the declaration.
3. Mark registration declaration shall contain the following points:

    a)   Name, national code number, address, postal code and nationality of the applicant. In case where an applicant is a legal entity, it is necessary to mention name, type of activity, domicile, registration place and number, nationality, principal office and if necessary, any other identification number.

    b)   Name, national number, address and postal code of legal representative of the applicant, if available.

    c)   Name, domicile and postal code of the person or persons who are qualified for receiving notices in Iran in case the applicant is not a resident of Iran.

    d)   Affixing a sample of that mark in the related cadre

    e)   Describing and determining components of the mark and determining the mark and specified letters in case the requested mark includes special letters.

    f)   Mentioning the goods and services for which the mark is used by determining class or classes requested in accordance with the international classification

    g)   Mentioning right of priority in case of request

    h)   Field of activity of the mark owner

    i)   Mentioning collective mark in case the registration is requested

    j)   In case the mark includes a word or words other than the Persian language, inserting a transcription and its translation

    k)   Mentioning color in case said color is regarded as specification of the mark

    l)   Mentioning that the mark is three-dimensional in the case of a request for its registration

    m)   Determination of appendices

    Note 1:   In case of submission of the declaration and other related documents by the legal entities, they shall be signed by the authorized signatories.

    Note 2:   In case of numerous applicants for registration, the person who has the right to refer to and correspond with the registration authority and performs other necessary administrative formalities as a representative of others, except for receipt of mark certificate, shall be appointed by mentioning domicile.

Note 3:   Name and address of the applicant abroad shall be in Latin, in addition to Persian script, and shall be registered and published with the same letters.

Note 4:   In all affairs relating to registration and publication of the marks, the registration authority investigates classification of the goods and services on the basis of international classification. In case of pictures in the mark, it is compulsory for the registration authority to observe its classification.

4. A separate declaration shall be used for the registration of each mark. Use of a declaration for registration of one mark for goods and services included in one or more classes is permissible.

5. A person who requests the registration of some marks simultaneously shall submit a separate declaration for each of them in accordance with this regulation. In this case, if the requests are done by the legal representative, original representation documents shall be attached to one of the declarations and its true certified copy shall be attached to each one of the other declarations.

6. The following documents shall be attached to the declaration:

a)   Original representation copy, in the case where the request has been submitted by the legal representative

b)   Presentation of 10 samples of the mark in graphical form which is equal to the mark affixed on the declaration and of which dimensions are at most 10 x 10 cm. If presentation of the mark is not graphical, 10 samples of the copy of the mark will be presented in the same dimensions and at the discretion of the Registration Authority.

c)   In case the mark is three dimensional, it is necessary to present the mark as graphical samples or two-dimensional pictures on paper and in such a manner that it can be viewed from six different angles and a unit sample which forms the same three-dimensional mark.

d)   Documents relating to right of priority shall be submitted simultaneously with submission of the declaration or within 15 days of that date (if priority right is requested)

e)   Presentation of documents including activity in the related field at the discretion of the Registration Authority

f)   Documents proving identity of the applicant

g)   Receipt relating to payment of legal expenses

7. Trade Mark registration phases are as follows:

a)   Collecting necessary information

b)   Filling in the application form (declaration)

c)   Checking the application and its related appendices: at this stage, staff of the registration office will review the declaration and its appendices and take one of the three kinds of decisions:

      (i)   If they find a defect in the submitted documents, a rectification notice will be issued and the applicant shall rectify the defect within the specified period.

      (ii)   If the application is rejected, a rejection notice will be issued.

      (iii)   Admission of application

d)   Publication of application: When the application is accepted, the registration office will ask the applicant to publish the application in the Official Gazette.

e)   Request for registration number: One month after the application has been published, the applicant may ask for the registration number by providing the office with a picture of the published application in the Official Gazette and paying the registration fee. Official registration of the Trade Mark must also be published.

f)   Request for registration certificate: One month after the publication of the official registration of the Trade Mark, the applicant may ask for the registration certificate.

7.1.3   Iran's Membership in International Trade Mark Conventions

7.1.3.1   Paris Convention for the Protection of Industrial Property (1883)

Iran has been a member of the Paris Convention for the Protection of Industrial Property since 1998.

7.1.3.2   Madrid Agreement (1891) and Protocol Relating to the Madrid Agreement (1989) Concerning the International Registration of Marks

On 25 September 2003, Iran acceded to both the Madrid Agreement and the Madrid Protocol on the International Registration of Marks with the World Intellectual Property Organization (WIPO). The Madrid Agreement and the Madrid Protocol came into force in Iran on 25 December, 2003.

7.2   Patent

In accordance with Article 1 of the Patents, Industrial Designs and Trademarks Registration Act (2008):

"An invention is the outcome of an individual(s) mind that produces a certain product or a process for the first time and provides for a solution to a specific problem in a certain line of specialty, technique, technology, industry and the like."

A patent is essentially a government grant to a person for the exclusive right to make, use, and sell his new and useful discovery, design, process, machine, manufacture, or other composition, or, any new and useful improvement on it.

Applying for a patent is not obligatory. But, obtaining of a patent gives the owner (patentee) the right and assurance to take legal action for preventing others from exploiting the patented invention or discovery without his consent.

7.2.1   Types of Patentable Discoveries and Inventions

According to Article 2 of the Patents, Industrial Designs and Trademarks Registration Act (2008),

"An invention shall be patentable if it includes a new innovation, and is industrially applicable. An innovation includes anything that has not been anticipated by prior art and would not be obvious to a person having ordinary skills in the art. An invention shall be considered industrially applicable if it may be made or used in a given line of industry. "Industry" may be construed in the broadest meaning of the word and shall include handicrafts, agriculture, fishery and services as well."

7.2.2   Un-patentable Discoveries and Inventions

Based on Article 4 of the Patents, Industrial Designs and Trademarks Registration Act (2008):

"The following shall be excluded from the scope of the protection of a patent:
1. *Discoveries, scientific theories, mathematical methods and works of art*
2. *Schemes, rules or methods for doing business, performing mental or social acts*
3. *Methods for treatment or diagnosis of human or animal diseases: This subsection shall not include products falling within the scope of definition of the patent and those used in the said methods*
4. *Genetic resources and genetic components comprising the same, as well as biological processes for the production of the same*
5. *Anything that has been already anticipated in industries and techniques"*

7.2.3   Documents Required for the Registration of an Invention or Discovery in Iran

The inventor or discoverer is required to make a written application to the Tehran Office for Industrial Property (patent office) and, together with the necessary fees, file what is known as a "declaration" with the following contents:
1. Patent declarations shall be drawn up in three copies and in a special form (A-1) and in Persian language and signed by the applicant or his legal representative after mentioning date.
2. In the case where deeds are attached to the declaration and other related documents are drawn up in another language other than Persian language, it is obligatory to submit the original documents with their unofficial translation. However, if perfect translation of these documents is not possible, one can attach their summary in Persian language. If necessary, the registration authority may request for an official translation of said documents while studying the declaration. In the case where technical and scientific

terms applied in the documents do not have a Persian equivalent, it is sufficient to mention the same terms.

3. The applicant shall submit, personally or by registered mail or on the basis of Article 167 of this regulation, the patent declaration to the registration authority. Date of collection of the declaration or date of giving message is regarded as date of declaration.

4. Patent declarations shall contain the following points:

   a) Name, national code number, address, postal code, nationality, position of the applicant and in the case where the applicant is a legal entity, it is necessary to mention name, type of activity, domicile, registration place and number, nationality, principal office and if necessary, any other identification number.

   b) Name, national number, address and postal code of the legal representative of the applicant, if available

   c) Name, domicile and postal code of the person or persons who are qualified for receiving notices in Iran in the case where the applicant is not a resident of Iran

   d) Name, address, and position of the inventor, in the case where the applicant is not the inventor

   e) Title of invention in such a manner that the invention specifies a claim and does not include any words such as "better" and so on. The title should preferably consist of between three and ten words.

   f) Date, place and number of declaration or invention certificate abroad at the request of the right of priority

   g) Information relating to the original declaration in the case where the invention is complementary

   h) Number of pages for description, claims, brief description of invention and plans

   i) Determination of the invention class on the basis of international classification of inventions

   j) Determination of appendices

   k) In the case of submission of the appendices and other related documents by the legal entities, they shall be signed by the authorized signatories

   l) Name and address of the applicant abroad shall be in Latin, in addition to Persian script, and shall be registered and published with the same letters.

5. The following documents shall be attached to the declaration:

   a) detailed description of invention

   b) claim or claims of invention

   c) brief description of invention

   d) design or designs, if necessary

   e) evidences affirming identity of the applicant and inventor

   f) written request for not mentioning the name of the inventor, in case the inventor does not want to mention his name

   g) documents relating to right of priority which shall be submitted simultaneously with submission of the declaration or within 15 days of that date

h)   receipt relating to payment of legal expenses

i)   representation documents, in the case where the legal representative applies.

Note 1:   In case the declaration is not qualified for conditions stipulated in Article 11 at the time of request, the registration authority will invite the applicant to perform the necessary corrections until the date of notification within 30 days and the date of application will be the same as the date of receiving the necessary corrections. If no correction is done at due date, the declaration will be null and void. The grace period is 60 days for persons residing abroad.

Note 2:   If some designs are referred to in this declaration that have not been included or attached, the registration authority will invite the applicant to present the designs within 30 days. In the case of submission, the date of receiving the designs will be regarded as the date of request. Otherwise, the registration authority will mention the date of request as the date of receiving the declaration and will regard reference to designs as null and void. The grace period is 60 days for those persons residing abroad.

j)   Any page of description, claim, brief description and the invention design shall be signed by the applicant or his legal representative.

k)   The declaration shall only relate to an invention or a group of the related inventions which comprises a general invention. Otherwise, the applicant can divide his invention declaration into two or more separate and independent declarations.

6. The registration authority, having received the declaration and the related appendices, investigates them within 6 months in terms of conformity with procedural and substantial conditions inserted in the law and this regulation.

Note 1:   The registration authority will consult concerned private or governmental authorities or specialists and experts about their views with regards to whether the substantial conditions of the invention are fulfilled. The grace period for answering the enquiry will be not later than 3 months.

Note 2:   The consulted authorities or experts and mentioned persons are obliged to answer such enquiries, but failure to do so will not prevent investigation and decision making by the registration authority.

Note 3:   Enquiring and asking said authorities and persons about their opinions may be based on contracts concluded with them.

7. In case it is necessary to correct or complete the declaration and its appendices after investigation of the declaration and its appendices, the registration authority asks the applicant in writing to take action regarding correction or completion of the document within 30 days of date of notification. Otherwise, the declaration will be null and void. The grace period determined in this article for the persons residing abroad is 60 days. The applicant will be notified of the decision of the registration authority regarding grant of patent certificate within 30 days of notification and the applicant shall take

action regarding registration of invention and publication of notice included in Article 32 of this regulation for payment of the related expenses. In case of failure to pay the expenses at due date, the declaration will be regarded null and void. The grace period for the applicants residing abroad will be 60 days.

8. Inventions are registered by mentioning the following information on the basis of form (A-2) in the patent register:

a) Number and date of declaration by mentioning hour, day, month and year
b) Number and date of patent
c) Name and address and nationality of inventor
d) Name and address and nationality of the applicant in case the applicant is not the inventor unless the inventor requests in writing not to mention his name in patent certificate.
e) Name and address of the legal representative of the inventor, if patent is requested by him
f) Title of invention
g) International classification of invention by mentioning the scientific field in which the invention is included
h) In case of a claim for right of priority and accepting it, date, number and place of submission of the prior declaration
i) Term of support

   Note 1:   Two pages are allocated to each invention in the patent register and any change and correction as well as transfers which are done partially or wholly regarding subject of the invention are mentioned in the said pages.

   Note 2:   Insertion of the said information shall be signed by the inventor or his legal representative as well as the head of the Patent Office after completion.

9. After registration, the notice of registration is published in the official Gazette within 30 days by mentioning the information mentioned in Article 31 of this regulation. The said notice is signed by the head of the Patent Office and is submitted to the official Gazette for publication.

10. After publication of patent notice and delivery of three copies published and reflected in the official Gazette to the registration authority, the patent certificate will be issued and submitted to the applicant or his representative. The patent certificate shall be prepared with use of updated technology and include a copy of description, claim, brief description and design and shall be punched and sealed and signed by the head of the Patent Office. The patent certificate shall contain the following points on the basis of form (A-3):

a) Number and date of declaration
b) Number and date of patent
c) Name and address and nationality of inventor
d) Name and address and nationality of the applicant unless the inventor requests in writing not to mention his name in patent certificate

e)   Title of invention
f)   International classification of invention
g)   In case of a claim for right of priority and accepting it, date, number and place of submission of the prior declaration
h)   Term of support

11. With regard to Article 16 of the Patents, Industrial Designs and Trademarks Registration Act (2008):

"Validity of a patent certificate is 20 years from the date of submission of the declaration. For keeping validity of the certificate, annual cost shall be paid within 2 months before expiry of a year from the date of submission of the declaration and every year afterwards until validity of the certificate in accordance with the table of costs; otherwise, the invention patent will be null and void."

7.2.4   Iran's Membership in International Patent Conventions

7.2.4.1   Paris Convention for the Protection of Industrial Property (1883)

Iran has been a member of the Paris Convention for the Protection of Industrial Property since 1998. Parties to this agreement undertake to grant each other's nationals patent and trademark rights identical to those of their own nationals. The right of priority is one of the major benefits of the Paris Convention. It allows for a person who has applied for a patent in one of the Convention countries to have the right to apply, within one year, for protection in any of the other Convention countries.

These later applications shall be regarded as if they had been filed on the same day as the first application. This provision is a major advantage for foreigners who wish to register and safeguard their patents in any number of countries, Iran included.

7.2.4.2   Patent Cooperation Treaty 1970 (PCT)

On 4 July 2013, the Islamic Republic of Iran deposited its instrument of ratification to the PCT, thus becoming the 148th Contracting State of the PCT, which came into force in Iran on 4 October 2013. Consequently, any international application filed after that date automatically includes the designation of the Islamic Republic of Iran.

Also, because the Islamic Republic of Iran is bound by Chapter II of the PCT, it is automatically elected in any demand for international preliminary examination filed in respect of an international application. Furthermore, nationals and residents of the Islamic Republic of Iran are entitled to file international applications under the PCT.

8.   Appendix

Table 8.1:   Important Iranian Websites

Ministry of Finance & Economy	www.mefa.gov.ir
Ministry of Industry & Mines	www.min.gov.ir
Ministry of Commerce	www.iranministryofcommerce.com
Iran Chamber of Commerce & Mines	www.iccim.org
Duties Islamic Republic	www.irica.gov.ir
Ministry of Foreign Affairs	www.mfa.gov.ir
Ministry of Oil	www.nioc.com
Ministry of Labour	www.irimlsa.ir
Organization of Managing & Planning	www.mpzog.ir
Value Added Tax Organization	www.vat.ir
Iranian Association of Certified Accountants	www.iacpa.ir
Tehran Stock Exchange Organization	www.tse.or.ir
Central Bank of Iran	www.cbi.ir
State Tax Organization	www.intamedia.ir
Iranian Privatization Organization	www.ipo.ir
Organization for Investment Economic & Technical Assistance of Iran (OIETAI)	www.investiniran.ir
Iran Foreign Investment Co.(IFIC)	www.ific.org.ir
Audit Organization	www.audit.org.ir
Electronic Visa for Iran	wvisa.mfa.gov.ir

Disclaimer

In the formulation of this guidebook, every effort has been made to offer current, correct and clearly stated information. Nevertheless, the information in the text is intended to provide general and legal guidelines only. This publication is circulated with the understanding that the authors are not responsible for the result of any actions taken on the groundwork of information in this publication, nor for any errors or omissions contained herein. The authors are not attempting, through this study, to render legal or financial advice. Readers are encouraged to consult with professional advisors for advice concerning specific matters before making any decisions.

Index

سرمایه‌گذاری در ایران

کتاب راهنمایی کاربردی به زبان آلمانی، انگلیسی و فارسی

فهرست مطالب

148

۱ فصل اول: مقدمه

۱-۱.   موقعیت جغرافیایی و جمعیت

جمهوری اسلامی ایران دارای مساحتی معادل ۱/۶۴۸/۱۹۵ کیلومتر مربع و جمعیتی بالغ بر ۸۰/۸ میلیون نفر دارد و در جنوب غربی آسیا واقع شده است. ایران از شمال با جمهوری آذربایجان، ارمنستان و ترکمنستان، از شرق با افغانستان و پاکستان و از غرب با ترکیه و عراق همسایه است. همچنین از شمال با دریای خزر، و از جنوب با کویت، عربستان سعودی، قطر، بحرین و امارات متحده عربی، خلیج فارس و دریای عمان محدود می‌شود که دو منطقه نخست از مناطق مهم استخراج نفت و گاز در جهان هستند.

ایران یکی از ثروتمندترین کشورهای دنیا در حوزه منابع هیدروکربن شناخته می‌شود به نحوی که دارای دومین ذخایر گاز جهان بوده و یکی از بزرگ‌ترین صادر کنندگان نفت به شمار می‌رود.

بر اساس گزارش‌های سازمان‌های جهانی نظیر بانک جهانی، ایران با داشتن ۷۰۰ بیلیون دلار تولید ناخالص داخلی، هجدهمین اقتصاد مطرح دنیا در میان ۲۰ اقتصاد برتر و دومین اقتصاد برتر خاورمیانه و شمال افریقا؛ هجدهمین کشور دنیا از حیث جمعیت و هفدهمین کشور جهان از نظر مساحت به شمار می‌رود. با در نظر گرفتن مساحت این کشور روشن می‌شود که ایران دومین کشور بزرگ خاورمیانه است. ایران همچنین با داشتن جمعیتی بالغ بر هشتاد میلیون نفر، دومین کشور پرجمعیت منطقه پس از مصر به شمار می‌رود.

۲-۱.   مزایای اقتصادی

بخش اعظم اقتصاد ایران نوعاً بر صنایع نفت و گاز و هیدروکربن و در مقیاس کوچک‌تر بر کشاورزی، خدمات و نیز حضور پُررنگ بخش دولتی در صنایع زیربنایی و مالی استوار است. ایران دومین دارندهٔ ذخایر گاز و چهارمین دارندهٔ ذخایر نفت خام در جهان است. تولید ناخالص داخلی و درآمدهای دولت تا اندازهٔ زیادی وابسته به درآمدهای نفتی است. در ایران، نفت و گاز طبیعی دو منبع از ذخایر زیرزمینی هستند که از جذابیت زیادی برای سرمایه‌گذاری و تجارت برخوردارند.

رشد اقتصادی ایران در سال‌های اخیر نوید ظهور یکی از بزرگ‌ترین اقتصادهای خاورمیانه و آسیا را می‌دهد. در ایران فرصت‌های سرمایه‌گذاری بی‌شماری برای سرمایه‌گذاران خارجی و تجّار به سبب وجود مناطق آزاد تجاری در سرتاسر کشور وجود دارد. در حال حاضر، بیش از بیست منطقه آزاد تجاری و منطقه ویژه اقتصادی در کشور ایجاد شده که مزایای بی‌شماری را برای سرمایه‌گذاران خارجی به همراه دارد.

۳-۱.   نگاهی گذرا به فرصت‌های تجاری و سرمایه‌گذاری

- تنوع اقتصادی سبب حضور بیش از چهل صنعت به طور مستقیم در بورس اوراق بهادار تهران شده است؛
- ایران دارای اقتصادی ثروتمند بر مبنای منابع طبیعی است؛
- ایران دارای اقتصادی ثروتمند از حیث نیروی کار است؛
- ایران دارای جمعیتی جوان و تحصیل‌کرده است؛
- بازار داخلی ایران بسیار گسترده است؛
- بازار خاورمیانه یکی از بازارهای اصلی و فرصتی برای صادرات غیرنفتی ایران است؛
- افزایش صنایع پیچیده و سرمایه‌های انسانی سبب پیدایش اقتصادی دانش‌محور در ایران شده است.

از سال ۲۰۰۶ و با گسترش تحریم‌ها علیه ایران، ایالات متحده امریکا تلاش‌های فراوانی کرد تا شرکت‌های فعال در بخش نفت و گاز و بخش‌های مالی را با تحریم‌های خود همراه کند. این امر موجب شد شرکت‌های خارجی از توسعهٔ میدان‌های گازی پارس جنوبی خارج شده یا سرمایه‌گذاری بیشتر خود در این میادین را به تأخیر بیاندازند و تأمین مالی پروژه‌ها با دشواری بسیار مواجه شود. از همین روی، دولت ایران به منظور توسعه میادین نفتی و گازی، تأمین مالی

پروژه‌ها و فروش اوراق مشارکت به مبلغ ۳/۵ میلیون دلار، به منابع داخلی و سرمایه‌گذاران ایرانی و همچنین شرکت‌های مهندسی داخلی روی آورد.

با وقوع برجام، تحریم‌های بین‌المللی علیه ایران لغو و فرصت‌های بی‌شماری برای سرمایه‌گذاران خارجی به منظور ورود به بازار ایران و یا بازگشت به فعالیت‌های پیشین فراهم شد. با توجه به این امر، شرکت‌های بین‌المللی باید تغییرات به‌وجودآمده را به منظور توسعه صنایع ایران و همچنین دریافت سود سرمایه‌گذاری مورد توجه قرار دهند. به منظور جذب سرمایه‌گذاری خارجی، قانون تشویق و حمایت از سرمایه‌گذاری خارجی (فیپا) در سال ۲۰۰۲ (۱۳۸۱) به تصویب مجلس شورای اسلامی رسید. برخی از مزایا و ویژگی‌های توسعه‌یافتۀ فیپا، به شرح زیر است:

۱. زمینه‌های سرمایه‌گذاری خارجی و فعالیت سرمایه‌گذاران خارجی در صنایع زیربنایی گسترش چشمگیری یافته است؛

۲. تعریف گسترده‌تر از سرمایه‌گذاری خارجی کلیه شیوه‌های سرمایه‌گذاری مستقیم خارجی و تأمین مالی پروژه‌ها و نیز ترتیبات قراردادی نظیر قراردادهای جوینت‌ونچر، ترتیبات بای‌بک و شیوه‌های مختلف قراردادهای ساخت، بهره‌برداری و انتقال را دربرمی‌گیرد؛

۳. این قانون سبب تسهیل و تسریع فرایند اخذ مجوز سرمایه‌گذاری خارجی و دیگر مجوزهای مربوطه در ایران شده است؛

۴. ایجاد یک مجموعه هماهنگ و جامع‌الابعاد به نام «مرکز خدمات سرمایه‌گذاری خارجی» در سازمان سرمایه‌گذاری خارجی با هدف حمایت از سرمایه‌گذاری و تسهیل فرایندهای مربوطه و کمک به سرمایه‌گذاران خارجی؛

۵. تسهیل و ایجاد مقررات ساده‌تر و منعطف‌تر به منظور دسترسی سرمایه‌گذاران خارجی به ارز و نیز انتقال سرمایه خارجی؛

۶. بهره‌مندی از حق خروج سرمایه و سود سرمایه‌گذاری به موجب مواد ۱۲، ۱۳، ۱۴ و ۱۵ قانون برای هر سرمایه‌گذار خارجی که سرمایه خود را به موجب فیپا ثبت نموده و مجوز سرمایه‌گذاری دریافت نموده است.

ماده ۱۲: نرخ ارز مورد عمل به هنگام ورود یا خروج سرمایه خارجی و همچنین کلیه انتقالات ارزی در صورت تک‌نرخی‌بودن ارز، همان نرخ رایج در شبکه رسمی کشور می‌باشد. در غیر این صورت، نرخ آزاد روز به تشخیص بانک مرکزی جمهوری اسلامی ایران ملاک خواهد بود.

گزینه‌های بسیاری برای شرکت‌های خارجی به منظور ورود به بازار سرمایه‌گذاری و تجارت ایران وجود دارد. صرف‌نظر از ایجاد روابط تجاری در قالب نمایندگی‌های بازرگانی، برای بسیاری از شرکت‌های بین‌المللی این مزیت متمایز به منظور حضور مستقیم و بدون واسطه وجود دارد. این امر سبب تسهیل تحقیق دربارۀ بازار، ایجاد روابط تجاری، برقراری ارتباط با مشتریان و نظارت بر جزئیات معاملات تجاری برای سرمایه‌گذاران خارجی می‌شود.

یکی دیگر از عناصر منطقه‌ای که به همراه حضور فیزیکی دارای اهمیت اساسی است، استفاده از نیروهای متخصص به عنوان مشاور در پروژه‌های سرمایه‌گذاری است.

۴-۱.   سیستم سیاسی

سیستم سیاسی ایران بر مبنای قانون اساسی ۱۹۷۹ استوار شده است. این سیستم از چند بخش تشکیل شده است. برخی از این بخش‌ها به صورت دموکراتیک و برخی از آنها به وسیله انتخابات دومرحله‌ای انتخاب می‌شوند. وجه ممتاز این سیستم سیاسی که در سال ۱۹۷۹ پایه‌گذاری شد، تلفیق سیستم دموکراتیک و سیستم مذهبی به عنوان نظام سیاسی است. سیستم سیاسی ایران از سه قوه تشکیل شده است که عبارتند از مقننه، مجریه، قضائیه. این سه قوه چارچوبی مشابه سیستم سیاسی سایر کشورها هستند. ایران کشوری با تنوع فرهنگی زیاد است که اقوام، فرهنگ‌ها و مذاهب آسمانی متعددی در آن حضور دارند. مذهب رسمی کشور، شیعه جعفری و زبان رسمی مردم ایران، فارسی است. زبان انگلیسی زبان رسمی در زمینه معاملات خارجی است.

۵-۱.   واحد پولی

واحد پولی ایران، ریال است که نرخ تبدیل آن نوعاً بر مبنای دلار امریکا تعیین می‌شود.

۶-۱.   ساعات کاری

هفته کاری در ایران از شنبه آغاز و تا پنج‌شنبه ادامه می‌یابد و روز جمعه، تعطیل عمومی است. وزارتخانه‌ها در روز پنج‌شنبه تعطیل است. ساعات کاری اداره‌های دولتی معمولاً ۸/۱۴ است. ساعات کار بانک‌ها از شنبه تا چهارشنبه معمولاً ۱۳/۳۰-۷/۳۰ و در روزهای پنج‌شنبه تا ۱۲ است.

مراکز خرید و بازارها در ایران در ساعات ۲۰/۳۰-۸/۳۰ بجز روزهای جمعه باز و مشغول فعالیت هستند.

۷-۱.   تعطیلات عمومی ایران در سال ۲۰۱۶

مناسبت	تاریخ
نوروز (سال نو)	۱ تا ۴ فروردین
روز جمهوری اسلامی ـ روز طبیعت	۱۲ و ۱۳ فروردین
ولادت امام علی(ع)	۲ اردیبهشت
عید مبعث	۱۶ اردیبهشت
ولادت امام مهدی(ع)	۲ خرداد
قیام ۱۵ خرداد	۱۵ خرداد
شهادت امام علی	۷ تیر
عید فطر	۱۶ تیر
عید فطر	۱۷ تیر
شهادت امام صادق(ع)	۹ مرداد
عید قربان	۲۲ شهریور
عید غدیر	۳۰ شهریور
تاسوعا	۲۰ مهر
عاشورا	۲۱ مهر
اربعین	۳۰ آبان
شهادت پیامبر و امام حسن(ع)	۸ آذر
شهادت امام رضا(ع)	۱۰ آذر
تولد پیامبر و امام صادق(ع)	۲۷ آذر
شهادت حضرت زهرا(ع)	۱۲ اسفند
ملی‌شدن صنعت نفت ایران	۲۹ اسفند

۸-۱.   ایران در یک نگاه

تهران	پایتخت
فارسی	زبان اصلی
اسلام ـ شیعه	مذهب اصلی
ریال	پول رایج
۱/۶۴۸/۱۹۵ کیلومتر مربع	مساحت
۸/۸۰ میلیون نفر (۲۰۱۴)	جمعیت
۹۸+	کد تلفن بین‌المللی

۲ فصل دوم: سرمایه‌گذاری خارجی در ایران

پس از گذشت ۴۸ سال از تصویب قانون اول سرمایه‌گذاری ایران، در سال ۱۳۸۱ قانون جدیدی با عنوان «قانون تشویق و حمایت سرمایه‌گذاری خارجی» که به اختصار «فیپا» نامیده می‌شود، به تصویب مجلس شورای اسلامی رسید. این قانون در مقایسه با قانون قبلی دارای ویژگی‌های منحصربه‌فردی برای سرمایه‌گذاری خارجی است که به اختصار به شرح آن می‌پردازیم.

۲-۱. شیوه‌های سرمایه گذاری خارجی

مطابق ماده ۳ قانون، شیوه‌های سرمایه‌گذاری عبارت است از:

۱. سرمایه‌گذاری مستقیم خارجی در زمینه‌هایی که فعالیت بخش خصوصی در آن مجاز می‌باشد؛

۲. سرمایه‌گذاری خارجی در همهٔ بخش‌ها در چارچوب روش‌های «جوینت‌ونچر»، «بیع متقابل»

و «ساخت، بهره‌برداری و واگذاری» امکان‌پذیر است که برگشت سرمایه و منافع حاصله، صرفاً از عملکرد اقتصادی طرح مورد سرمایه‌گذاری ناشی شود و متکی به تضمین دولت یا بانک‌ها یا شرکت‌های دولتی نباشد.

۲-۱-۱. سرمایه‌گذاری مستقیم خارجی

سرمایه‌گذاری مستقیم خارجی نوعی از سرمایه‌گذاری برون‌مرزی است که به‌وسیله یک شخص حقیقی یا حقوقی مقیم در کشور (سرمایه‌گذار مستقیم)، با هدف دستیابی به «سود بلندمدت»در یک بنگاه اقتصادی در کشوری دیگر، صورت می‌پذیرد. عمدتاً در این نوع سرمایه‌گذاری کنترل و مدیریت بنگاه اقتصادی سرمایه‌پذیر به صورت کلی یا جزئی در اختیار سرمایه‌گذار خارجی قرار خواهد گرفت.

مطابق قانون، سرمایه‌گذاری مستقیم نوعی از سرمایه‌گذاری خارجی است که با به‌کارگیری اقلام سرمایه در بنگاه اقتصادی سرمایه‌پذیر، به‌وسیله اشخاص حقیقی یا حقوقی خارجی و یا ایرانی با سرمایهٔ دارای منشأ خارجی، با هدف دستیابی به کنترل بنگاه اقتصادی سرمایه‌پذیر و سود بلندمدت، صورت می‌پذیرد.

به موجب این قانون، سرمایه‌گذاری مستقیم خارجی به شیوه‌های زیر محقق می‌شود:

الف) از طریق به‌کارگیری سرمایه خارجی در شرکت ایرانی جدید یا خرید سهام شرکت ایرانی موجود توسط سرمایه‌گذار خارجی؛

ب) از طریق ترتیبات قراردادی که با تشکیل شرکت یا بدون تشکیل شرکت، به‌وسیله توافقات قراردادی فی‌مابین طرفین محقق شود.

بدیهی است سرمایه‌گذاری مستقیم خارجی در بخش خصوصی مطابق تمامی روش‌های مقرر در قانون از قبیل تشکیل شرکت ایرانی جدید، خرید سهام شرکت ایرانی موجود و ترتیبات قراردادی مجاز است.

از ماده ۳ قانون و دیگر قوانین مرتبط، چنین استنباط می‌شود که سرمایه‌گذاری خارجی در بخش‌های اقتصادی که در انحصار دولت قرار دارد، صرفاً در چارچوب روش‌های قراردادی که برگشت سرمایه و منافع حاصله از عملکرد اقتصادی طرح مورد سرمایه‌گذاری حاصل و متکی به تضمین دولت یا بانک‌ها یا شرکت‌های دولتی نباشد، مجاز است. درواقع این ماده در دو بند، ضوابط سرمایه‌گذاری خارجی در بخش خصوصی و دولتی اقتصاد ایران را بیان می‌کند. مطابق اصل ۴۴ قانون اساسی:

«نظام اقتصادی جمهوری اسلامی ایران بر پایه سه بخش دولتی، تعاونی و خصوصی با برنامه‌ریزی منظم و صحیح استوار است.

الف) بخش دولتی شامل همهٔ صنایع بزرگ، صنایع مادر، بازرگانی خارجی، معادن بزرگ، بانکداری، بیمه، تأمین نیرو، سدها و شبکه‌های بزرگ آب‌رسانی، رادیو و تلویزیون، پست و تلگراف و تلفن، کشتیرانی، راه‌آهن و مانند اینهاست که به صورت مالکیت عمومی در اختیار دولت است.

ب) بخش تعاونی شامل شرکت‌ها و مؤسسات تعاونی تولید و توزیع است که در شهر و روستا طبق ضوابط اسلامی تشکیل می‌شود.

پ) بخش خصوصی شامل آن قسمت از کشاورزی، دامداری، صنعت، تجارت و خدمات می‌شود که مکمل فعالیت‌های اقتصادی دولتی و تعاونی است.

مالکیت در این سه بخش تا جایی که با اصول دیگر این فصل مطابق باشد و از محدوده قوانین اسلام خارج نشود و موجب رشد و توسعه کشور شود و مایه زیان جامعه نشود، مورد حمایت قانون جمهوری اسلامی است. تفصیل ضوابط و قلمرو و شرایط هر سه بخش را قانون معین می‌کند».

به موجب بند «الف» ابلاغیه سیاست‌های کلی اصل ۴۴ قانون اساسی:

«سرمایه‌گذاری، مالکیت و مدیریت در زمینه‌های یادشده در صدر اصل ۴۴ قانون اساسی به شرح ذیل، توسط بنگاه‌ها و نهادهای عمومی غیردولتی و بخش‌های تعاونی و خصوصی مجاز است:

- صنایع بزرگ، صنایع مادر (از جمله صنایع پایین‌دستی نفت و گاز) و معادن بزرگ (به استثنای نفت و گاز)؛
- فعالیت بازرگانی خارجی در چارچوب سیاست‌های تجاری و ارزی کشور؛
- بانکداری توسط بنگاه‌ها و نهادهای عمومی غیردولتی و شرکت‌های تعاونی و شرکت‌های سهامی عام مشروط به تعیین سقف سهام هر‌یک از سهام‌داران با تصویب قانون؛
- بیمه؛
- تأمین نیرو شامل تولید و واردات برق برای مصارف داخلی و صادرات؛
- کلیه امور پست و مخابرات به استثنای شبکه‌های مادر مخابراتی، امور واگذاری فرکانس و شبکه‌های اصلی تجزیه و مبادلات و مدیریت توزیع خدمات پایه پستی؛
- راه و راه‌آهن؛
- هواپیمایی (حمل‌ونقل هوایی) و کشتیرانی (حمل‌ونقل دریایی).

سهم بهینۀ بخش‌های دولتی و غیردولتی در فعالیت‌های صدر اصل (۴۴)، با توجه به حفظ حاکمیت دولت و استقلال کشور و عدالت اجتماعی و رشد و توسعه اقتصادی طبق قانون تعیین می‌شود».

بند «الف» سیاست‌های کلی اصل ۴۴ قانون اساسی، آن دسته از فعالیت‌های اقتصادی را برشمرده که بخش خصوصی قادر است در این زمینه‌ها به سرمایه‌گذاری، مالکیت و مدیریت بپردازد. درنتیجه، به موجب سیاست‌های کلی این اصل، سرمایه‌گذاری مستقیم خارجی در زمینه‌های هشت‌گانه فوق توسط سرمایه‌گذاری خارجی مجاز است.

۲-۱-۲. ترتیبات قراردادی

به موجب بند «ب» ماده ۳ قانون، سرمایه‌گذاری خارجی در همۀ بخش‌ها در چارچوب روش‌های «جوینت‌ونچر»، «بیع متقابل» و «ساخت، بهره‌برداری و واگذاری» که برگشت سرمایه و منافع

حاصله صرفاً از عملکرد اقتصادی طرح مورد سرمایه‌گذاری ناشی شود و متکی به تضمین دولت یا بانک‌ها یا شرکت‌های دولتی نباشد، امکان‌پذیر است.

در ادامه به بیان کلیاتی از هریک از این قراردادها پرداخته و بحث تفصیلی دربارهٔ هرکدام از این موضوعات را به فصول بعدی کتاب واگذار می‌کنیم.

۲-۱-۲. جوینت‌ونچر

اصطلاح مشارکت در گسترهٔ حقوق سرمایه‌گذاری خارجی کاربرد فراوانی دارد و این قالب قراردادی در بیشتر سیستم‌های حقوقی به‌وسیلهٔ سرمایه‌گذاران و در تحقق سرمایه‌گذاری مورد استفاده قرار می‌گیرد.

اگرچه، مدل مشارکت به عنوان یک ترتیب قراردادی مطلوب و مناسب، در راستای تسهیم ریسک‌ها و هزینه‌های سرمایه‌گذاری همواره مورد توجه سرمایه‌گذاران قرار داشته، اما چگونگی به‌کارگیری این قرارداد منوط به رعایت الزام‌هایی است که معمولاً به‌واسطهٔ قوانین و مقررات حاکم بر قرارداد تعیین می‌شوند.

در برخی موارد، بر حسب قوانین و مقررات کشور سرمایه‌پذیر، موضوع پروژه و الزامات اجرایی آن، مشارکت در قالب تشکیل شرکتی توصیه می‌شود که دارای شخصیت حقوقی مستقل از شرکاست و به جوینت‌ونچر شرکتی موسوم است. گاهی اوقات نیز مشارکت بدون تشکیل شرکت و به صورت قراردادی، گزینه مناسبی برای سرمایه‌گذاری است که از آن به جوینت‌ونچر قراردادی تعبیر می‌شود.

انتخاب مناسب‌ترین چارچوب با پیش‌بینی شروط مناسب و دقیق قراردادی به‌منظور سرمایه‌گذاری، یکی از مهم‌ترین موضوعاتی است که سرمایه‌گذاران در مراحل ابتدایی و تکوین پروژه، با انجام بررسی‌های مقدماتی و لحاظ الزامات اجرایی پروژه مورد توجه قرار می‌دهند. مشارکت به عنوان یکی از چارچوب‌های قراردادها، هدفِ سرمایه‌گذاری محسوب نمی‌شود، بلکه شیوه و طریقی است که سرمایه‌گذاران خارجی به‌وسیله آن به اهداف خود از سرمایه‌گذاری ـ همان‌گونه که در طرح تجاری پیش‌بینی شده است ـ نائل می‌شوند.

در سیستم‌های حقوقی مختلف این شیوه سرمایه‌گذاری دارای عناوین متنوعی است. گاهی از آن به «Joint Venture»، «Partnership»، «Consortium» و گاهی نیز «Shareholder Agreement» یاد می‌شود. در پاره‌ای از سیستم‌های حقوقی این عناوین دارای تفاوت‌هایی نیز هستند که ورود به جزئیات این مباحث از حوصلهٔ این دفتر خارج است.

در ادبیات حقوقی ایران نیز، قالب حقوقی مشارکت هم در قانون مدنی (مواد ۵۷۱ تا ۶۰۶)، هم قانون تجارت (مبحث شرکت‌ها) و هم در آیین‌نامهٔ عملیات بانکی بدون ربا (ماده ۱۸) مورد اشاره قرار گرفته است.

همان‌طورکه بند «ب» ماده ۳ قانون مقرر کرده، مشارکت مدنی به عنوان یکی از ترتیبات قراردادهای سرمایه‌گذاری به همراه مشارکت حقوقی، تشکیل‌دهندهٔ مشارکت انتفاعی یا جوینت‌ونچر به شمار می‌روند.

در جوینت‌ونچر شرکتی طرفین مشارکت، به تشکیل شرکتی از اقسام شرکت‌های تجاری دارای شخصیت حقوقی اقدام کرده و هرکدام درصدی از سهام آن را تملک می‌کنند. در این صورت، طرفین مشارکت سهام‌دار نامیده شده و شرکت مسئول اجرای طرح مربوط به مشارکت یا پروژه موضوع جوینت‌ونچر خواهد بود.

در جوینت‌ونچر قراردادی، طرفین مشارکت به دلایلی از تشکیل شرکت به نحو یادشده اجتناب کرده و با انعقاد قراردادی که حاکم بر روابط فیمابین خواهد بود، خود شرکا مستقیماً به اجرای طرح سرمایه‌گذاری اقدام می‌کنند.

۲-۲-۱-۲.   قراردادهای نفتی

در پی تحولات قانونی طی چند سال گذاشته در قوانین نفتی ایران، قرارداد جدید در کنار قرارداد بای‌بک یا بیع متقابل، تحت عنوان «قرارداد نفتی ایران» پا به عرصه وجود نهاد. در این بخش این دو قرارداد به اختصار مورد بررسی قرار خواهند گرفت.

۲-۲-۱-۲-۱.   قرارداد بای‌بک

دومین روش سرمایه‌گذاری خارجی که در بند «ب» ماده ۳ قانون عنوان شده، «بیع متقابل» است. در سال‌های اخیر قراردادهای بیع متقابل به عنوان یکی از ترتیبات قراردادی سرمایه‌گذاری، نقش برجسته‌ای در اقتصاد ایران داشته‌اند. شهرت این قرارداد بیشتر به دلیل کاربرد آن در توسعهٔ میادین نفتی و گازیِ کشف‌شده است. پروژه‌های متعددی در صنایع نفت و گاز، با مبالغ کلان به‌وسیله این قالب قراردادی در کشور اجرا شده و یا در حال اجراست. افزون بر صنایع نفت و گاز، قالب قرارداد بیع متقابل در دیگر صنایع و بخش‌ها نیز قابلیت به‌کارگیری دارد. در این بخش به بیان کلیاتی از این قرارداد پرداخته می‌شود.

بیع متقابل برگردان عبارت لاتین «Buy Back» است که در ترجمه دقیق به معنای «توافق بازخرید محصول» است. «بیع متقابل» یا «توافق بازخرید محصول» یکی از اقسام «تجارت متقابل» است.

«بیع متقابل» یا «بای‌بک»، قراردادی چندجزئی و از جمله شیوه‌های «تجارت متقابل» است که مطابق آن سرمایه‌گذار اقلام نقد و غیرنقد سرمایه مانند ماشین‌آلات، تجهیزات، دانش فنی، خدمات تخصصی و تکنولوژی را در ایجاد، توسعه، بازسازی و اصلاح یک واحد تولیدی به کار می‌گیرد. استهلاک هزینه‌های سرمایه‌ای و غیرسرمایه‌ای سرمایه‌گذار و نیز پرداخت سود سرمایه‌گذاری، از محل محصولات واحد تولیدی صورت می‌پذیرد. در ایران، به سبب الزامات موجود در قانون اساسی و قانون نفت، قراردادهای بیع متقابل اغلب با هدف توسعه میادین نفتی و گازی منعقد می‌شوند.

در حوزه نفت و گاز، اگر مرحله اکتشاف نیز تحت شمول خدمات قرار گیرد، بیع متقابل یکی از اقسام قراردادهای خدماتی «خطرپذیر» با شیوه پرداخت ویژه است. در این شیوه، پیمانکار با انعقاد قرارداد با دولت سرمایه‌پذیر اقلام نقد و غیرنقد سرمایه را به‌منظور توسعه میادین نفت و گاز به کار گرفته و استهلاک هزینه‌های سرمایه‌ای، غیرسرمایه‌ای و حق‌الزحمه پیمانکار که از پیش تعیین شده است با فروش نفت یا گاز تولیدی میدان و به موجب «قرارداد بلندمدت فروش نفت یا گاز» به عنوان یکی از ضمائم قرارداد بای‌بک، محقق می‌شود.

۲-۲-۱-۲-۲. قرارداد نفتی ایران

یکی از بحث‌هایی که این روزها در محافل علمی و تخصصی مطرح است، بهینه‌سازی سازوکار قراردادی اجرای پروژه در بخش بالادستی صنایع نفت و گاز در ایران است. بدین منظور سمیناری نیز در فوریه ۲۰۱۴ در تهران برگزار شد و برخی از شروط قرارداد نفتی جدیدی که «کمیته بازنگری قراردادهای نفتی» تدوین نموده است، تحت عنوان «قرارداد نفتی ایران»، (قرارداد نوع چهارم) رونمایی شد. این قرارداد که در پاسخ به نارسایی‌ها و خلأهای موجود در نسل‌های مختلف قرارداد بیع متقابل تهیه شده، تلاشی است که در شروع ایجاد یک تحول در قراردادهای نفتی ایران مؤثر خواهد بود. از سوی دیگر مجلس شورای اسلامی نیز در قوانینی که در چند سال گذشته تصویب نموده به‌ویژه قانون «وظایف و اختیارات وزرات نفت» مصوب ۱۳۹۱/۲/۱۹، نقش مهمی در این تحول داشته است.

قرارداد نفتی ایران، از حیث ماهوی بیانگر نوع جدیدی از قراردادهای نفتی در ردیف قراردادهای امتیازی، مشارکت در تولید، خدمت و جوینت‌ونچر نبوده و حداکثر قراردادی هیبرید است که از برخی عناصر جوینت‌ونچر (در ارتباط با نحوه اجرای عملیات نفتی) و سازوکار بازیافت هزینه‌ها در قراردادهای مشارکت در تولید (تخصیص نفت هزینه‌ای به پیمانکار) تشکیل یافته است.

مطابق قرارداد IPC در مرحله اکتشاف، شرکت ملی نفت ایران و پیمانکار به منظور اجرای عملیات، اقدام به تشکیل شرکت عملیاتی اکتشافی نموده و عملیات اکتشاف با سرمایه‌گذاری و ریسک‌پذیری انحصاری پیمانکار، تحت هدایت و راهبری او اجرایی می‌شود. شرکت ملی نفت ایران نیز به عنوان شریک فنی و بدون آنکه در هزینه‌ها و ریسک‌های این عملیات شریک شود، در کنار پیمانکار قرار خواهد گرفت. در صورتی‌که عملیات اکتشاف به کشف میدان تجاری منجر نشود، هزینه‌هایی که پیمانکار در راستای اجرای عملیات متحمل شده بازپرداخت نخواهد شد، ولی در صورت کشف میدان تجاری، هزینه‌های پیمانکار در مرحله اکتشاف به مرحله توسعه منتقل و در دوره استهلاک، بازیافت می‌شود.

با اجرای عملیات ارزیابی و احراز کشف میدان تجاری، پروژه وارد مرحله توسعه می‌شود. در این مرحله نیز به منظور اجرای عملیات، شرکت عملیاتی توسعه‌ای تشکیل شده و کلیه هزینه‌ها و ریسک‌های عملیات توسعه در این مرحله، بر عهده شرکت نفتی بین‌المللی یا پیمانکار بوده و این عملیات تحت هدایت و راهبری او اجرایی می‌شود. شرکت ملی نفت ایران نیز به عنوان شریک فنی و بدون آنکه در هزینه‌ها و ریسک‌های این عملیات شریک شود، در کنار پیمانکار قرار خواهد گرفت. کلیه هزینه‌های سرمایه‌ای مستقیم و هزینه‌های غیرمستقیم عملیات توسعه که به وسیله پیمانکار و از طرف شرکت ملی نفت ایران تعهد و پرداخت شده است، به همراه هزینه‌های پول (هزینه‌های بانکی)، از محل تولیدات قابل تخصیص به شرکت مزبور، مستهلک خواهد شد؛ بنابراین برخلاف مرحله اکتشاف که مشارکت شرکت ملی نفت ایران صرفاً جنبه عملیاتی و انتقال دانش فنی، مدیریتی و تکنولوژیک داشته و مشارکت در سرمایه‌گذاری محقق نمی‌شود. در مرحله توسعه، به‌رغم اینکه کلیه ریسک‌ها و هزینه‌های اجرای عملیات با پیمانکار است، برحسب میزان سهام شرکت ملی نفت در این عملیات، پیمانکار سهم سرمایه‌گذاری شرکت مزبور را متقبل شده و متعاقباً این هزینه‌ها را از محل تولیدات قابل تخصیص به این شرکت مستهلک خواهد نمود.

سازوکار اجرای عملیات تولید، در مقایسه با عملیات اکتشاف و توسعه از تنوع بیشتری برخوردار است. بر این اساس ممکن است: ۱) عملیات تولید با حمایت‌ها و مساعدت‌های فنی و مالی لازم از سوی پیمانکار، به وسیله شرکت ملی نفت ایران یا یکی از شرکت‌های وابسته به او اجرا شود؛ ۲) شرکت عملیاتی توسعه‌ای، اجرای عملیات تولید را نیز برعهده گیرد؛ ۳) به منظور اجرای عملیات تولید و اداره میدان، یک شرکت عملیاتی تولیدی تأسیس شود و شرکت عملیاتی توسعه‌ای که قبلاً در مرحله توسعه ایجاد شده، شرکت مزبور را از حیث مالی و فنی حمایت کند.

سرانجام مطابق پانل‌های سمینار، اجرای عملیات نگهداشت ظرفیت تولید و ارتقا و بهبود بازیافت نفت بر عهده شرکت عملیاتی تولیدی خواهد بود و این شرکت گزارش مربوط به این عملیات را به شرکت عملیاتی توسعه‌ای که قبلاً در مرحله توسعه ایجاد شده، ارائه و شرکت اخیر

از حیث مالی و فنی مساعدت‌های لازم را به عمل خواهد آورد. با اتمام دوره پرداخت که بر حسب شرایط هر میدان بین ۱۵ تا ۲۰ سال از تاریخ آغاز تولید اولیه از میدان متغیر است، قرارداد خاتمه خواهد یافت.

در پانل‌ها راجع به نوع شرکت‌های اکتشافی و توسعه‌ای مشترک سخنی گفته نشده است، ولی شرکت تولیدی مشترک، به صورت یک شرکت عملیاتی مشترک غیرانتفاعی تشکیل می‌شود.

۳-۲-۱-۲.   قرارداد ساخت، بهره‌برداری و انتقال

یکی دیگر از ترتیبات قراردادی مطابق قانون، قرارداد ساخت، بهره‌برداری و واگذاری است. این شیوهٔ سرمایه‌گذاری در پروژه‌های زیربنایی مانند نیروگاهی، مخابراتی، فرودگاهی و بزرگراه‌های ایران کاربرد دارد، ولی به‌کارگیری آن در پروژه‌های تفریحی مانند ساخت تله‌کابین نیز امکان‌پذیر است. در سیستم بی.او.تی که در پروژه‌های معظم زیربنایی کاربرد دارد، سازمانی دولتی امتیاز ساخت و بهره‌برداری از پروژه‌ای معین را به کنسرسیوم اعطا می‌کند و کنسرسیوم در مقابل، تأمین مالی، طراحی، تأمین تجهیزات، ساخت، نصب، آزمایش، راه‌اندازی و مدیریت پروژه را ظرف مدت مشخص بر عهده گرفته و طی دوره بهره‌برداری، هزینه‌ها و سود سرمایه‌گذاری خود را از فروش محصولات یا خدمات پروژه مستهلک و دریافت می‌کند. پس از پایان دوره بهره‌برداری، تأسیسات بدون پرداخت هیچ‌گونه مبلغی، به سازمان دولتیِ اعطاکنندهٔ امتیاز منتقل خواهند شد.

مبنای اصلی شکل‌گیری یک پروژه زیربنایی به شیوه بی.او.تی، اراده دولت یا شرکتی دولتی در ایجاد تأسیسات و اعطای امتیاز ساخت و بهره‌برداری از تأسیسات مزبور به بخش خصوصی است. همان‌طورکه پیش‌تر گفته شد، پروژه‌های موضوع قراردادهای بی.او.تی نوعاً تأسیسات زیربنایی هستند که در اختیار بخش عمومی قرار دارند. به همین دلیل، از بی.او.تی به عنوان یکی از ترتیبات همکاری و مشارکت بخش عمومی و خصوصی یاد می‌شود.

پس از طی مراحل و تشریفات مقتضی و برگزاری مناقصه، شرکت دولتی و کنسرسیوم برنده مناقصه اقدام به امضای موافقت‌نامه اصلی پروژه خواهند کرد. به موجب موافقت‌نامه مزبور امتیاز ساخت و بهره‌برداری از پروژه‌ای مشخص به کنسرسیوم اعطا و کنسرسیوم متعهد به تأمین مالی، طراحی، ساخت، نصب، راه‌اندازی، آزمایش و بهره‌برداری از تأسیسات طی مدت مشخص در قرارداد خواهد شد.

توافق‌نامهٔ پروژه مبنای اصلی ایجاد رابطهٔ قراردادی بین بخش عمومی و خصوصی بوده و همهٔ قراردادهای بعدی اعتبار خود را از این موافقت‌نامه می‌گیرند. در این موافقت‌نامه حقوق و تعهدات سازمان یا شرکت دولتی شامل تأمین تسهیلات ضروری به‌منظور اجرای پروژه مانند

زمین، آب، برق، کسب مجوزهای لازم، تأمین سوخت مورد نیاز پروژه وغیره به تفصیل بیان می‌شوند.

۴-۲-۱-۲.   سرمایه‌گذاری در پروژه‌های ساختمانی ایران

با توجه به افزایش قیمت اموال در ایران در مقایسه با کشورهای هم‌طراز خود، این کشور جهش قابل ملاحظه‌ای را در بازار املاک و مستغلات در چند سال اخیر شاهد بوده است. با توجه به جمعیت جوان کشور، سرمایه‌گذاران خارجی تمرکز خود را بر بازار مستغلات متمرکز نموده‌اند که در طول زمان نشان داده بازاری ایمن و ثابت است. از سوی دیگر، پیمانکاران و مشاوران تمرکز خود را به تهیه املاک برای توریست‌ها و ساکنان محلی که به دنبال خانه‌های راحت و مدرن هستند، معطوف نموده‌اند. سرمایه‌گذاران نیز به سرمایه‌گذاری در این پروژه‌ها مشتاق هستند زیرا از یک سو، تقاضای روبه‌رشد در بازار را پاسخگوست و از سوی دیگر، بازگشت سرمایه را در سال‌های پیش رو تضمین می‌کند. وانگهی، رشد در پروژه‌های ساختمانی، به پروژه‌های زیربنایی کشور نیز راه یافته است. دولت ایران در بخش عمومی به دنبال ساخت و نوسازی زیرساخت‌هاست که این امر فرصت‌های سرمایه‌گذاری بسیاری را برای سرمایه‌گذاران در این پروژه‌ها بر مبنای مشارکت بخش عمومی و خصوصی (بی.او.تی) جوینت‌ونچر و... فراهم می‌کند. این پروژه‌ها دربرگیرندهٔ نرخ سود مطلوبی برای سرمایه سرمایه‌گذاران است. در سال‌های اخیر، صنعت ساخت‌وساز به سبب افزایش سرمایه‌گذاری‌های ملی و بین‌المللی، رشد کرده و در حال حاضر، بزرگ‌ترین صنعت در خاورمیانه به شمار می‌رود.

۴-۲-۱-۲-۱.   قراردادهای ساخت

انتخاب نوع قرارداد در صنعت ساخت‌وساز ایران به جایگاه کارفرما (مالک) وابسته است. اگر کارفرما شخص یا شرکت خصوصی باشد، انعقاد هر نوع قراردادی ساختی بین کارفرما و پیمانکار، امکان‌پذیر است. در این فرض طرفین قرارداد قادرند در خصوص هرگونه سیستم‌های تحویل پروژه نظیر طراحی، مناقصه، ساخت، طراحی و ساخت، مهندسی، تأمین تجهیزات و ساخت، و شیوهٔ کلید در دست توافق کنند. از سوی دیگر، چنانچه کارفرما متعلق به یک سازمان یا شرکت دولتی باشد، محدودیت‌هایی در خصوص انتخاب نوع قرارداد ساخت وجود دارد. دولت و بخش‌های دولتی در ایران ملزمند، قراردادهای از پیش تنظیم‌شده‌ای را که از سوی دولت طراحی و تدوین شده است در پروژه‌های ساخت برحسب مورد و موضوع به کار گیرند.

۲-۴-۲-۱-۲.   انتخاب پیمانکار

در بخش خصوصی ایران، کارفرمایان قادرند به صورت مستقیم، با پیمانکاران وارد مذاکره شده و پیمانکار باصلاحیت را که دانش فنی و منابع کافی برای اجرای پروژه را در اختیار دارد، برگزینند. به‌هرحال، مؤسسه‌ها و شرکت‌های دولتی موظفند از شیوه مناقصه به منظور انتخاب پیمانکار برای اجرای پروژه‌های مناقصه عمومی استفاده کنند. قانون مناقصات ایران که در سال ۲۰۰۵ تصویب شد، در ماده اول خود، مقرر داشته:

«قوای سه‌گانه جمهوری اسلامی ایران اعم از وزارتخانه‌ها، سازمان‌ها و مؤسسات و شرکت‌های دولتی، مؤسسات انتفاعی وابسته به دولت، بانک‌ها و مؤسسات اعتباری دولتی، شرکت‌های بیمه دولتی، مؤسسات و نهادهای عمومی غیردولتی (درمواردی که آن بنیادها و نهادها از بودجه کل کشور استفاده می‌نمایند)، مؤسسات عمومی، بنیادها و نهادهای انقلاب اسلامی، شورای نگهبان قانون اساسی و هم‌چنین دستگاه‌ها و واحدهایی که شمول قانون بر آنها مستلزم ذکر یا تصریح نام است، اعم از این‌که قانون خاص خود را داشته یا از قوانین و مقررات عام تبعیت نمایند نظیر وزارت جهاد کشاورزی، شرکت ملی نفت ایران، شرکت ملی گاز ایران، شرکت ملی صنایع پتروشیمی ایران، سازمان گسترش و نوسازی صنایع ایران، سازمان بنادر و کشتیرانی جمهوری اسلامی ایران، سازمان توسعه و نوسازی معادن و صنایع معدنی ایران، سازمان صدا و سیمای جمهوری اسلامی ایران و شرکت‌های تابعه آنها موظفند در برگزاری مناقصه مقررات این قانون را رعایت کنند».

فرایند مناقصه در سازمان‌های دولتی و عمومی ایران به صورت باز نیست بلکه مشروط به احراز صلاحیت قبلی است و پس از آن شرکت‌کنندگان در مناقصه، دارای فهرستی کوتاه خواهند بود و پیشنهادهای خود را برای اجرای پروژه ارائه خواهند داد. بر مبنای ماده ۱۲ قانون مناقصات:

الف) در ارزیابی کیفی مناقصه‌گران، موارد زیر باید لحاظ شود:

- تضمین کیفیت خدمات و محصولات؛
- داشتن تجربه و دانش در زمینه مورد نظر؛
- حُسن سابقه؛
- داشتن پروانه کار یا گواهینامه‌های صلاحیت در صورت لزوم؛
- توان مالی متقاضی برای انجام کار در صورت لزوم.
- ب) مراحل ارزیابی کیفی مناقصه‌گران به شرح زیر است:
- تعیین معیارهای ارزیابی و اهمیت نسبی معیارها؛

- تهیه اسناد ارزیابی؛
- دریافت، تکمیل و ارسال اسناد ارزیابی از سوی متقاضیان؛
- ارزیابی اسناد دریافت‌شده و تعیین امتیاز هریک از مناقصه‌گران و رتبه‌بندی آنها؛
- اعلام اسامی مناقصه‌گران صلاحیت‌دار به کارفرما و امتیازات و رتبۀ آنها (تهیه لیست کوتاه)؛
- مستندسازی ارزیابی کیفی مناقصه‌گران.

پ) سازمان مدیریت و برنامه‌ریزی کشور مکلف است با همکاری دستگاه‌های اجرایی حداکثر سه ماه پس از تصویب این قانون، آیین‌نامه اجرایی ارزیابی کیفی مناقصه‌گران را با رعایت موازین مقرر در این ماده که بیانگر شاخص‌های اندازه‌گیری و روش ارزیابی مناقصه‌گران باشد تهیه و به تصویب هیئت وزیران برساند».

۳-۴-۲-۱-۲. شیوه‌های قیمت‌گذاری

طرفین قرارداد در بخش خصوصی قادرند هر نوع شیوه قیمت‌گذاری را به منظور اجرای پروژه برگزینند. بر مبنای شرایط سایت پروژه و سایر فاکتورها، طرفین قادرند یکی از شیوه‌های مقطوع، ساعتی و تخمینی به علاوه سود را برگزینند. به‌هرحال، در بخش‌های دولتی و عمومی کارفرما شیوۀ قیمت‌گذاری را که نوعاً بر مبنای قیمت واحد تعیین می‌شود، اعمال می‌کند. این شیوه قراردادی، بر مبنای تخمین مقادیر کار در پروژه و قیمت هر واحد کار تعیین می‌شود. قیمت نهایی یک پروژه، بر مبنای مقادیر مورد نیاز برای اجرای کارها تعیین خواهد شد.

۴-۴-۲-۱-۲. حل‌وفصل اختلافات

سیستم حل‌وفصل اختلافات در قراردادهای ساخت ایران مانند بسیاری از کشورهای دیگر بر مبنای تکنیک‌های ADR یا شیوه‌های جایگزین حل‌وفصل اختلافات طراحی شده است. مراحل ابتدایی این شیوه بر مذاکره و میانجیگری استوار است. اگر طرفین نتوانند دربارۀ اختلاف پیش‌آمده ظرف مدت مشخصی به تفاهم و سازش برسند، شیوۀ داوری یا مراجعه به دادگاه به جریان خواهد افتاد. اگر کارفرما از بخش عمومی یا دولتی باشد، سیستم حل‌وفصل اختلافات از سازوکار مشخص و از پیش تعیین‌شده‌ای برخوردار است و طرفین به الزامات قانونی در این راستا ملتزمند. اگرچه در قراردادهای ساخت بخش عمومی و دولتی نیز تکنیک‌های ADR وجود دارد ولی این تکنیک‌ها در مقایسه با پروژه‌های بخش خصوصی دارای تفاوت‌های عمده‌ای است که همین امر، مشاوره متخصصان حقوقی را در این پروژه‌ها اجتناب‌ناپذیر می‌سازد.

۳-۱-۲.   سرمایه‌گذاری خارجی در اوراق بهادار (FPI)

۲-۱-۳-۱.   بورس اوراق بهادار ایران

بورس اوراق بهادار تهران که در سال ۱۹۶۸ تأسیس شده است، از نخستین بازارهای اوراق بهادار در ایران است. در سال ۲۰۰۵، قانون جدید بازار سرمایه ایران به تصویب مجلس رسید. طبق این قانون، بورس تهران تغییر شکل داد و به عنوان شرکت سهامی عام با شش هزار سهامدار تشکیل شد. از زمان آغاز، بورس تهران مشهور به بازار سامان‌یافته و منظم بوده که امکان معاملات مقرون‌به‌صرفه در آن وجود دارد. سیستم معاملاتی کاملاً کامپیوتری‌شده به افزایش ظرفیت و کارایی این بورس کمک کرده است. در سال ۱۹۹۴ سیستم مبادلات الکترونیکی آغاز به کار کرد و در سال ۲۰۰۷، بورس تهران به سمت سیستم معاملاتی قدرتمندی حرکت کرد تا بتواند حجم زیاد معاملات را پوشش دهد. بورس تهران گواهی ISO۹۰۰۱ را برای کیفیت سیستم، و در سال ۲۰۰۹ گواهی ISO۲۷۰۰۱ را برای سیستم مدیریت امنیتی فناوری اطلاعات دریافت نموده است.

بورس اوراق بهادار تهران اقدامات اصلاحی زیادی را در چند سال گذشته انجام داده تا با رویه جهانی هماهنگ شود و نیازهای متفاوت سرمایه‌گذاران را پاسخ دهد. بورس تهران همچنان آمادهٔ ادامه به سمت پیشرفت، آزادسازی و جهانی‌شدن است. بورس اوراق بهادار تهران، با سیستم معاملاتی تمام اتوماتیک و روش‌های ثبت دفتری، یکی از فعال‌ترین بورس‌های منطقه خاورمیانه به حساب می‌آید. در پایان مارس ۲۰۱۵ کل سرمایهٔ ۳۱۴ شرکت عضو بورس اوراق بهادار تهران بیش از ۱۷۲ میلیارد دلار بوده است. سهم کل سرمایه این بازار به تولید ناخالص ملی حدود ۶۰ درصد در سال ۲۰۱۵ بوده است. در این سال، ارزش کل معاملات برابر با ۱۸۰ میلیاد دلار بوده که نشان‌دهندهٔ حجم معاملاتی برابر با ۱۳۲/۵ درصد بوده است. نسبت قیمت به درآمد در بورس تهران ۵/۴ بوده است.

برای افزایش قدرت رقابتی بورس اوراق بهادار تهران و با هدف حرکت سریع‌تر به سمت آزادسازی و جهانی‌شدن، مقامات مربوطه اقدام به تشویق و معرفی ابزارهای مالی جدیدی نموده‌اند و مؤسسات مالی اقدامات اصلاحی متعددی را در این زمینه انجام داده‌اند نظیر افزودن معاملات آتی سهام، کاهش محدودیت‌های سرمایه‌گذاری خارجی، منظم‌تر شدن رویه ثبت خارجی، و تنظیم سیستم‌ها و روش‌های مختلف معاملاتی با هدف مطابقت بیشتر با استانداردهای جهانی.

۲-۳-۱-۲.   سرمایه‌گذاری خارجی در بورس اوراق بهادار تهران

مانند سایر بازارهای نوظهور، بورس اوراق بهادار تهران نیز در گذشته محدودیت‌های مختلفی را برای سرمایه‌گذاری خارجی وضع کرده بود. با رشد بورس اوراق بهادار ایران و توسعه اقتصادی، مسئولان بورس به‌تدریج این محدودیت‌ها را کاهش دادند. از آوریل ۲۰۱۰، روند سرمایه‌گذاری خارجی در بورس اوراق بهادار از سیستم «اجازه‌ای» به سیستم «بازگشت به وطن» تغییر یافته است. در ۱۸ آوریل ۲۰۱۰ با پیشنهاد وزارت امور اقتصاد و دارایی و طبق بند ۳ از ماده ۴ قانون بورس اوراق بهادار ایران مصوب ۲۰۰۵، هیئت وزیران «آیین‌نامه سرمایه‌گذاری خارجی در بورس‌ها و بازارهای خارج از بورس» را تصویب نمود. این آیین‌نامه متعاقباً روند درخواست سرمایه‌گذاری خارجی در بورس اوراق بهادار تهران را تسهیل نمود.

بر اساس ماده ۷ این آیین‌نامه، محدودیت‌های حاکم بر مالکیت سهام توسط سرمایه‌گذاران خارجی غیراستراتژیک، در هر بورس یا بازار خارج از بورسی به ترتیب ذیل مقرر گردید:

تعداد سهام تملک‌شده توسط مجموع سرمایه‌گذاران خارجی نباید از بیست درصد (۲۰%) کل تعداد سهام شرکت‌های عضو بورس یا بازار خارج از بورس، بیشتر شود، یا از بیست درصد (۲۰%) از تعداد سهام هر شرکت حاضر در بورس یا بازار خارج از بورس. تعداد سهام تملک‌شده توسط هر سرمایه‌گذار خارجی در هر شرکت عضو بورس یا بازار خارج از بورس، نباید از ده درصد (۱۰%) تعداد سهام چنین شرکت‌هایی بیشتر باشد.

بر اساس ماده ۴ این آیین‌نامه، اشخاص یا شرکت‌های خارجی باید اطلاعات و مدارک لازم به همراه تقاضای خود را در فرم‌های تعیین‌شده به سازمان بورس ارائه کنند تا مجوز معامله در هر بورس یا بازار خارج از بورس را دریافت کنند.

۳-۳-۱-۲.   خرید و فروش سهام

۱.   **انتخاب کارگزار**: در انتخاب کارگزار باید توجه شود که آیا آن کارگزار (شخص یا شرکت) دارای جایگاه حرفه‌ای و دارای مجوز فعالیت در بورس اوراق بهادار تهران است، یا خیر. فهرست کاملی از کارگزاران عضو بورس تهران در بخش عضویت بورس تهران، منعکس شده است. اعتماد شما نسبت به کارگزار خود و همچنین رضایت شما نسبت به خدمات وی، دارای اهمیت است. خدمات کارگزاران عبارت است از گزارش‌های بازار، توصیه در مورد انتخاب سهام و زمان خرید و فروش، انجام معامله، تحویل به‌موقع مدارک مهم مانند رسیدهای تأییدیه و سایر فعالیت‌های مرتبط با معامله که مورد نیاز مشتریان است.

۲.   **افتتاح حساب کارگزاری**: هنگامی که سرمایه‌گذار، شرکت کارگزاری خود را انتخاب کرد،

باید یک حساب کارگزاری افتتاح شود. این حساب به مشتری امکان می‌دهد که معاملات اوراق بهادار (خرید و فروش سهام) را در هر زمان انجام دهد؛ همانند یک حساب بانکی که اجازه می‌دهد مبلغی پول را واریز، منتقل یا برداشت نمایید. باز کردن حساب کارگزاری نسبتاً آسان است و بیشتر از افتتاح یک حساب بانکی طول نمی‌کشد. برای این کار، یک کارت نمونه امضا باید تکمیل شود که مشتمل بر نام، آدرس (کاری و شخصی)، شماره تماس، و مهم‌تر از همه امضای مشتری است.

۳. هنگامی که یک حساب بازگشایی شد، مشتری می‌توانند بر اساس دستورالعمل معاملاتی بین سرمایه‌گذار و کارگزار، به‌سرعت اقدام به خرید و فروش کند. دستورالعمل معاملاتی می‌تواند بر اساس اهداف سرمایه‌گذار متفاوت باشد؛ خواه کوتاه‌مدت یا بلندمدت باشد، حداقل یا حداکثر ارزش معاملات باشد (محدودیت معاملاتی) و غیره. همه مبادلات به صورت محرمانه انجام می‌شود و کارگزار جزئیات خرید و فروش را برای مشتری برای هیچ‌کس آشکار نمی‌کند.

۴. **سفارش به کارگزار:** پس از گشایش حساب، یک معامله‌گر به سرمایه‌گذار معرفی می‌شود. معامله‌گر فروشنده‌ای دارای مجوز است که اجازهٔ خرید و فروش اوراق بهادار را در بورس تهران دارد. معامله‌گر معرفی‌شده، شخص محل رجوع شما در کلیه معاملات خواهد بود. وی دستورات شما را به احتمال زیاد از طریق تلفن (مگر ترتیب دیگری مقرر شود) دریافت می‌کند و این دستورات را از طریق ترمینال معاملاتی که متصل به سیستم اصلی بورس است، اجرا می‌کند؛ بنابراین، هنگام سفارش خرید یا فروش، باید با معامله‌گر خود تماس بگیرید و جزئیات سفارش را تشریح کنید. معامله‌گر باید از این جزئیات مطلع شود: سفارش خرید یا فروش، کدام سهام را بخرید یا بفروشد، تعداد سهامی که باید بخرید یا بفروشد، و همچنین ترجیحاً قیمت پیشنهادی (هنگام خرید) و قیمت تقاضاشده (هنگام فروش).

۵. **انجام معامله:** خرید و فروش از طریق ثبت دفتری انجام می‌شود. بدین معنا که مالکیت سهام و وجه نقد به صورت الکترونیکی به حساب کارگزار منتقل می‌شود، بدون اینکه گواهی سهام و وجه نقد به صورت فیزیکی تحویل داده شود. حساب مورد نظر در هنگام خرید سهام، طلبکار و در هنگام فروش سهام، بدهکار می‌شود. بورس اوراق بهادار تهران شروع به استفاده از معاملات بدون کاغذ یا بدون نوشته کرده است که منجر به حذف تحویل فیزیکی گواهی سهام در هنگام خرید یا فروش شده است. این سیستم جایگزین روش نوشتاری شده که در آن گواهی سهام برای انتقال به مالک بعدی، تحویل داده می‌شد. به جای این کار، گواهی‌های سهام قابل جابه‌جایی نبوده و در محل امنی (شرکت سپرده‌گذاری

مرکزی اوراق بهادار و تسویه وجوه) نگهداری می‌شود. مزیت سیستم ثبت دفتری نسبت به سیستم کاغذی کاملاً واضح است. این روش منجر به کاهش چشمگیر کاغذبازی شده، معاملات را تسهیل نموده و اتلاف یا جعل سهم را از بین برده است.

امروزه بورس تهران، معاملات را به روش (T+۳) انجام می‌دهد که به معنای چهار روز پس از تاریخ انجام معامله است؛ بنابراین پرداخت یا تحویل سهم به کارگزار باید در روز معامله انجام شود. برای کسب نتیجه بهتر، همیشه آخرین فرصت تسویه با کارگزار خود برای معاملات در آینده را بررسی کنید.

۴-۳-۱-۲.   ارتباطات بین‌المللی

بورس اوراق بهادار تهران از سال ۱۹۹۲ تا ۲۰۱۰ عضو کامل فدراسیون جهانی بورس‌ها (WFE)، و همچنین یکی از مؤسسان و عضو فدراسیون بورس‌های اروپایی ـ آسیایی (FEAS) از سال ۱۹۹۵ تاکنون می‌باشد. به علاوه، مشترک و امضاکننده شبکه بین‌المللی مدیریت شرکتی (ICGN) می‌باشد. بورس تهران یک شرکت‌کنندهٔ فعال در اتاق بورس اعضای سازمان همکاری اسلامی است.

۴-۱-۲.   صدور مجوز سرمایه‌گذاری خارجی

الف) مدارک مورد نیاز جهت صدور مجوز سرمایه‌گذاری خارجی

نظر به ضرورت تسهیل در امر اطلاع‌رسانی به متقاضیان سرمایه‌گذاری خارجی در سطح استان و همچنین تسهیل و تسریع در امور مربوط به اخذ مجوز سرمایه‌گذاری خارجی، مدارک مورد نیاز جهت صدور مجوز سرمایه‌گذاری خارجی در هر پروژه به منظور انعکاس به متقاضیان به شرح زیر به استحضار می‌رسد:

۱.   فرم تکمیل‌شدهٔ درخواست سرمایه‌گذاری خارجی؛

۲.   درخواست کتبی صدور مجوز سرمایه‌گذاری خارجی توسط سرمایه‌گذار/سرمایه‌گذاران خارجی

۳.   تصویر موافقت اصولی صادره از وزارتخانه یا دستگاه اجرایی ذی‌ربط جهت اجرای پروژه

ب) مراحل صدور مجوز سرمایه‌گذاری خارجی

بر اساس قانون تشویق وحمایت سرمایه‌گذاری خارجی، رویه اداری درخواست مجوز

سرمایه‌گذاری خارجی به صورتی بسیار کوتاه و ساده طراحی شده است. همان‌گونه که در نمودار زیر مشاهده می‌شود، کل فرایند صدور مجوز سرمایه‌گذاری در چهار مرحله به ترتیب زیر می‌باشد.

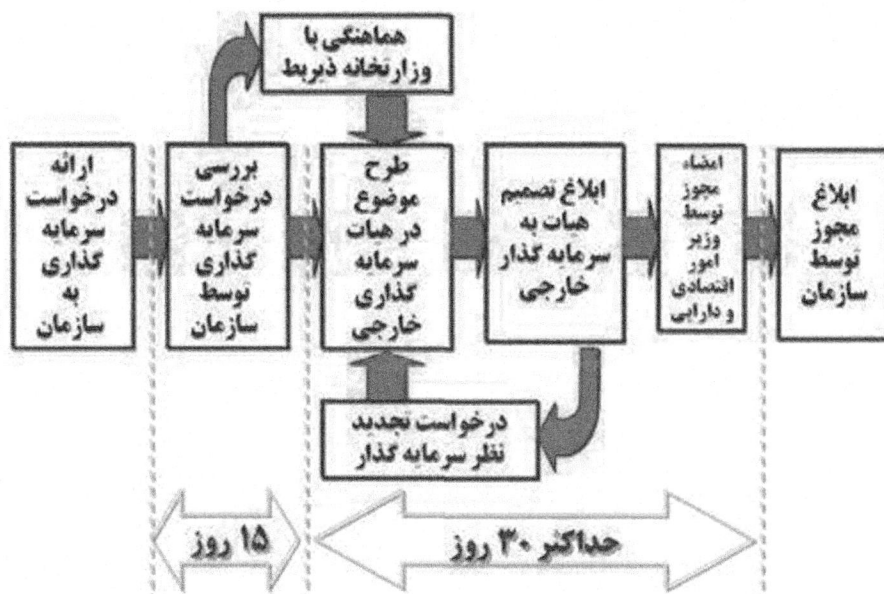

مرحله اول: ارائه درخواست پذیرش سرمایه‌گذاری به سازمان

به متقاضیان توصیه می‌شود اطمینان حاصل نمایند که اطلاعات مندرج در فرم درخواست پذیرش مجدانه و ترجیحاً با استفاده از مطالعات توجیه فنی و اقتصادی طرح و در صورت نبود چنین مطالعاتی، به کمک آخرین اطلاعات و داده‌های طرحی که مایل به سرمایه‌گذاری در آن هستند، تنظیم شده باشد. به همین منظور در طول تدارک درخواست پذیرش، کارکنان اداره کل سرمایه‌گذاری‌های خارجی سازمان می‌توانند طرف مشورت قرار گیرند.

مرحله دوم: بررسی درخواست پذیرش سرمایه‌گذاری توسط هیئت سرمایه‌گذاری خارجی

متعاقب ارائه درخواست، سازمان گزارشی درخصوص درخواست مزبور به منظور بررسی و اخذ تصمیم از سوی هیئت سرمایه‌گذاری خارجی تهیه می‌نماید. این فرایند معمولاً ۱۵ روز کاری از زمان دریافت درخواست پذیرش به طول می‌انجامد. معمولاً از نمایندگان سرمایه‌گذاران خارجی نیز برای شرکت در جلسه هیئت سرمایه‌گذاری خارجی دعوت به عمل می‌آید. در هر صورت

هیئت سرمایه‌گذاری خارجی باید طی حداکثر یک ماه دربارهٔ درخواست پذیرش، تصمیم‌گیری کند.

مرحله سوم: ارسال پیش‌نویس مجوز سرمایه‌گذاری برای سرمایه‌گذار خارجی

به منظور حصول اطمینان از رضایت سرمایه‌گذار خارجی از تصمیم هیئت، پیش‌نویس مجوز سرمایه‌گذاری پیش از صدور برای سرمایه‌گذار خارجی ارسال می‌شود. این کار فرصت آن را برای سرمایه‌گذار خارجی فراهم می‌سازد تا جزئیات محتوای مجوز سرمایه‌گذاری را بررسی نموده و پیش از صدور نهایی آن، موافقت یا مخالفت خود را ابراز دارد.

سازمان از هرگونه اظهار نظر مخالف با تصمیمات هیئت سرمایه‌گذاری خارجی استقبال نموده و آماده است تا موضوع را به منظور بررسی دوباره در هیئت مطرح نماید.

مرحله چهارم: صدور مجوز سرمایه‌گذاری

پیش از آنکه سازمان رسماً از موافقت سرمایه‌گذار خارجی با محتوای پیش‌نویس مجوز اطلاع حاصل نماید، مجوز نهایی در هیچ شرایطی صادر نمی‌شود. متعاقب دریافت تائیدیهٔ سرمایه‌گذار دربارهٔ پیش‌نویس مجوز، مجوز نهایی با امضای وزیر امور اقتصادی و دارایی صادر می‌شود.

۳ فصل سوم: مناطق آزاد تجاری ـ صنعتی و مناطق ویژه اقتصادی ایران

در تعریف سازمان ملل متحد (یونیدو) از مناطق آزاد به عنوان «محرکه»ای در جهت تشویق صادرات صنعتی یاد شده است. همچنین در برداشت جدید که به منطقه آزاد پردازش صادرات معروف است، مناطق آزاد به ناحیهٔ صنعتی ویژهای در خارج از مرز گمرکی گفته میشود که تولیداتش جهتگیری صادراتی دارند. فلسفه این اصطلاح را میتوان در تغییر استراتژی واردات به استراتژی توسعه صادرات دانست. همچنین مناطق ویژه تجاری ـ صنعتی را میتوان به صورت زیر تعریف کرد: «به محدوده جغرافیایی مشخصی که قوانین گمرکی محدوده گمرکی کشور در آن اجرا نمیشود و به منظور تسهیل در امر واردات و صادرات کالا و حمایت از صنعت داخلی کشور و همچنین جذب فناوریهای نوین در امر تولید و توسعه منطقهای در مبادی گمرکات و نقاط مرزی کشور ایجاد میشود، مناطق ویژه تجاری ـ صنعتی گفته میشود».

برخی از مهمترین تفاوتهای مناطق آزاد و ویژه اقتصادی را میتوان در موارد زیر خلاصه کرد:

- معافیت مالیاتی به مدت ۱۵ سال در مناطق آزاد وجود دارد و در مناطق ویژهٔ اقتصادی تخفیف مالیاتی طبق مقررات داخل کشور است
- خردهفروشی کالا در مناطق ویژه اقتصادی فقط برای اتباع خارجی امکانپذیر است، ولی در مناطق آزاد، خردهفروشی برای اتباع خارجی و داخلی امکانپذیر است؛
- مقررات روادید برای اتباع خارجی در مناطق ویژه بر اساس ضوابط داخل کشور است، ولی در مناطق آزاد روادید در مرزهای ورودی اعطا میشود؛
- مقررات کار و بیمه اجتماعی در استخدام اتباع خارجی در مناطق آزاد تابع مقررات خاص مناطق است ولی در مناطق ویژه اقتصادی تابع مقررات داخل کشور است.

۳.۱. مناطق آزاد تجاری ـ صنعتی

مهمترین اهداف ایجاد مناطق آزاد عبارتند از: توسعه صادرات و کمک به کشور برای ورود به بازارهای جهانی و آشنایی با تجارت خارجی و گسترش و متنوع ساختن صادرات، دستیابی به بازارهای پولی جهان، شتاب بخشیدن به ورود سرمایههای خارجی به کشور بهویژه در بخشهای

مولد، جذب و انتقال تکنولوژی و فناوری به درون اقتصاد کشور، افزایش کارایی اقتصادی و تربیت نیروی انسانی ماهر، افزایش تولید و ارزش افزوده بخش‌های اقتصادی بهویژه بخش صنعت، کمک به ورود کالاهای واسطه‌ای و سرمایه‌ای با شرایط و قیمت مناسب‌تر، افزایش درآمد کشور ناشی از فعالیت‌های خدماتی (حمل‌ونقل، بارگیری و تخلیه، بانکداری، بیمه‌گری و توریسم)، ایجاد فرصت‌های اشتغال در داخل کشور.

۳-۱-۱.   مزایا و جذابیت‌های سرمایه‌گذاری خارجی در مناطق آزاد تجاری ـ صنعتی

- معافیت مالیاتی برای بیست سال از روز اجرای کلیه فعالیت‌های اقتصادی؛
- آزادی ورود و خروج سرمایه و سود سرمایه‌گذاری؛
- حمایت و تضمین سرمایه‌گذاری خارجی؛
- حذف روادید ورود و سهولت صدور مجوز اقامت برای اشخاص خارجی؛
- مقررات مناسب برای کارکنان، کارفرما و نیز تأمین اجتماعی؛
- انتقال کالای ساخته‌شده به سرزمین اصلی بدون پرداخت هیچ‌گونه عوارض گمرکی؛
- حذف پرداخت عوارض گمرکی بر واردات از خارج از منطقه و بالعکس؛
- استخدام نیروی کار ماهر و آموزش‌دیده در کلیه سطوح مهارتی و حرفه‌ای؛
- استفاده از مواد اولیه نفت و گاز به عنوان خوراک و سوخت برای کلیه فعالیت‌های صنعتی.

۳-۱-۲.   لیست مناطق آزاد تجاری ـ صنعتی ایران

- منطقه آزاد تجاری ـ صنعتی قشم
- منطقه آزاد تجاری ـ صنعتی چابهار
- منطقه آزاد تجاری ارس
- منطقه آزاد تجاری انزلی
- منطقه آزاد تجاری اروند
- منطقه آزاد تجاری کیش
- منطقه آزاد تجاری ماکو

۳-۱-۳.   مقررات مربوط به سرمایه‌گذاری در مناطق آزاد تجاری ـ صنعتی

- قانون اداره مناطق آزاد تجاری ـ صنعتی؛
- مناطق آزاد تجاری ـ صنعتی تازه تأسیس‌شده؛
- آیین‌نامه اجرایی صدور ویزا برای اشخاص خارجی در مناطق آزاد تجاری ـ صنعتی؛
- مقررات ورود و اقامت اتباع خارجی؛
- آیین‌نامه اجرایی عملیات پولی ـ بانکی در مناطق آزاد تجاری ـ صنعتی؛
- دستورالعمل اجرایی عملیات پولی ـ بانکی در مناطق آزاد تجاری ـ صنعتی؛
- مقررات تأسیس مؤسسه‌های بیمه در مناطق آزاد تجاری ـ صنعتی؛
- ضوابط ثبت شرکت‌ها و مالکیت صنعتی ـ معنوی در مناطق آزاد تجاری ـ صنعتی؛
- مقررات واردات، صادرات و امور گمرکی مناطق آزاد تجاری ـ صنعتی؛
- آیین‌نامه نحوه استفاده از زمین و منابع ملی در مناطق آزاد تجاری ـ صنعتی؛
- تسهیلات ویژه برای انتقال کالاهای تولیدشده در مناطق آزاد به سایر نقاط کشور؛
- مقررات واردات اتومبیل در مناطق آزاد.

۳-۲.   مناطق ویژه اقتصادی

منطقه ویژه اقتصادی منطقه حراست‌شده‌ای است که در مبادی ورودی کشور با محدوده‌های گمرکی تأسیس می‌شود و هدف از ایجاد آنها پشتیبانی از تولیدات داخلی و توسعه صادرات غیرنفتی و ایجاد تحرک در اقتصادهای منطقه‌ای است. به همین منظور مقررات خاصی نیز در آنها به اجرا درمی‌آید.

۳-۲-۱.   مزایا و جذابیت‌های سرمایه‌گذاری خارجی در مناطق ویژه اقتصادی

۱.   ورود کالا از مناطق مذکور جهت مصرف داخلی، تابع مقررات صادرات و واردات خواهد بود و صدور کالا از این مناطق بدون هیچ‌گونه تشریفاتی انجام خواهد شد؛

۲.   ورود کالا از خارج از کشور یا مناطق آزاد تجاری ـ صنعتی به منطقه با کمترین تشریفات گمرکی انجام شده و ترانزیت داخلی کالای واردشده به منطقه بر اساس مقررات مربوطه انجام خواهد شد؛

۳.   ورود کالای موضوع این ماده به مناطق واقع در مبادی ورودی کشور بدون هرگونه تشریفات گمرکی انجام خواهد شد؛

۴.   کالاهایی که از خارج یا از مناطق آزاد تجاری ـ صنعتی یا مناطق دیگر به منطقه وارد می‌شوند می‌توانند بدون هرگونه تشریفات از کشور خارج شوند؛

۵.   مدیریت منطقه می‌تواند پس از طبقه‌بندی و ارزش‌گذاری منطقه، حق استفاده از قسمت‌های آن را به اشخاص حقیقی یا حقوقی واجد شرایط واگذار کند؛

۶.   صاحبان کالاهای واردشده به منطقه می‌توانند تمام یا قسمتی از کالای خود را به منظور ورود موقت به داخل کشور به گمرک اظهار و با انجام مقررات مربوطه ترخیص نمایند؛

۷.   در صورتی‌که پردازش کالاهای واردشده به منطقه به میزانی باشد که به موجب تغییر تعرفه گمرکی کالاهای مذکور شود، میزان سود بازرگانی مربوط به کالاهای فوق برای ورود به سایر نقاط کشور تنها معادل سود بازرگانی مواد اولیه و قطعات وارداتیِ به‌کاررفته در آن، محاسبه و دریافت خواهد شد؛

۸.   واردکنندگان کالا به مناطق می‌توانند تمام یا قسمتی از کالای خود را در مقابل قبض انبار تفکیکی قابل معامله که توسط مدیریت منطقه صادر خواهد شد، به دیگران واگذار کنند. در این صورت دارندهٔ قبض انبار تفکیکی، صاحب کالا محسوب خواهد شد؛

۹.   مدیریت هر منطقه مجاز است با تأیید گمرک ایران، حسب درخواست متقاضی نسبت به صدور گواهی مبدأ برای کالاهایی که از منطقه خارج می‌شوند اقدام نماید؛

۱۰. کلیه کالاهایی که برای تولید یا ارائه خدمات مورد نیاز منطقه وارد می‌شوند، از شمول مقررات عمومی صادرات واردات مستثنی هستند. واردات کالاهای مذکور به سایر نقاط کشور تابع مقررات صادرات و واردات خواهد بود؛

۱۱. واردات درصدی از کالاهای تولیدشده در مناطق موضوع بند (د) تبصره ۲۵ قانون برنامه دوم توسعه اقتصادی، اجتماعی و فرهنگی جمهوری اسلامی ایران به داخل کشور، معادل نسبتی از مجموع ارزش افزوده و مواد و قطعات داخلیِ به‌کاررفته به قیمت کل کالای تولیدی، بدون هرگونه محدودیتی مجاز است و علاوه بر عدم نیاز به ثبت سفارش و گشایش، مشمول ممنوعیتی نخواهد بود؛

۱۲. کالاهای تولیدشده در مناطق ویژه اقتصادی، همچنین مواد اولیه و قطعات منفصلهٔ واردشده از منطقهٔ یادشده به داخل کشور، به دلیل عدم استفاده از منابع و سهمیه ارزی کشور، مشمول ضوابط قیمت‌گذاری نیست.

۳-۲-۲.   لیست مناطق ویژه اقتصادی ایران

- منطقه ویژه اقتصادی سلماس
- منطقه ویژه اقتصادی پیام
- منطقه ویژه اقتصادی بوشهر
- منطقه ویژه اقتصادی عسلویه
- منطقه ویژه اقتصادی انرژی پارس
- منطقه ویژه اقتصادی پتروشیمی
- منطقه آزاد اقتصادی سرخس
- منطقه ویژه اقتصادی سبزوار
- منطقه ویژه اقتصادی شیراز
- منطقه ویژه اقتصادی سلفچگان
- منطقه ویژه اقتصادی سیرجان
- منطقه ویژه اقتصادی ارگ جدید
- منطقه ویژه اقتصادی اسلام‌آباد غرب
- منطقه ویژه اقتصادی لرستان
- منطقه ویژه اقتصادی امیرآباد
- منطقه ویژه اقتصادی خلیج فارس
- منطقه ویژه اقتصادی شهید رجایی
- منطقه ویژه اقتصادی یزد

۳-۲-۳.   مقررات مربوط به سرمایه‌گذاری در مناطق ویژه اقتصادی

۱.   قانون تشکیل و اداره مناطق ویژه اقتصادی جمهوری اسلامی ایران

۴   فصل چهارم: شیوه‌های ورود سرمایه‌گذار خارجی به ایران

سه شیوهٔ عمدهٔ ورود و استقرار سرمایه‌های خارجی به وسیله سرمایه‌گذاران، عبارتند از تأسیس شرکت فرعی، تأسیس شعبه، و دایر کردن دفتر نمایندگی در ایران. در ادامه به بررسی هریک از سه شیوه فوق و بیان نکات کلیدی و کاربردی در این راستا پرداخته می‌شود.

۴-۱.   تأسیس شرکت فرعی (ایرانی)

۴-۱-۱.   کلیات

۱.   **تعاریف**

به موجب ماده ۱ لایحه اصلاحی قسمتی از قانون تجارت مصوب ۱۳۴۷: «شرکت سهامی شرکتی است که سرمایه آن به سهام تقسیم شده و مسئولیت صاحبان سهام محدود به مبلغ اسمی سهام آنهاست. شرکت‌های سهامی به دو نوع سهامی خاص و سهامی عام تقسیم می‌شوند. تفاوت عمده این دو نوع شرکت در این امر خلاصه می‌شود که برخلاف شرکت سهامی خاص، در شرکت سهامی عام می‌توان سهام را عرضه عمومی نمود. به عبارت دیگر مطابق ماده ۴ لایحه اصلاحی قانون تجارت، شرکت سهامی به دو نوع تقسیم می‌شود:

نوع اول: شرکت‌هایی که مؤسسین آنها قسمتی از سرمایهٔ شرکت را از طریق فروش سهام به مردم تأمین می‌کنند. این‌گونه شرکت‌ها شرکت سهامی عام نامیده می‌شوند.

نوع دوم: شرکت‌هایی که تمام سرمایه آنها در موقع تأسیس منحصراً توسط مؤسسین تأمین شده است. این‌گونه شرکت‌ها شرکت سهامی خاص نامیده می‌شوند.

تبصره: در شرکت‌های سهامی عام عبارت «شرکت سهامی عام» و در شرکت‌های سهامی خاص عبارت «شرکت سهامی خاص» باید قبل از نام شرکت یا بعد از آن بدون فاصله با نام شرکت در کلیه اوراق و اطلاعیه‌ها و آگهی‌های شرکت به طور روشن و خوانا قید شود.

۲.   **سایر انواع شرکت‌های تجاری در ایران**

مطابق قانون تجارت ایران، علاوه بر شرکت‌های سهامی، شرکت‌های تجاری دیگری نیز وجود دارند که عبارتند از: شرکت با مسئولیت محدود، شرکت تضامنی، شرکت مختلط غیرسهامی، شرکت مختلط سهامی، شرکت نسبی و شرکت تعاونی تولید و مصرف.

در حقوق ایران، تفاوت عمدهٔ انواع شرکت‌های تجاری در مسئولیت سهامداران خلاصه می‌شود. در شرکت با مسئولیت محدود همچون شرکت سهامی، مسئولیت سهامداران تا میزان سهام آنها در شرکت است ولی برخلاف شرکت‌های سهامی، در شرکت با مسئولیت محدود، سرمایه شرکت به سهام تقسیم نمی‌شود و در نقل و انتقال سهام، تشریفات متفاوتی بر این شرکت‌ها حاکم است. سایر انواع شرکت‌های تجاری به دلیل مسئولیت بالایی که قانون برای سهامداران در نظر گرفته است، نوعا مورد استقبال سرمایه‌گذاران خارجی قرار نمی‌گیرد. از این رو، در این بخش صرفاً به مقررات شرکت‌های سهامی که بیشتر مورد استقبال و استفادهٔ سرمایه‌گذاران خارجی قرار می‌گیرند، پرداخته می‌شود.

۳. **ویژگی‌های کلی**

سهامداران شرکت سهامی عام در مالکیت، سود و زیان، و همچنین در اموال شرکت در زمان تسویه بر اساس میزان سهام خود، مشارکت می‌کنند. همان‌طور که در بالا اشاره شد، مسئولیت هر سهامدار به میزان ارزش اسمی سهام وی است، و به غیر از مواردی مثل کلاهبرداری یا اعمال متقلبانه، برای مسئولیت شرکت به سهامداران رجوع نخواهد شد. شرکت بر اساس قانون دارای شخصیت حقوقی مستقل است و به نام خود می‌تواند طرح دعوا کند یا مورد شکایت واقع شود. سهامداران دارای حقوق متداول سهامداری هستند که به طور کلی شامل شرکت در جلسات سهامداران، دریافت گزارش مالی، انتخاب و جایگزینی هیئت مدیره، و رأی‌دهی در تصمیمات مهم شرکت می‌شود.

۴. **تعداد سهامداران**

در شرکت سهامی عام، حداقل تعداد سهامداران پنج نفر است، درحالی‌که شرکت سهامی خاص باید دارای سه شریک باشد.

۵. **تابعیت سهامداران**

در مورد تابعیت اشخاصی که شرکت سهامی را تشکیل می‌دهند، محدودیت قانونی وجود ندارد اما از جهت عملی، دولت ایران معمولاً حضور سهامداران ایرانی را در فعالیت‌های مهم و مرتبط با برنامه‌های توسعه ملی الزامی می‌نماید.

۶. **سهام**

شرکت سهامی می‌تواند سهام عادی یا ممتاز به صورت در وجه حامل یا ثبت‌شده، منتشر نماید. درحالی‌که قانون به طور خاص امتیازات مربوط به سهام ممتاز را بیان نکرده است، رویه این گونه است که رجحان در سود و اموال شرکت در زمان تسویه و قدرت رأی‌دهی چند برابر، توسط قانون به رسمیت شناخته می‌شود. تفاوت اصلی در سهام در وجه حامل و ثبت‌شده به نحوه انتقال سهام و آثار مالیاتی آن مربوط است.

٧. **مدیریت**

مدیریت شرکت سهامی بر عهده هیئت مدیره است که با مجموعی از آرای سهامداران و حداقل دو سال یک بار، انتخاب می‌شوند.

٨. **انحلال و تسویه**

مقررات کلی ناظر بر انحلال و تسویه شرکت‌های سهامی در قانون مشخص شده است و شرکت‌ها می‌توانند در اساسنامه شرایط دلخواه خود را در این مورد بیان کنند؛ مشروط بر اینکه مخالف با قانون نباشد. ازآنجاکه مقررات قانونی در این باب ماهیتاً کلی است، توصیه می‌شود در هنگام نوشتن اساسنامه، روشی برای انحلال و تسویه بیان شود.

٢-١-۴.   سرمایه

١. **سهم سرمایه**

در زمان تأسیس شرکت، حداقل سرمایه‌ای معادل با ١/۰۰۰/۰۰۰ ریال برای سهامی خاص و ۵/۰۰۰/۰۰۰ ریال برای سهامی عام لازم است. پرداخت برای سهم شرکت می‌تواند به صورت نقد یا غیرنقد باشد. اگر پرداخت به صورت آوردهٔ غیرنقدی باشد، ارزش اموالِ آورده‌شده باید توسط کارشناس رسمی قوه قضاییه ارزیابی شود. در صورت پرداخت نقدی، تنها ۳۵ درصد آن باید در زمان تأسیس پرداخت شود و مبلغ باقی‌مانده در طول پنج سال و با اعلام هیئت مدیره یا سهامداران، پرداخت می‌شود. در صورت پرداخت به صورت غیرنقد، کل مال مورد نظر باید در زمان تأسیس به شرکت منتقل شود. سرمایه سهامی می‌تواند در هر زمان با دو سومِ آرای اخذشده در مجمع عمومی فوق‌العاده، افزایش یابد. کاهش سرمایه نیز می‌تواند در هر زمان با دو سوم آرای اخذشده در مجمع عمومی فوق‌العاده، رخ دهد. همچنین الزامی قانونی برای کاهش سرمایه در هنگام از بین رفتن نیمی از سرمایه شرکت وجود دارد.

٢. **پذیره‌نویسی**

اگرچه تنها ۳۵ درصد از سرمایهٔ شرکت باید در زمان تأسیس پرداخت شود، ولی ۱۰۰ درصد سرمایه باید پذیره‌نویسی شود. به‌رغم وجود الزام مبنی بر پذیره‌نویسی ۱۰۰ درصد سهام، در عمل رویه‌ای برای «سهام اجازه داده شده و منتشرنشده» ایجاد شده که امکان اجرای برنامه خرید سهام توسط کارکنان را فراهم می‌کند. به طور کلی، این روش شامل برگزاری مجمع عمومی فوق‌العاده است که در آن سهامداران افزایش سرمایه را در زمان و به میزانی که هیئت مدیره تعیین می‌کند، تأیید می‌نمایند.

۳. **ارزش اسمی**

باید برای سهام شرکت سهامی یک ارزش اسمی تعیین شود. برای شرکت‌های سهامی عام، قانون حداکثر ارزش اسمی را ۱۰/۰۰۰ ریال برای هر سهم تعیین نموده است. اما حداقل و حداکثری برای ارزش اسمی سهام شرکت‌های سهامی خاص وجود ندارد. الزامی برای هر دو نوع شرکت سهامی عام و خاص وجود دارد که همهٔ سهام باید دارای ارزش اسمی برابری باشند و به نظر می‌رسد این الزام برای هر دو نوع سهام عادی و ممتاز باشد. هنگامی که هر دو نوع سهام عادی و ممتاز منتشر می‌شود، ظاهراً هر دوی آنها باید ارزش یکسانی داشته باشند. همچنین الزام مشابهی وجود دارد که درخواست پرداخت قسمت پرداخت‌نشده از ارزش سهام باید بدون هیچ‌گونه تبعیضی انجام شود. اگر مقرراتی برای صدور سهام کوچک وضع شود، ارزش اسمی آنها باید برابر باشد.

۴. **گواهی سهم**

در مورد شکل و محتوای گواهی سهم، الزامات خاصی در قانون ذکر شده است. گواهی سهم باید متحدالشکل، چاپ‌شده، دارای شماره سریال، و امضاشده توسط حداقل دو نفر از صاحبان امضای مجاز باشند. هر گواهی باید شامل موارد زیر باشد:

- نام و شکل شرکت و شماره ثبت آن در اداره ثبت شرکت‌ها؛
- سرمایه ثبت‌شده و میزان پرداخت‌شده از آن؛
- نوع سهام؛
- ارزش اسمی سهام و قسمت پرداخت‌شده از آن به صورت حروف و عدد؛
- تعداد سهامی که گواهی نشان‌دهندهٔ آن است.

۵. **گواهی سهم موقت**

قانون مقرر می‌دارد هنگامی که گواهی‌های سهم صادر نشده است، شرکت باید گواهی‌های موقت برای سهامداران صادر کند که نشان‌دهندهٔ تعداد سهام و مبلغ پرداخت‌شده است. قانون همچنین مقرر می‌دارد تا زمانی که کلیه مبلغ اسمی سهام در وجه حامل پرداخت شود، صدور گواهی در وجه حامل (بی‌نام) ممنوع است، اما می‌توان برای پذیره‌نویسان چنین سهامی، پیش از پرداخت کل مبلغ اسمی گواهی‌های ثبت‌شده صادر کرد. در این شرایط، مقررات قانونی در مورد انتقال سهام ثبت‌شده در مورد این نوع سهام، قابل اِعمال است.

۶. انتقال سهام

سهام در وجه حامل می‌تواند با تحویل فیزیکی آن منتقل شود، درحالی‌که انتقال سهام ثبت‌شده تا زمانی که انتقال در دفتر ثبت شرکت ذکر نشود، انجام نمی‌شود. در مورد سهام ثبت‌شده، امکان وضع محدودیت‌هایی برای نقل و انتقال در اساسنامه شرکت وجود دارد.

۷. اندوخته‌ها

اندوختهٔ قانونی شرکت با ذخیره ۵ درصد از سود خالص شرکت سهامی در هر سال تا رسیدن آن به ۱۰ درصد سرمایه شرکت، ضروری است. سود خالص عبارت است از درآمد سالانه منهای هزینه‌ها، استهلاک، و هرگونه اندوختهٔ دیگر (به غیر از ۵ درصد از سود خالص).

۸. سود سهام

پرداخت سود سهام باید توسط سهامداران در مجمع عمومی اجازه داده شود و تنها از سود قابل تقسیم قابل پرداخت است. سود قابل تقسیم عبارت است از سود خالص به‌دست‌آمده در یک سال با کسر: الف) ضررهای ایجادشده در سال‌های قبل؛ ب) سایر اندوخته‌های اختیاری، به علاوه سود قابل تقسیم سال‌های قبل که قبلاً تقسیم نشده است.

۹. حق اولویت

سهامداران برای خرید سهام جدید دارای حق اولویت هستند. این حق ممکن است با اخذ دو سوم آرای مجمع عمومی فوق‌العاده کنار گذاشته شود.

۳-۱-۴.   تشکیل شرکت

۱. اساسنامه

سند تأسیس شرکت سهامی که اساسنامه نامیده می‌شود، تقریباً برابر است با مجموعه‌ای از مقررات و ضوابط داخلی شرکت‌های تشکیل‌شده در سایر کشورها. سهامداران پذیره‌نویسی‌شده یا مؤسسان شرکت باید پیش از ثبت شرکت تأسیس‌شده، اساسنامه را بپذیرند و آن را امضا کنند.

۲. پرداخت مبلغ تعهدشده

میزانی مشخص و الزامی از مبلغ تعهدشده باید پیش از تأسیس شرکت در حساب افتتاح‌شده به نام شرکت، پرداخت شود. رسید این پرداخت بانکی یکی از اسنادی است که باید در هنگام ثبت شرکت در اداره ثبت شرکت‌ها، ارائه شود.

٣. **مجمع مؤسسین**

تشکیل جلسه سهامداران متعهدشده یا مؤسسین در شرکت‌های سهامی عام به موجب قانون الزامی است، اما در شرکت سهام خاص الزامی نیست. با این وجود، حتی در شرکت‌های سهامی خاص نیز تشکیل چنین جلسه‌ای توصیه می‌شود، زیرا آسان‌ترین راه برای انجام کلیه اقدامات لازم برای تشکیل شرکت است. کلیه سهامداران مؤسس شرکت باید:

- اساسنامه را بپذیرند و آن را امضا کنند؛
- تعهدات و پرداخت بر اساس آن را تأیید کنند؛
- مدیران و بازرسان را انتخاب کنند؛
- قبول مدیران و بازرسان را دریافت کنند؛
- یک روزنامه کثیرالانتشار را برای انتشار اعلامیه‌های شرکت انتخاب کنند.

٤. **اولین جلسه هیئت مدیره**

پیش از شروع به فعالیتِ شرکت سهامی، هیئت مدیره باید به دلایل ذیل تشکیل جلسه دهد:

- انتخاب رئیس هیئت مدیره و نایب رئیس؛
- انتخاب مدیر عامل و تعیین وظایف وی؛
- تأیید شکل گواهی سهام و تعیین نماینده شرکت برای امضای آنها؛
- انتخاب دارندهٔ حق امضای مجاز از طرف شرکت.

علاوه بر این توصیه می‌شود که در اولین جلسه هیئت مدیره، بانک یا بانک‌هایی برای ذخیره سرمایه شرکت مشخص شود.

٥. **ثبت**

برای تشکیل یک شرکت سهامی خاص، اسناد زیر باید به اداره ثبت شرکت‌ها ارائه شود:

١. **نسخه‌ای از اساسنامه شرکت که توسط همه سهامداران امضا شده است؛**

٢. **اعلامیه‌ای مبنی بر اینکه سهام شرکت پذیره‌نویسی شده به همراه رسید بانکی مبنی بر اینکه مبلغ لازم پرداخت شده است؛**

٣. **قبولی امضاشده توسط مدیران و بازرسان؛**

٤. **بیانیه‌ای مبنی بر انتخاب روزنامه کثیرالانتشاری که اعلامیه‌های شرکت در آن منتشر می‌شود؛**

٦. **اظهارنامه (در فرم مخصوص منتشرشده توسط اداره ثبت شرکت‌ها).**

شرکت سهامی عام زمانی تشکیل می‌شود که اساسنامهٔ آن توسط سهامداران در جلسه مؤسسین پذیرفته شود و به همراه صورت‌جلسه انتخاب مدیران و بازرسان و قبولی امضاشدهٔ آنها، به اداره ثبت شرکت‌ها ارائه شود. مؤسسین شرکت سهامی عام که باید حداقل ۲۰ درصد سرمایه شرکت را تعهد نمایند، با ارائه اساسنامه، اعلامیه و اظهارنامه، روند ثبت شرکت را در اداره ثبت شرکت‌های تهران آغاز می‌نمایند. اظهارنامه باید بیان‌کنندهٔ:

- نام شرکت؛

- هویت و اقامتگاه مؤسسین؛

- اهداف شرکت؛

- سرمایه که شامل تعیین جداگانه سهام پرداخت‌شده و آوردهٔ نقدی و غیرنقدی است؛

- تعداد سهام ثبت‌شده در وجه حامل به همراه ارزش اسمی آنها و تعداد سهام ممتاز به همراه توصیفی از حقوق سهامداران ممتاز؛

- آوردهٔ نقد یا غیرنقد مؤسسین؛

- محل شرکت؛

- مدت.

هنگامی که ادارهٔ ثبت شرکت‌ها نسبت به اطلاعات ارائه‌شده توسط مؤسسین اطمینان حاصل نماید، اجازهٔ انتشار اطلاعیه شرکت را می‌دهد که باید شامل اطلاعات و دستورالعمل‌هایی در مورد چگونگی و محل پذیره‌نویسی سهام شرکت توسط سرمایه‌گذاران علاقه‌مند باشد. هنگامی که کل سهام شرکت پذیره‌نویسی شد و حداقل ۳۵ درصد مبلغ آن پرداخت شد، مؤسسین باید سهام را به سهامداران پذیره‌نویسی‌شده تسلیم کنند و سپس برای تشکیل جلسه مؤسسین دعوت به عمل آورند. در این جلسه، اساسنامه توسط سهامداران پذیره‌نویسی‌شده بررسی می‌شود، اولین مدیران و بازرسان انتخاب می‌شوند، و روزنامه‌ای برای انتشار اعلامیه‌های شرکت تعیین می‌شود. با تأیید اساسنامه توسط سهامداران، این سند به همراه صورت‌جلسه به ادارهٔ ثبت شرکت‌ها ارائه می‌شود.

۶. انتشار

اعلامیه تشکیل شرکت باید در روزنامه رسمی و روزنامه کثیرالانتشار تعیین‌شده توسط سهامداران منتشر شود. هزینهٔ چاپ این اعلامیه توسط شرکت پرداخت می‌شود و معمولاً شامل موارد زیر است:

- نام و شکل؛

- اهداف؛

- آدرس دفتر مرکزی؛

- مدت و تاریخ تشکیل؛

- ملیت؛

- سهم سرمایه، ارزش اسمی سهام، و نوع سهام؛

- میزان پرداخت‌شده از سهم سرمایه و شماره رسید یا رسیدهای بانکی که مدرک این پرداخت هستند؛

- هویت مؤسسین و تعداد سهام متعلق به آنها؛

- اسامی اولین اعضای هیئت مدیره و مدیر عامل؛

- اختیارات مدیر عامل؛

- اشخاص دارای حق امضا از طرف شرکت؛

- روزنامه کثیرالانتشاری که اعلامیه‌های شرکت در آن منتشر می‌شود؛

- نام اولین بازرس قانونی و علی‌البدل؛

- روش تسویه.

٧. **آغاز شخصیت حقوقی**

اگرچه انجام الزامات ثبتی و انتشار آن برای تکمیل روند تشکیل ضروری است، اما شخصیت حقوقی شرکت از تاریخ قبول سِمت کتبی مدیران و بازرسان آغاز می‌شود.

٨. **هزینه‌ها**

در ارتباط با تشکیل شرکت، باید هزینه‌های زیر پرداخت شود:

- هزینه‌های ثبتی بر اساس سرمایه شرکت که باید به اداره ثبت شرکت‌ها پرداخت شود؛

- هزینه‌های انتشار اعلامیه ثبت شرکت در روزنامه رسمی که باید به اداره ثبت شرکت‌ها پرداخت شود؛

- هزینه انتشار در روزنامه کثیرالانتشار به نرخ روز؛

- مالیات تمبر بر روی گواهی‌های سهام.

۹.   **مسئولیت مؤسسین**

بر اساس قانون، مؤسسین شرکت به صورت انفرادی و تضامنی مسئول کلیه اعمالی هستند که در ارتباط با تشکیل شرکت انجام می‌دهند.

۴-۱-۴.   هیئت مدیره

۱.   **تعداد**

اگرچه قانون مقرر می‌دارد که شرکت سهامی عام باید دارای حداقل پنج مدیر باشد، حداقلی برای شرکت سهامی خاص ذکر نشده است، اما ازآنجایی‌که هیئت مدیره شرکت سهامی خاص و عام باید یک مدیر و نائب رئیس انتخاب کنند، و داشتن هیئت مدیره به موجب قانون الزامی است، هیئت مدیره شرکت سهامی خاص باید دارای حداقل دو عضو باشد.

۲.   **انتخاب و عزل**

مدیران باید حداقل هر دو سال یک بار از بین سهامداران انتخاب شوند. لازم است که این انتخاب به صورت رأی‌گیری جمعی و در مجمع عمومی عادی انجام شود. یک یا همهٔ مدیران ممکن است توسط سهامداران عزل شوند. انتخاب مجدد مدیران بلامانع است. اشخاص حقوقی نیز می‌توانند به عنوان مدیر انتخاب شوند.

۳.   **مدت مدیریت**

مدت مدیریت مدیران باید در اساسنامه تعیین شود، اما این مدت نباید از دو سال بیشتر باشد. با وجود این، اگر این مدت پیش از انتخاب جانشین تمام شود، مدیر حاضر می‌تواند به وظایف خود در مدیریت و اداره امور شرکت تا زمان انتخاب مدیر جدید ادامه می‌دهد.

۴.   **سهام وثیقه**

مدیران باید تعداد سهامی را که توسط اساسنامه تعیین می‌شود، دارا باشند و این میزان نباید کمتر از تعدادی باشد که برای رأی دادن در مجامع عمومی لازم است. هر مدیر ملزم است تعداد مشخصی از سهام را در طول مدیریت خود، در شرکت به وثیقه بگذارد تا تضمینی برای ضررهای وارده به شرکت ناشی از تخلف مدیران نسبت به وظایف خود باشد. این سهام وثیقه باید از جمله سهام ثبت‌شده باشند. طبق قانون، تخلف از این مقررات موجب می‌شود تا مدیر متخلف در معرض عزل از سمت خود قرار گیرد.

۵.   **حدود اختیارات**

مطابق لایحه اصلاحیه قانون تجارت، هیئت مدیره شرکت سهامی در حدود موضوع شرکت چنان‌که در اساسنامه مقرر شده است، از کلیه اختیارات لازم به منظور مدیریت شرکت برخوردار است. به‌هرحال هیئت مدیره ممکن است کلیه اختیاراتی را که صراحتاً به مجامع

عمومی سهامداران تفویض شده است، اعمال نکند. با این حال محدودیت‌های ناظر به اختیارات هیئت مدیره صرفاً بین مدیران و سهامداران معتبر بوده و در مقابل اشخاص ثالث اعتباری ندارد.

۶. **مسئولیت**

مدیران نه‌تنها مطابق لایحه اصلاحیه قانون تجارت و نیز قانون تجارت در مقابل شرکت، سهامداران و اشخاص ثالث مسئولیت دارند بلکه منفرداً و متضامناً ممکن است برای فعل یا ترک فعلشان تحت تعقیب کیفری قرار گیرند.

۷. **جلسات هیئت مدیره**

به منظور تشکیل جلسات هیئت مدیره باید اکثریت مدیران در جلسه حاضر باشند. شیوه تشکیل و دعوت از هیئت مدیره شامل آگهی، باید در اساسنامهٔ شرکت تعیین شود. به‌هرحال مطابق قانون، رئیس هیئت مدیره و تعدادی از مدیران که یک سوم مدیران را تشکیل می‌دهند می‌توانند برای تشکیل هیئت مدیره از مدیران دعوت به عمل آورند. تصمیمات هیئت مدیره با اکثریت مدیران حاضر در جلسه معتبر خواهد بود مگر اینکه اکثریت بیشتری در اساسنامه مقرر شده باشد. صورت جلسات هر جلسه باید به وسیله اکثریت مدیران حاضر در جلسه امضا شود. این صورت‌جلسه‌ها باید حاوی نام مدیرانی که در جلسه حضور داشتند و نیز مدیران غایب، خلاصه‌ای از تصمیمات اتخاذشده و تاریخ جلسه باشد.

۸. **اقدامات بدون تشکیل جلسه**

کلیه اقدامات هیئت مدیره بدون تشکیل جلسه معتبر خواهد بود؛ اگر این اقدامات به صورت کتبی به تصویب و امضای کلیه مدیران برسد.

۹. **نمایندگی**

اگرچه در لایحه اصلاحیه قانون تجارت هیچ مقرره‌ای دربارهٔ نماینده مدیر وجود ندارد، این امر در عمل اتفاق می‌افتد و مدیران قادرند نماینده‌ای به جای خود معرفی کنند.

۱۰. **مدیران علی‌البدل**

ایجاد مدیران علی‌البدل مطابق قانون تجارت مورد شناسایی قرار گرفته ولی حضورشان اجباری نیست.

۱۱. **مدیر عامل**

مطابق قانون حداقل یک شخص حقیقی باید به وسیله هیئت مدیره به عنوان مدیر عامل انتخاب و عملیات روزانه و اجرایی شرکت را بر عهده گیرد. این شخص ممکن است عضو هیئت مدیره یا خارج از هیئت مدیره باشد ولی نمی‌تواند در عین حال رئیس هیئت مدیره هم باشد مگر اینکه سه چهارم اعضای هیئت مدیره موافقت کنند. حدود اختیارات مدیر

عامل باید به وسیله هیئت مدیره و در زمان انتصاب او تعیین شود. در این صورت، مدیر عامل به عنوان نماینده قانونی شرکت تلقی و دارای اختیارات لازم به منظور اقدام از جانب شرکت خواهد بود.

۱۲. **حق‌الزحمه**

مدیران در راستای اجرای وظایف مدیریت و حضور در جلسات مستحق دریافت حق‌الزحمه و همچنین پاداش از سود شرکت پس از تصویب سهامداران خواهند بود. برای شرکت سهامی خاص این پاداش محدود به ده درصد سود و برای شرکت‌های سهامی عام پنج درصد خواهد بود. مدیران ممکن است به عنوان کارمندان شرکت انجام وظیفه کنند که در این صورت نیز حقوق خود را دریافت خواهند کرد.

۱۳. **انجام معامله با شرکت**

اعضای هیئت مدیره و مدیر عامل شرکت و همچنین مؤسسه‌ها و شرکت‌هایی که اعضای هیئت مدیره یا مدیر عامل شرکت، شریک یا عضو هیئت مدیره یا مدیر عامل آنها باشند، نمی‌تواند بدون اجازه هیئت مدیره در معاملاتی که با شرکت یا به حساب شرکت می‌شود، به طور مستقیم یا غیرمستقیم طرف معامله واقع و یا سهیم شوند و در صورت اجازه نیز مفاد ماده ۱۲۹ لایحه قانونی اصلاح قسمتی از قانون تجارت، لازم‌الرعایه می‌باشد.

به موجب این ماده: «اعضای هیئت مدیره و مدیر عامل شرکت و همچنین مؤسسات و شرکت‌هایی که اعضای هیئت مدیره و یا مدیر عامل شرکت شریک یا عضو هیئت مدیره یا مدیر عامل آنها باشند، نمی‌توانند بدون اجازه هیئت مدیره در معاملاتی که با شرکت یا به حساب شرکت می‌شود به طور مستقیم یا غیرمستقیم طرف معامله واقع و یا سهیم شوند و در صورت اجازه نیز هیئت مدیره مکلف است بازرس شرکت را از معامله‌ای که اجازهٔ آن داده شده، بلافاصله مطلع نماید و گزارش آن را به اولین مجمع عمومی عادی صاحبان سهام بدهد. بازرس نیز مکلف است ضمن ارائه گزارشی خاص حاوی جزئیات معامله، نظر خود را دربارهٔ چنین معامله‌ای به همان مجمع تقدیم کند. عضو هیئت مدیره یا مدیر عامل ذی‌نفع در معامله، در جلسه هیئت مدیره و نیز در مجمع عمومی عادی، هنگام اخذ تصمیم نسبت به معامله مذکور حق رأی نخواهد داشت».

۱۴. **رقابت با شرکت**

اگر هرکدام از مدیران یا مدیر عامل، معامله‌ای در رقابت با شرکت منعقد کنند و شرکت متحمل ضرر یا تفویت منفعت شود، مدیر یا مدیر عامل مربوطه مسئول جبران خسارت شرکت خواهد بود.

۵-۱-۴.   مجامع عمومی سهامداران

۱.   انواع

مجامع سهامداران که به اصطلاح مجامع عمومی خوانده می‌شوند، به سه نوع تقسیم می‌شوند. نوع اول عبارت است از مجمع عمومی مؤسس که فقط تشکیل آن در شرکت‌های سهامی عام الزامی است. نوع دوم مجمع عمومی عادی خوانده می‌شود که باید هر یک سال یک بار تشکیل شود و نوع سوم مجمع عمومی فوق‌العاده خوانده می‌شود که برحسب مورد تشکیل می‌شود. به علاوه دو مجمع دیگر سهامداران وجود دارد: مجمع اول یک مجمع تخصصی است که به منظور تغییر امتیازات سهام ممتازه تشکیل می‌شود. در این مجمع، صاحبان سهام ممتازه به منظور تصمیم‌گیری دربارهٔ تغییر در امتیازات وابسته به سهام دعوت می‌شوند. مجمع بعدی مجمع عمومی عادی به طور فوق‌العاده است که ممکن است به وسیله هیئت مدیره یا بازرسان و یا بیست درصد از سهامداران شرکت تشکیل شود و در خصوص موضوعی که در صلاحیت مجمع عمومی عادی است، در زمانی غیر از زمان تشکیل این مجمع تصمیم‌گیری کنند.

۲.   صلاحیت مجمع عمومی عادی

صلاحیت مجمع عمومی عادی شامل کلیه امور شرکت به غیر از مواردی که در صلاحیت مجمع عمومی مؤسس و مجمع عمومی فوق‌العاده است. این موارد شاملِ: الف) بررسی و تصویب اساسنامه و حساب سود و زیان و نیز گزارش‌های مالی شرکت؛ ب) بررسی و تصویب گزارش سالانه مدیران؛ پ) بررسی و تصویب گزارش سالیانه بازرسان؛ ت) انتخاب بازرسان در صورتی‌که مدت مأموریت آنها پایان پذیرفته باشد و انتخاب بازرس و بازرس علی‌البدل؛ ث) انتخاب روزنامه کثیرالانتشار که آگهی‌های قانونی شرکت در آن منتشر می‌شود.

۳.   صلاحیت مجمع عمومی فوق‌العاده

مجمع عمومی فوق‌العاده صلاحیت هرگونه تغییر در اساسنامه یا سرمایه شرکت و یا انحلال آن را خواهد داشت.

۴.   ریاست مجامع عمومی سهامداران

مطابق قانون، مجامع عمومی سهامداران به وسیله هیئتی شامل رئیس، رئیس مجمع، یک منشی و دو ناظر تشکیل می‌شود. لازم نیست منشی از سهامداران باشد اما ناظر باید از سهامداران شرکت باشد.

۵.   آگهی

آگهی دعوت به جلسات مجامع عمومی باید حداقل ده و حداکثر چهل روز از تاریخ جلسه

منتشر شود و این آگهی باید در روزنامه کثیرالانتشار تعیین‌شده برای شرکت منتشر شود. این آگهی باید حاوی دستور جلسه، تاریخ، ساعت و مکان جلسه باشد. اگر کلیه سهامداران در جلسه حاضر باشند، احتیاجی به انتشار این آگهی نیست.

۶. **حد نصاب**

حد نصاب لازم برای تشکیل مجمع عمومی عادی و فوق‌العاده حضور بیش از پنجاه درصد سهمی است که حق رأی دارد.

۷. **صورت جلسات**

منشی جلسه کلیه صورت جلسات را تهیه و تصمیمات اتخاذشده را یادداشت می‌کند. این صورت جلسات باید به وسیله رئیسه هیئت امضا شده و یک نسخه از آن در مرکز اصلی شرکت نگهداری شود.

۸. **ثبت صورت جلسات**

در صورتی‌که موضوع صورت جلسات یکی از موضوعات زیر باشد صورت‌جلسه باید در اداره ثبت شرکت‌ها به ثبت برسد: الف) انتخاب مدیران و بازرسان؛ ب) تصویب ترازنامه؛ پ) افزایش و کاهش سرمایهٔ شرکت و هرگونه تغییر در اساسنامه؛ ت) انحلال شرکت و نحوه تسویه.

۹. **انتشار صورت جلسات**

علاوه بر ثبت صورت جلسات، در صورتی‌که این صورت جلسات حاوی یکی از موضوعات زیر باشد باید در روزنامه کثیرالانتشار شرکت و روزنامه رسمی منتشر شود: الف) انتخاب مدیران و بازرسان؛ ب) کاهش و افزایش سرمایه و هرگونه تغییر در اساسنامه؛ پ) انحلال شرکت و نام و مشخصات مدیران تصفیه؛ ت) نام و اختیارات مدیر عامل؛ ث) تعیین روزنامه‌ای که کلیه آگهی‌های قانونی شرکت در آن منتشر خواهد شد.

۱۰. **تعویق جلسات**

مجامع عمومی ممکن است به مدت دو هفته با پیشنهاد هیئت رئیسه و تصویب مجمع به تأخیر بیفتد. در این مورد نیاز به انتشار هیچ‌گونه آگهی جدیدی برای دعوت نیست و حد نصاب لازم برای تشکیل جلسهٔ به تأخیر افتاده همان است که در جلسه اصلی بوده است.

۱۱. **دعوت سهامداران اقلیت**

سهامداران اقلیتی که در مجموع حداقل یک پنجم سهام شرکت را مالک‌اند، می‌توانند در هر زمانی از هیئت مدیره و بازرسان، دعوت از مجمع عمومی را درخواست نمایند. در صورتی‌که هیئت مدیره یا بازرسان از دعوت مجمع خودداری کنند، این سهامداران می‌تواند خود اقدام به دعوت از مجمع کنند.

6-1-4.   مقررات متفرقه

١.   بازرسان شرکت

مطابق قانون تجارت، انتخاب بازرس اصلی و بازرس علی‌البدل سالیانه یک بار و به وسیله سهامداران در مجمع عمومی عادی خواهد بود. انتخاب بیشِ از یک بازرس اصلی و یک بازرس علی‌البدل اختیاری است. به طور کلی وظیفه بازرس، نظارت بر منافع سهامداران و اشخاص ثالث است و در صورت تخلف از این وظیفه ممکن است تحت تعقیب کیفری قرار گیرند. برخی از اشخاص نظیر مجرمان، مدیران، و خویشاوندان آنها و اشخاصی که با شرکت معامله می‌کنند، صلاحیت اخذ این پست و انتخاب شدن به عنوان بازرس را ندارند. علاوه بر سایر وظایف، بازرسان موظفند هرساله گزارش عملکرد خود را به مجمع عمومی عادی ارائه دهند.

٢.   حساب‌های شرکت

شرکت‌های سهامی عام و خاص ملزم به نگهداری دفاتر قانونی شرکت هستند. این دفاتر مبنایی برای تعیین مالیات شرکت است و در صورت تخلفِ شرکت از این تعهد، مقامات مالیاتی ممکن است به شکل علی‌الرأس مالیات شرکت را تعیین کنند.

٣.   نام شرکت

مطابق قانون، عبارت شرکت سهامی خاص باید به همراه نام شرکت در کلیه اوراق شرکت قید شود. در عمل، اداره ثبت شرکت‌ها صرفاً اسامی ایرانی را به منظور ثبت می‌پذیرد و از ثبت اسامی که با نام شرکت‌های از قبل تأسیس‌شده مشابهت دارد، خودداری می‌ورزد.

7-1-4.   تفاوت‌های شرکت سهامی عام با خاص

١.   حداقل سرمایه در شرکت‌های سهامی خاص یک میلیون ریال و در شرکت‌های سهامی عام پنج میلیون ریال است؛

٢.   سهامداران شرکت‌های سهامی عام ملزمند حداقل بیست درصد سرمایهٔ اولیه شرکت را تعهد و ٣۵ درصد این میزان را نقداً پرداخت نمایند، درحالی‌که مؤسسان شرکت‌های سهامی خاص باید ١٠٠ درصد سرمایه را تعهد و حداقل ٣۵ درصد سرمایه نقدی و ١٠٠ درصد سرمایه نقدی را پرداخت کنند؛

۳. هیئت مدیره شرکت‌های سهامی عام می‌باید از پنج عضو تشکیل شود درحالی‌که در شرکت‌های سهامی خاص تعداد مدیران باید سه نفر باشد؛
۴. مدیران شرکت‌های سهامی خاص حق دریافت پاداش به میزان ده درصد سود را دارند درحالی‌که در شرکت‌های سهامی عام، این میزان پنج درصد است؛
۵. تشکیل مجمع عمومی مؤسس در شرکت‌های سهامی عام الزامی و در شرکت‌های سهامی خاص غیرالزامی است؛
۶. گزارش مالی سالیانه شرکت‌های سهامی عام باید به وسیله حسابدار رسمی تأیید شود درحالی‌که چنین الزامی برای شرکت‌های سهامی خاص وجود ندارد.

۸-۱-۴. فهرست عناوین مواد اساسنامه

- نام شرکت؛
- نوع شرکت؛
- مدت شرکت؛
- موضوع شرکت؛
- مرکز اصلی شرکت و شعب آن در صورت وجود؛
- ترکیب سرمایه شرکت و تعیین میزان نقد و غیر نقد آن؛
- تعیین نوع سهام اعم از با نام و بی‌نام و ممتازه (و تعیین امتیازات آن)؛
- تعیین میزانی از مبلغ سهم که پرداخت شده است و تعیین شخصی که گواهی سهم را امضا می‌کند؛
- تعیین مدت زمانی که مابقی مبلغ اسمی سهم باید پرداخت شود؛
- تعیین نحوه تبدیل سهام؛
- شیوه و شرایط افزایش و کاهش سرمایه شرکت؛
- دوره و شیوه تشکیل مجامع عمومی؛
- مقررات حاکم بر حد نصاب مجامع عمومی و شیوه اداره این جلسات؛
- شیوه انجام معاملات و نیز تعداد سهام لازم به منظور اعتباربخشی به مجامع عمومی؛
- تعداد مدیران و شیوه انتخاب آنان و نیز انتخاب مدیران علی‌البدل؛
- تعیین قلمرو اختیارات و وظایف هیئت مدیره؛

- شیوه تشکیل جلسات هیئت مدیره؛

- مقررات حاکم بر تشکیل جلسات هیئت مدیره؛

- شیوه انتخاب رئیس و نایب رئیس هیئت مدیره؛

- شیوه معاملات شرکت و تعداد سهام لازم به منظور اعتباربخشی به اقدامات هیئت مدیره؛

- تعداد سهام و وثیقه مدیران که باید در شرکت نگهداری شود؛

- تعداد بازرسان شرکت و شیوه انتخاب آنها؛

- نحوه انتخاب مدیر عامل؛

- تاریخ و خاتمه سال مالی و محدوده زمانی به منظور تعیین ترازنامه و حساب سود و زیان شرکت و ارائه آن به بازرسان و مجمع عمومی عادی سالیانه؛

- شیوه انحلال اختیاری شرکت؛

- نحوه اصلاح اساسنامه شرکت.

۲-۴. شعب و نمایندگی شرکت‌های خارجی

به موجبِ «قانون اجازه ثبت شعبه یا نمایندگی شرکت‌های خارجی» که به شکل ماده‌واحده تنظیم شده است: «شرکت‌های خارجی که در کشور محل ثبت خود شرکت قانونی شناخته می‌شوند، مشروط به عمل متقابل از سوی کشور متبوع، می‌توانند در زمینه‌هایی که توسط دولت جمهوری اسلامی ایران تعیین می‌شود در چارچوب قوانین و مقررات کشور به ثبت شعبه یا نمایندگی خود اقدام کنند».

ماده ۲ آیین‌نامه اجرایی قانون فوق نیز در تعریف شعبه این‌چنین بیان داشته است: «شعبه شرکت خارجی، واحد محلی تابع شرکت اصلی است که مستقیم موضوع و وظایف شرکت اصلی را در محل، انجام می‌دهد. فعالیت شعبه در محل تحت نام و با مسئولیت شرکت اصلی خواهد بود». از اهداف و جهات تأسیس شعبه می‌توان به این موارد اشاره کرد: نگهداری اسناد و مدارک مربوط به شرکت و رسیدگی به دفاتر مالیاتی، ثبت و ضبط حساب‌ها، تسهیل فرایند حسابداری، ارتباط با مراکز اداری و رسمی دولت سرمایه‌پذیر، تسهیل امر سرمایه‌گذاری در مرحلۀ پیش از استقرار سرمایه، مرحله پس از استقرار سرمایه و ارائه خدمات فنی و مهندسی پس از اتمام پروژه به دولت سرمایه‌پذیر. در برخی قراردادها نیز طرف خارجی ملزم به تأسیس شعبه در قلمرو طرف سرمایه‌پذیر می‌شود.

شرکت‌های خارجی افزون بر تأسیس شعبه، برخی مواقع به اعطای نمایندگی در کشور میزبان می‌اندیشند. اعطای نمایندگی و به عبارت دیگر داشتن دفتر نمایندگی دارای تفاوت‌های ماهوی و شکلی با تأسیس شعبه توسط شرکت خارجی است. از جمله تفاوت اساسی شعبه شرکت خارجی و نمایندگی آن، در اهداف تأسیس آنها نهفته است. اصولاً اعطای نمایندگی و تأسیس دفتر نمایندگی به‌منظور انجام امور بازاریابی، بازرگانی، تجاری و خدماتی است. در مقابل، شعب شرکت‌های خارجی افزون بر امور بازرگانی و تجاری، در راستای موضوع‌های سرمایه‌گذاری و برای پیگیری امور مربوط به اجرای پروژه‌های سرمایه‌گذاری نیز تأسیس می‌شوند. شرکت‌های خارجی به‌منظور سازماندهی و بسط فعالیت‌های بازرگانی، تجاری و اقتصادی خود در دیگر کشورها، معمولاً اقدام به اعطای نمایندگی می‌کنند.

به موجب ماده ۴ آیین‌نامه اجرایی قانون اجازه ثبت شعبه و نمایندگی شرکت‌های خارجی: «نماینده شرکت خارجی، شخصی حقیقی یا حقوقی است که بر اساس قرارداد نمایندگی، انجام بخشی از موضوع و وظایف شرکت طرف نمایندگی را در محل بر عهده گرفته است. نمایندگی شرکت خارجی نسبت به فعالیت‌هایی که تحت نمایندگی شرکت طرف نمایندگی در محل انجام می‌پذیرد، مسئولیت خواهد داشت».

برخلاف شعبه که فاقد شخصیت حقوقی بوده و به عنوان بخشی از شرکت اصلی در دیگر کشورها فعالیت می‌کند و فعالیتش تحت نام و با مسئولیت شرکت اصلی است، نماینده شرکت خارجی، طرف قرارداد شرکت اصلی بوده و با داشتن شخصیت حقوقی مستقل (در مورد شرکت‌ها) انجام بخشی از موضوع و وظایف شرکت اصلی را با مسئولیت خود مطابق قرارداد نمایندگی بر عهده می‌گیرد.

۱-۲-۴.   شرکت‌های مجاز به ثبت شعبه یا نمایندگی در ایران

به موجب «قانون اجازه ثبت شعبه یا نمایندگی شرکت‌های خارجی» که به شکل ماده‌واحده تنظیم شده است: «شرکت‌های خارجی که در کشور محل ثبت خود شرکت قانونی شناخته می‌شوند، مشروط به عمل متقابل از سوی کشور متبوع، می‌توانند در زمینه‌هایی که توسط دولت جمهوری اسلامی ایران تعیین می‌شود در چارچوب قوانین و مقررات کشور به ثبت شعبه یا نمایندگی خود اقدام کنند».

همچنین ماده ۱ آیین‌نامه اجرایی قانون فوق مقرر داشته: «شرکت‌های خارجی که در کشور محل ثبت خود، شرکت قانونی شناخته می‌شوند، مشروط به عمل متقابل در کشور متبوع، می‌توانند

برای فعالیت در ایران در موارد و زمینه‌های زیر بر اساس مقررات این آیین‌نامه و سایر قوانین و مقررات مربوط نسبت به ثبت شعبه یا نمایندگی خود اقدام کنند»:

- ارائه خدمات بعد از فروش کالاها یا خدمات شرکت خارجی؛

- انجام عملیات اجرایی قراردادهایی که بین اشخاص ایرانی و شرکت خارجی منعقد می‌شود؛

- بررسی و زمینه‌چینی برای سرمایه‌گذاری شرکت خارجی در ایران؛

- مشارکت با شرکت‌های فنی و مهندسی ایرانی برای انجام کارها در کشورهای ثالث؛

- افزایش میزان صادرات غیرنفتی ایران؛

- ارائه خدمات فنی و مهندسی و انتقال دانش فنی و فناوری بین طرفین؛

- انجام فعالیت‌هایی که مجوز آن توسط دستگاه‌های دولتی که به طور قانونی مجاز به صدور مجوز هستند، صادر شده از قبیل ارائه خدمات در زمینه‌های حمل‌ونقل، بیمه و بازرسی کالا، بانکی، بازاریابی و غیره.

۴-۲-۲.   تفاوت‌های شعبه و نمایندگی شرکت‌های خارجی

آیین‌نامه اجرایی «قانون اجازه ثبت شعبه یا نمایندگی شرکت‌های خارجی» برای اولین بار سعی در تفکیک نمایندگی شرکت خارجی از شعبه شرکت خارجی داشته است. این امر به‌صراحت در ماده ۲ و همین‌طور در ماده ۴ آیین‌نامه اجرایی قانون قید شده و مسئولیت هرکدام به طور مجزا بیان شده است؛ به این شرح که فعالیت شعبه در محل، تحت نام و با مسئولیت شرکت اصلی بوده و بالعکس، نمایندگی شرکت خارجی نسبت به فعالیت‌های تحت نمایندگی تحت شرکت طرف نمایندگی، خود مسئولیت خواهد داشت. در واقع می‌توان این آیین‌نامه را مرجع قانونیِ تفکیک ماهوی این دو نهاد قلمداد کرد. وانگهی برخلاف شعبه که فاقد شخصیت حقوقی بوده و بخشی از وجود شرکت اصلی در دیگر کشورها به حساب می‌آید و فعالیتش تحت نام و با مسئولیت شرکت اصلی است، نماینده شرکت خارجی، طرف قرارداد شرکت اصلی بوده و با داشتن شخصیت حقوقی مستقل (در مورد شرکت‌ها) انجام بخشی از موضوع و وظایف شرکت اصلی را با مسئولیت خود مطابق قرارداد نمایندگی بر عهده می‌گیرد.

۴-۲-۳.   زمینه‌های فعالیت شعب و نمایندگی شرکت‌های خارجی

با وجود تفاوت‌های شعبه شرکت خارجی با نمایندگی شرکت خارجی، قانون‌گذار در ماده ۱ آیین‌نامه اجرایی قانون ثبت شعبه یا نمایندگی، زمینه‌های فعالیت شعبه و نمایندگی را به صورت

مشترک بیان کرده است. با وجود این باید خاطرنشان ساخت، هدف قانون‌گذار به‌کارگیری یکسان این دو نبوده و برحسب شرایط خاص هرکدام از زمینه‌های فعالیت مندرج در ماده فوق‌الذکر، شعبه یا نمایندگی مورد استفاده قرار خواهد گرفت.

الف) ارائه خدمات بعد از فروش کالاها یا خدمات شرکت خارجی

در پروژه‌های سرمایه‌گذاری، از لوازم و مقدمات اساسی اجرای پروژه تهیه ماشین‌آلات، تجهیزات و قطعات یدکی و مصرفیِ مورد نیاز پروژه توسط سرمایه‌گذار خارجی است.

سرمایه‌گذار خارجی به‌منظور تهیه و تدارک این اقلام سرمایه یا به خرید تجهیزات از خارج از کشور و واردات آنها اقدام می‌کند یا از طریق شعبه یا نمایندگی شرکت‌های خارجی در ایران که تهیه‌کننده یا ارائه‌کنندهٔ این محصولات هستند، اقلام مورد نیاز را در اختیار می‌گیرد.

ب) انجام عملیات اجرایی قراردادهایی که بین اشخاص ایرانی و شرکت خارجی منعقد می‌شوند

این بند در پروژه‌های سرمایه‌گذاری ناظر به نقش شعبه شرکت خارجی در مرحلهٔ پس از استقرار سرمایه و انعقاد قرارداد سرمایه‌گذاری است؛ بنابراین در عمل، انجام عملیات اجرایی قراردادهای منعقدهٔ شرکت خارجی در کشور میزبان، عمدتاً از طریق شعبه یا نماینده‌ای که نقش شعبه را ایفا می‌کند، صورت می‌پذیرد و عملاً نمایندگی مرسوم در این موارد به کار گرفته نمی‌شود.

پ) بررسی و زمینه‌سازی برای سرمایه‌گذاری شرکت خارجی در ایران

یکی از مواردی که شرکت خارجی اقدام به ثبت شعبه در ایران می‌کند، استفاده از شعبه برای بررسی و زمینه‌سازی سرمایه‌گذاری در کشور است. آنچه در این بند از ماده ۱ آیین‌نامه اجرایی قانون ثبت شعبه یا نمایندگی شرکت‌های خارجی بدان اشاره شده، ناظر به فعالیت متقاضیان سرمایه‌گذاری در مرحلهٔ پیش از استقرار سرمایه و انعقاد قرارداد مربوط به سرمایه‌گذاری است.

ت) همکاری با شرکت‌های فنی و مهندسی ایرانی برای انجام کار در کشورهای ثالث

در برخی موارد، شرکت‌های فنی ـ مهندسی ایرانی ترجیح می‌دهند برای انجام پروژه‌های صنعتی و زیربنایی در دیگر کشورها (به‌ویژه کشورهای همسایه) با همکاری و از طریق مشارکت شرکت‌های خارجی، کنسرسیومی تشکیل و اقدام به انجام کار و اجرای پروژه کنند. بدین‌منظور، شرکت‌های خارجی برای مشارکت با شرکت‌های فنی ـ مهندسی ایرانی چه در مرحلهٔ پیش از

شرکت در مناقصه و چه در مرحلهٔ پس از آن و انعقاد قرارداد، ممکن است اقدام به ثبت شعبه در ایران کنند.

ث) افزایش صادرات غیرنفتی جمهوری اسلامی ایران

مطابق این بند، یکی از مواردی که شرکت خارجی قادر به ثبت شعبه در ایران است، فرضی است که فعالیت شرکت خارجی منجر به افزایش صادرات غیرنفتی شود؛ بنابراین، موضوع فعالیت شرکت خارجی که در ایران به‌واسطه شعبه به انجام آن مبادرت می‌ورزد، باید پروژه‌های غیرنفتی باشد.

آنچه در این بند مقرر شده، برخلاف دیگر بندها، به نوعی دربردارندهٔ هدف از ثبت شعبه است و زمینهٔ فعالیت شعبه شرکت خارجی را شامل نمی‌شود؛ ازاین‌رو باید گفت شرکت‌های خارجی در اجرای پروژه‌های غیرنفتی در تمام بخش‌ها از جمله پتروشیمی، کشاورزی، صنایع، نساجی، خدمات وغیره می‌توانند اقدام به ثبت شعبه در ایران کنند.

ج) ارائه خدمات فنی و مهندسی و انتقال دانش فنی و فناوری

یکی دیگر از زمینه‌هایی که شرکت‌های خارجی قادرند توسط شعبه یا نمایندگی خود در ایران فعالیت کنند، ارائه خدمات فنی ـ مهندسی، انتقال دانش فنی و فناوری است.

چ) انجام فعالیت‌هایی که مجوز آن توسط دستگاه‌های دولتیِ مجاز به صدور مجوز، صادر می‌شود، از قبیل ارائه خدمات در زمینه‌های حمل‌ونقل، بیمه و بازرسی کالا، بانکی، بازاریابی وغیره.

با توجه به اهمیت و حساسیت پاره‌ای از فعالیت‌های اقتصادی، حسب قوانین و مقررات خاص، اقدام به این فعالیت‌ها مستلزم صدور مجوز از مراجع ذی‌صلاح است. طبق این بند، شرکت‌های خارجی می‌توانند در چنین فعالیت‌هایی، اقدام به تأسیس شعبه یا نمایندگی کرده و راه را برای حضور در ایران هموار سازند. از جمله این فعالیت‌ها می‌توان به امکان تأسیس شعبه بانک خارجی با اخذ مجوز از بانک مرکزی اشاره کرد.

۴-۲-۴.   شعبه شرکت خارجی

به موجب «قانون اجازه ثبت شعبه یا نمایندگی شرکت‌های خارجی» که به شکل ماده‌واحده تنظیم شده است: «شرکت‌های خارجی که در کشور محل ثبت خود شرکت قانونی شناخته می‌شوند، مشروط به عمل متقابل از سوی کشور متبوع، می‌توانند در زمینه‌هایی که توسط دولت جمهوری اسلامی ایران تعیین می‌شود در چارچوب قوانین و مقررات کشور به ثبت شعبه یا نمایندگی خود اقدام کنند».

ماده ۲ آیین‌نامه اجرایی قانون فوق‌الذکر نیز، در تعریف شعبه این‌چنین بیان داشته است: «شعبه شرکت خارجی، واحد محلی تابع شرکت اصلی است که مستقیماً موضوع و وظایف شرکت اصلی را در محل، انجام می‌دهد. فعالیت شعبه در محل تحت نام و با مسئولیت شرکت اصلی خواهد بود». از اهداف و جهات تأسیس شعبه می‌توان به این موارد اشاره کرد: نگهداری اسناد و مدارک مربوط به شرکت و رسیدگی به دفاتر مالیاتی، ثبت و ضبط حساب‌ها، تسهیل فرایند حسابداری، ارتباط با مراکز اداری و رسمی دولت سرمایه‌پذیر، تسهیل امر سرمایه‌گذاری در مرحلهٔ پیش از استقرار سرمایه، مرحلهٔ پس از استقرار سرمایه و ارائه خدمات فنی و مهندسی بعد از اتمام پروژه به دولت سرمایه‌پذیر. در برخی از قراردادها نیز طرف خارجی ملزم به تأسیس شعبه در قلمرو طرف سرمایه‌پذیر می‌شود.

۴-۲-۵.   مدارک مورد نیاز برای ثبت شعبه

به استناد آیین‌نامه اجرایی قانون اجازه ثبت شعبه یا نمایندگی شرکت‌های خارجی، شرکت‌های خارجی متقاضی ثبت شعبه در ایران باید اسناد و مدارک زیر را به اداره کل ثبت شرکت‌ها و مالکیت صنعتی ارائه کنند: ۱) درخواست کتبی شرکت؛ ۲) تصویر مصدق اساسنامه شرکت، آگهی تأسیس و آخرین تغییرات ثبت‌شده در مراجع ذی‌ربط؛ ۳) آخرین گزارش مالی تأییدشده شرکت؛ ۴) گزارش توجیهی حاوی اطلاعات مربوط به فعالیت‌های شرکت مشتمل بر:

الف) اطلاعات مربوط به فعالیت‌های شرکت؛ ب) تبیین دلایل و ضرورت ثبت شعبه در ایران؛ پ) تبیین نوع و حدود اختیارات و محل فعالیت شعبه؛ ت) برآورد نیروی انسانیِ ایرانی و خارجی مورد نیاز؛ ث) نحوه تأمین منابع وجوه ارزی و ریالی برای اداره امور شعبه.

۵) ارائه معرفی‌نامه از دستگاه دولتی در صورتی‌که با آن دستگاه قرارداد داشته باشند؛ ۶) اظهارنامه ثبت شعبه شرکت خارجی؛ ۷) تصدیق ثبت شرکت خارجی؛ ۸) اختیارنامهٔ نماینده یا نمایندگان شرکت خارجی؛ ۹) ارائه تعهدنامه دایر بر اینکه چنانچه مجوز فعالیت آن‌ها از سوی

مراجع ذی‌صلاح لغو شود، ظرف مدت معینی که توسط اداره ثبت شرکت‌ها و مالکیت صنعتی ابلاغ می‌شود، نسبت به انحلال شعبه و معرفی مدیر تصفیه اقدام کنند.

لازم به یادآوری است که همهٔ اسناد شرکت که در کشور خارجی تهیه می‌شوند، پس از تأیید مراجع ذی‌ربط (نظیر مرجع ثبت شرکت‌ها) و تأیید وزارت خارجه آن کشور، باید به تأیید سفارت یا نمایندگی جمهوری اسلامی ایران در آن کشور برسد و پس از ترجمه رسمی به زبان فارسی و تأیید اداره فنی دادگستری اصل و ترجمه آن به اداره ثبت شرکت‌ها ارائه شود.

۶-۲-۴. مسئولیت‌های شرکت خارجی در قبال شعبه و نمایندگی

فعالیت شعبه در محل، تحت نام و با مسئولیت شرکت اصلی بوده و بالعکس، نمایندگی شرکت خارجی نسبت به فعالیت‌های تحت نمایندگی شرکت طرف نمایندگی، خود مسئولیت خواهد داشت. به عبارت دیگر همان‌طور که ماده ۲ «آیین‌نامه اجرایی قانون اجازه ثبت شعب و نمایندگی شرکت‌های خارجی» مقرر کرده است، مسئولیت کلیه فعالیت‌های شعبه شرکت خارجی بر عهده شرکت اصلی نهاده شده است. این در حالی است که در خصوص نمایندگی، تمام فعالیت‌ها با نام و با مسئولیت نماینده صورت می‌گیرد و شرکت اصلی خارجی هیچ مسئولیت و تکلیف قانونی طبق قوانین ایران بر عهده ندارد.

۷-۲-۴. نمایندگی شرکت خارجی

شرکت‌های خارجی افزون بر تأسیس شعبه، برخی مواقع به اعطای نمایندگی در کشور میزبان می‌اندیشند. اعطای نمایندگی و به عبارت دیگر داشتن دفتر نمایندگی با تأسیس شعبه توسط شرکت خارجی، دارای تفاوت‌های ماهوی و شکلی است. از جمله اینکه تفاوت اساسی شعبه شرکت خارجی و نمایندگی آن در اهداف تأسیس آنها نهفته است. اصولاً اعطای نمایندگی و تأسیس دفتر نمایندگی به‌منظور انجام امور بازاریابی، بازرگانی، تجاری و خدماتی است. در مقابل، شعب شرکت‌های خارجی افزون بر امور بازرگانی و تجاری، در راستای موضوع‌های سرمایه‌گذاری و برای پیگیری امور مربوط به اجرای پروژه‌های سرمایه‌گذاری نیز تأسیس می‌شوند. شرکت‌های خارجی به‌منظور سازماندهی و گسترش فعالیت‌های بازرگانی، تجاری و اقتصادی خود در دیگر کشورها، معمولاً اقدام به اعطای نمایندگی می‌کنند.

به موجب ماده ۴ آیین‌نامه اجرایی قانون اجازه ثبت شعبه و نمایندگی شرکت‌های خارجی: «نماینده شرکت خارجی، شخصی حقیقی یا حقوقی است که بر اساس قرارداد نمایندگی، انجام بخشی از موضوع و وظایف شرکت طرف نمایندگی را در محل بر عهده گرفته است. نمایندگی

شرکت خارجی، نسبت به فعالیت‌هایی که تحت نمایندگی شرکت طرف نمایندگی در محل انجام می‌پذیرد، مسئولیت خواهد داشت».

برخلاف شعبه که فاقد شخصیت حقوقی بوده و به عنوان بخشی از شرکت اصلی در دیگر کشورها فعالیت می‌کند و فعالیتش تحت نام و با مسئولیت شرکت اصلی است، نماینده شرکت خارجی، به عنوان طرف قرارداد شرکت اصلی بوده و با داشتن شخصیت حقوقی مستقل (در مورد شرکت‌ها) انجام بخشی از موضوع و وظایف شرکت اصلی را با مسئولیت خود مطابق قرارداد نمایندگی بر عهده می‌گیرد.

۸-۲-۴.   مدارک مورد نیاز برای ثبت نمایندگی

شرایط ثبت نمایندگی شرکت خارجی در ایران

الف) شخص حقیقی

۱) تصویر مصدق قرارداد نمایندگی با شرکت خارجی؛ ۲) تصویر شناسنامه؛ ۳) آدرس محل سکونت نماینده و محل نمایندگی؛ ۴) ارائه سابقه فعالیت شخص متقاضی ثبت نمایندگی در زمینه امور پیش‌بینی‌شده در قرارداد نمایندگی؛ ۵) تصویر مصدق اساسنامه شرکت خارجی طرف نمایندگی، آگهی تأسیس و آخرین تغییرات ثبت‌شده در مراجع ذی‌ربط؛ ۶) گزارش فعالیت‌های شرکت خارجی طرف نمایندگی و تبیین دلایل و ضرورت اخذ نمایندگی؛ ۷) آخرین گزارش مالی تأییدشده شرکت خارجی طرف نمایندگی؛ ۸) ارائه معرفی‌نامه وزارتخانه ذی‌ربط (در صورتی‌که قرارداد با دستگاه مربوطه منعقد شده باشد)؛ ۹) اظهارنامه ثبت نمایندگی شرکت خارجی؛ ۱۰) تصدیق ثبت شرکت خارجی؛ ۱۱) اختیارنامه نماینده یا نمایندگان عمده شرکت خارجی.

ب) شخص حقوقی

۱) تصویر مصدق قرارداد نمایندگی با شرکت خارجی؛ ۲) تصویر مصدق اساسنامه شرکت متقاضی ثبت نمایندگی؛ ۳) روزنامه رسمی حاوی آگهی تأسیس شرکت؛ ۴) روزنامه رسمی در خصوص آخرین تغییرات ثبت‌شده خصوصاً در مورد مدیران؛ ۵) ارائه سابقه فعالیت شخص حقوقی متقاضی ثبت نمایندگی در زمینه امور پیش‌بینی‌شده در قرارداد نمایندگی؛ ۶) همهٔ مدارک مندرج در شماره‌های ۵ لغایت ۱۱ یادشده در بند «الف».

لازم به یادآوری است همهٔ اسناد باید به تأیید مراجع ذی‌ربط و وزارت امور خارجه کشور اصیل و همچنین به تأیید سفارت یا نمایندگی جمهوری اسلامی ایران در کشور مربوطه برسد و متعاقب آن ترجمهٔ رسمی فارسی مدارک نیز مورد تأیید ادارهٔ فنی دادگستری قرار بگیرد.

۴-۲-۹. مسئولیت‌ها و وظایف نمایندگی و شعبه شرکت خارجی

نماینده و شعبه شرکت خارجی نسبت به فعالیت‌هایی که به نام این شرکت انجام می‌شود به شرح ذیل مسئول هستند:

الف) اشخاصی که مجوز فعالیت آنها از سوی مراجع ذی‌ربط لغو می‌شود مکلفند در مهلت تعیین‌شده توسط اداره ثبت شرکت‌ها و مالکیت‌های صنعتی، نسبت به انحلال شعبه یا نمایندگی و انجام امور تصفیه آن اقدام کنند. شرکت‌هایی که مجوز فعالیت آنها تمدید نمی‌شود، شش ماه مهلت دارند تا نسبت به انحلال شرکت ثبت‌شده و انجام امور تصفیه آن اقدام نمایند؛

ب) شعبه شرکت‌های خارجی که نسبت به ثبت شعبه خود در ایران اقدام نموده و به فعالیت می‌پردازند موظفند، هر سال گزارش سالانه شرکت اصلی مشتمل بر گزارش‌های مالی حسابرسی‌شده توسط حسابرسان مستقل مقیم در کشور متبوع را به دستگاه ذی‌ربط ارائه کنند؛

پ) کلیه اشخاص حقیقی و حقوقی مشمول آیین‌نامه اجرایی «قانون اجازه ثبت شعبه یا نمایندگی شرکت‌های خارجی» موظفند گزارش فعالیت شعبه یا نمایندگی در ایران را همراه با صورت‌های مالی حسابرسی‌شدهٔ خود ظرف مدت چهار ماه پس از پایان سال مالی به دستگاه‌های ذی‌ربط ارسال دارند. حسابرسی مذکور تا زمانی که آیین‌نامه اجرایی تبصره ۴ ماده‌واحده قانون استفاده از خدمات تخصصی و حرفه‌ای حسابداران ذی‌صلاح به عنوان حسابدار رسمی (مصوب ۱۳۷۲) اعلام نشده است، توسط سازمان حسابرسی و مؤسسات حسابرسی مورد قبول دستگاه ذی‌ربط که شرکای آن افراد حقیقی تأییدشده توسط اداره نظارت سازمان حسابرسی باشند، انجام می‌گیرد؛

ت) اداره امور شعبه یا نمایندگی، باید توسط یک یا چند شخص حقیقی مقیم ایران انجام گیرد.

۴-۲-۱۰. مدیریت امور شعبه یا نمایندگی شرکت خارجی

به موجب ماده ۹ آیین‌نامه اجرایی قانون اجازه ثبت شعبه یا نمایندگی شرکت‌های خارجی: «اداره امور شعبه یا نمایندگی ثبت‌شده طبق این آیین‌نامه، باید توسط یک یا چند شخص حقیقی مقیم ایران انجام گیرد».

۴-۲-۱۱. ارائه گزارش

به موجب ماده ۸ آیین‌نامه اجرایی قانون اجازه ثبت شعبه یا نمایندگی شرکت‌های خارجی: «کلیه اشخاص حقیقی و حقوقی مشمول این آیین‌نامه موظفند گزارش فعالیت شعبه یا نمایندگی در

ایران را همراه با صورت‌های مالی حسابرسی‌شدهٔ خود ظرف مدت چهار ماه پس از پایان سال مالی به دستگاه‌های ذی‌ربط ارسال دارند. حسابرسی مذکور تا زمانی که آیین‌نامه اجرایی تبصره ۴ ماده‌واحده قانون استفاده از خدمات تخصصی و حرفه‌ای حسابداران ذی صلاح به عنوان حسابدار رسمی (مصوب ۱۳۷۲) اعلام نشده است، توسط سازمان حسابرسی و مؤسسات حسابرسی مورد قبول دستگاه ذی‌ربط که شرکای آن افراد حقیقی تأییدشده توسط اداره نظارت سازمان حسابرسی باشند، انجام می‌گیرد».

۱۲-۴-۲-۴.   مقررات مالیاتی شعبه و نمایندگی شرکت‌های خارجی

از لحاظ مالیاتی اگرچه قانون‌گذار ایران صرفاً درآمدهای مالیاتی حاصل در ایران را مأخذ مالیاتی اعلام کرده، ولی با عنایت به «آیین‌نامه اجرایی ثبت شعب و نمایندگی شرکت‌های خارجی» و همچنین دستورالعمل سازمان مالیاتی در خصوص شعب و نمایندگی شرکت‌های خارجی، شعب شرکت‌های خارجی مکلفند هر سال گزارش سالانه شرکت اصلی مشتمل بر گزارش‌های مالی حسابرسی‌شده توسط حسابرسان مستقل مقیم در کشور متبوع را به دستگاه ذی‌ربط کشور محل شعبه ارائه کنند. درحالی‌که نمایندگی شرکت‌های خارجی دارای چنین تعهدی نیستند.

به موجب تبصره ۳ ماده ۱۰۷ قانون مالیات‌های مستقیم: «شعب و نمایندگی‌های شرکت‌ها و بانک‌های خارجی در ایران که بدون داشتن حق انجام دادن معامله به امر بازاریابی و جمع‌آوری اطلاعات اقتصادی در ایران برای شرکت مادر اشتغال دارند و برای جبران مخارج خود از شرکت مادر وجوهی دریافت می‌کنند، نسبت به آن مشمول مالیات بر درآمد نخواهند بود». بنابراین شعبه شرکت خارجی که در ایران با توجه به ماده فوق صرفاً به امر بازاریابی و جمع‌آوری اطلاعات اقتصادی در ایران برای شرکت مادر اشتغال دارند، مشمول مالیات نخواهند شد.

باین‌حال به منظور رعایت الزامات مقررات قانون تجارت ایران، توجه به نکات زیر به منظور انجام فعالیت توسط شعبه در ایران توصیه می‌شود:

۱) در اجرای قانون ثبت شرکت‌های خارجی در ایران، باید بابت فعالیت موضوع شعبه دفاتر شعبه شرکت خارجی تهیه شود؛

۲) هرچند طبق حکم تبصره ۳ ماده ۱۰۷ قانون مالیات‌های مستقیم، شعبه شرکت خارجی در ایران که بدون داشتن حق انجام دادن معامله، به امر بازاریابی و جمع‌آوری اطلاعات اقتصادی در ایران برای شرکت مادر اشتغال دارند و برای جبران مخارج خود از شرکت مادر وجوهی دریافت می‌کنند، نسبت به آن وجوه مشمول مالیات نخواهند بود، ولی توجه به نکات ذیل در انجام رسیدگی‌ها دربارهٔ فعالیت آنها در ایران ضروری است.

• برخی از شعب و نمایندگی شرکت‌های خارجی علاوه بر انجام امور بازاریابی و جمع‌آوری

اطلاعات برای شرکت اصلی (شرکت مادر) اقدام به امور بازاریابی و جمع‌آوری اطلاعات جهت سایر اشخاص خارجی نیز می‌نمایند. در این صورت فعالیت‌های انجام‌شده بابت سایر اشخاص خارجی مشمول مالیات خواهد بود.

- برخی از شعب و نمایندگی‌های شرکت خارجی در ایران علاوه بر بازاریابی و جمع‌آوری اطلاعات در زمینه خدمات پس از فروش نیز فعالیت دارند. در این صورت، موضوع فعالیت خدمات پس از فروش از مصادیق تبصره ۳ ماده ۱۰۷ نبوده و شعبه شرکت خارجی علاوه بر درآمد حاصل از خدمات پس از فروش که احتمالاً در برخی موارد عاید آن خواهد شد در زمینه کمیسیونری خارجی نیز مشمول پرداخت مالیات است.

۳. مأموران مالیاتی در اجرای تبصره ۳ ماده ۱۰۷ با رسیدگی به اسناد و مدارک شرکت و جمع‌آوری اطلاعات لازم از نحوه و چگونگی انجام فعالیت شرکت در ایران اطمینان حاصل می‌کنند. در هر حال اگر جمع‌آوری اطلاعات منجر به کشف این امر شود که شرکت اصلی اقدام به فروش کالا و خدمات می‌نماید (فروش مستقیم)، در چنین حالتی وضعیت شعبه همانند قبل نخواهد بود بلکه وارد فعالیت انتفاعی شده و شعبه مزبور باید شخص حقیقی یا حقوقی دیگری را معرفی کند که امور نمایندگی فروش مستقیم را بر عهده دارد.

۵   فصل پنجم: مالیات؛
مروری بر سیستم مالیاتی ایران

۵-۱.   مبانی مالیات و نرخ آن

بر اساس بررسی سازمان سرمایه‌گذاری و کمک‌های اقتصادی و فنی ایران (OIETAI)، نظام مالیاتی ایران به دو دسته کلی مالیات مستقیم و غیرمستقیم تقسیم شده است. سهم مالیات‌های مستقیم از کل درآمدهای مالیاتی در حال حاضر تقریباً ۶۸ درصد است. دو نوع عمده از مالیات‌های مستقیم از جمله مالیات بر درآمد و مالیات بر املاک وجود دارد. هر دسته از مالیات‌های مستقیم، به نوبه خود به زیرمجموعه‌هایی تقسیم شده است. مالیات‌های غیرمستقیم شامل مالیات بر واردات و مالیات بر ارزش افزوده (VAT) است. مالیات بر واردات در حال حاضر توسط گمرک ایران جمع‌آوری شده و در حوزه صلاحیت اداره مالیاتی ایران نیست. جدول زیر به اختصار انواع مختلفی از مالیات در سیستم مالیاتی ایران را نشان می‌دهد:

جدول ۱-۵. مالیات بر درآمد

نرخ مالیاتی	اشخاص مشمول مالیات	درآمد مشمول مالیات	مبنای مالیاتی
۱۵-۳۵ درصد	مالکانی که املاک خود را به دیگران اجاره داده‌اند	درآمد به‌دست‌آمده افراد از نقل و انتقال حقوق مربوط به اموال غیرمنقول واقع در ایران، پس از کسر معافیت‌ها: اجاره کامل، کسر ۲۵% برای هزینه‌ها، و تعهدات مالک نسبت به اموال	مالیات بر درآمد املاک و مستغلات
۱۰ درصد برای کارمندان دولت و ۱۰- ۳۵ درصد برای دیگران	اشخاص حقیقی	حقوق، دستمزد و یا هر پاداش دیگری که توسط افراد در رابطه با خدمات اشتغال آن‌ها دریافت شده است. پرداخت برای کارهایی که خارج از ایران انجام شده است نیز مشمول مالیات خواهد بود، مشروط بر اینکه پرداخت‌کننده مقیم ایران باشد	مالیات بر درآمد استخدامی

نرخ مالیاتی	اشخاص مشمول مالیات	درآمد مشمول مالیات	مبنای مالیاتی
۱۵-۳۵ درصد	اشخاص حقیقی	فعالیت‌های تجاری غیرشرکتی (فروش کل از کالا و خدمات) به غیر از موارد استثناشده در موافقت‌نامه مالیات مضاعف	مالیات بر درآمد تجارت انفرادی
۲۵ درصد	اشخاص حقوقی	سود کل شرکت و سود حاصل از فعالیت‌های سودآور دیگر اشخاص حقوقی، برگرفته از منابع در ایران یا خارج از کشور، به غیر از ضرر و زیان ناشی از منابع معاف‌نشده و منهای معافیت‌های مشروط	مالیات بر درآمد شرکتی
۱۵-۳۵ درصد	اشخاص حقیقی یا حقوقی	درآمد به‌دست‌آوردهٔ بلاعوض و یا از طریق پارتی‌بازی و یا به عنوان جایزه	مالیات بر درآمد اتفاقی

جدول ۲-۵. مالیات بر اموال

نرخ مالیاتی	اشخاص مشمول مالیات	درآمد مشمول مالیات	مبنای مالیاتی
۵ درصد و ۲ درصد	اشخاص حقیقی یا حقوقی	انتقال نهایی املاک و مستغلات و سرقفلی منوط به پرداخت مالیات در تاریخ انتقال است	مالیات بر نقل و انتقال املاک و مستغلات
۰.۵ درصد و ۴ درصد	شرکت‌های سهامی خاص و سایر شرکت‌ها	مالیات بر نقل و انتقال سهام ارزش اسمی انتقال سهام	مالیات بر انتقال سهام
۵-۶۵ درصد	اشخاص حقیقی	هرگونه املاک به‌جامانده از متوفی	مالیات بر ارث
بر اساس مقررات مواد ۴۴ تا ۵۱	اشخاص حقیقی یا حقوقی	هر ورق از چک چاپ‌شده توسط بانک‌ها (ریال ۲۰۰)، برات، سفته (۰.۳ درصد)، و سایر اسناد و برگه‌های قابل مذاکره با مبلغی مشخص	تمبر مالیاتی

جدول ۵-۳. مالیات بر واردات

نرخ مالیاتی	درآمد مشمول مالیات	اشخاص مشمول مالیات	مبنای مالیاتی
مالیات بر واردات: مالیات بر واردات در حال حاضر توسط گمرک ایران جمع‌آوری می‌شود			

جدول ۵-۴. مالیات بر ارزش افزوده

نرخ مالیاتی	اشخاص مشمول مالیات	درآمد مشمول مالیات	مبنای مالیاتی
هم‌اکنون ۹ درصد است و معمولاً به طور سالانه یک درصد افزایش می‌یابد	اشخاص حقیقی و حقوقی	ارزش افزوده ناشی از فروش کالاها، خدمات و واردات آنها، به غیر از ۱۷ موردی که در ماده ۱۲ قانون مالیات بر ارزش افزوده به عنوان استثناها بیان شده است.	ارزش افزوده

۵-۲.   مالیات سرمایه‌گذاران خارجی در ایران

همه سرمایه‌گذاران خارجی که مشغول کسب‌وکار در ایران هستند، یا از منابعی در ایران درآمد کسب می‌کنند، مشمول مالیات هستند. بر اساس نوع فعالیت سرمایه‌گذار خارجی در ایران، مالیات‌ها و معافیت‌های متفاوتی اعمال می‌شود؛ از جمله مالیات بر سود، مالیات بر درآمد، مالیات بر اموال و غیره.

۵-۲-۱.   مالیات‌های مستقیم

همه اشخاص حقیقی یا حقوقی غیر ایرانی برای درآمد به‌دست‌آمده در ایران و همچنین برای درآمد به‌دست‌آمده از طریق اعطای مجوز یا حقوق دیگر، کمک‌فنی و آموزشی، یا قرارداد فیلم‌سازی در قلمرو ایران، مشمول مالیات هستند. بسته به نوع فعالیت سرمایه‌گذار خارجی، مالیات و معافیت‌های مختلفی قابل اجرا هستند، از جمله مالیات بر سود، مالیات بر درآمد، مالیات بر دارایی، و غیره.

سرمایه‌گذاران خارجی در ایران از همان حمایت‌ها و امتیازاتی بهره‌مند می‌شوند که برای سرمایه‌گذاران ایرانی وجود دارد. این بدین معناست که هر دو سرمایه‌گذار ایرانی و خارجی به مقدار یکسان مالیات پرداخت می‌کنند. تخفیفات و معافیت‌های مالیاتی نیز به طور یکسان به سرمایه‌گذاران داخلی و خارجی اعطا می‌شود. ازآنجاکه سرمایه‌های خارجی معمولاً به صورت

اشخاص حقوقی فعال هستند، در ادامه بر قوانین و مقررات مالیات بر درآمد شرکتی تمرکز می‌کنیم.

۵-۲-۲.   مالیات بر درآمد شرکتی

۱.   **مسائل کلی**

اشخاص حقوقی خارجی مقیم خارج از کشور برای درآمدهای مشمول مالیات به‌دست‌آمده از عملیات سرمایه‌گذاری خود در ایران یا فعالیت‌های انجام‌شده توسط آنها، به طور مستقیم و یا از طریق نمایندگان خود در ایران، مشمول مالیات با نرخ ثابت ۲۵ درصد هستند. اشخاص حقوقی مشمول مالیات دیگری از جمله مالیات بر سود سهام و مالیات بر سود مشارکت که ممکن است از طرف شرکت‌های سرمایه‌پذیر دریافت کنند، نخواهند بود.

اشخاص حقوقی ملزم هستند حتی در دوره معافیت مالیاتی، اظهارنامه مالیاتی و ترازنامه سود و زیان خود را که بر اساس دفاتر رسمی آنها تهیه شده، تا حداکثر چهار ماه بعد از سال مالیاتی (از ۲۱ مارس هر سال تا ۲۰ مارس سال بعد)، به همراه لیست همکاران و سهامداران، سهام و آدرس آنها، به اداره مالیاتی و بخش مربوط به فعالیت آن شخص حقوقی ارائه کنند. اگر اشخاص حقوقی در دورۀ زمانیِ مشخص‌شده، اسناد خود را ارائه نکنند، معافیت مالیاتی باطل می‌شود.

۲.   **معافیت‌ها**

قانون مالیات‌های مستقیم و آیین‌نامه‌های مرتبط با آن، برخی معافیت‌های مالیاتی را برای اشخاص حقوقی در نظر گرفته‌اند که در جدول زیر نشان داده شده است.

جدول ۵-۵. مهم‌ترین معافیت‌های مالیاتی

نوع تشویقی	مدت معافیت	میزان معافیت	فعالیت
معافیت دائم	دائمی	۱۰۰ درصد	کشاورزی
تعطیلات مالیاتی	۴ سال	۸۰ درصد	صنایع و معادن
تعطیلات مالیاتی	۲۰ سال	۱۰۰ درصد	صنایع و معادن در مناطق کمترتوسعه‌یافته
اعتبار مالیاتی	دائمی	۵۰ درصد	توریست
تعطیلات مالیاتی	در طول برنامه پنج‌ساله توسعه	۱۰۰ درصد	صادرات خدمات و کالاهای غیرنفتی
معافیت دائم	دائمی	۱۰۰ درصد	صنایع دستی
معافیت دائم	دائمی	۱۰۰ درصد	خدمات آموزشی و ورزشی
معافیت دائم	دائمی	۱۰۰ درصد	فعالیت‌های فرهنگی
اعتبار مالیاتی	دائمی	۵۰ درصد	دستمزد در مناطق کمترتوسعه‌یافته
تعطیلات مالیاتی	۲۰ سال	۱۰۰ درصد	تمام فعالیت‌های اقتصادی در مناطق آزاد
اعتبار مالیاتی	دائمی	۵۰ درصد	سود شرکت‌های خصوصی و همکاری‌کننده که در جهت توسعه، بازسازی و نوسازی واحدهای صنعتی و معدنی موجود استفاده می‌شود

۳. **کسورات**

هزینه‌هایی که در ارزیابی درآمد مشمول مالیات قابل کسر هستند، در قانون مالیات‌های مستقیم بیان شده است. این مخارج تا حد معقولی باید توسط مدارک مستند حمایت شوند و به طور انحصاری مرتبط با درآمد به‌دست‌آمده در سال مورد نظر باشند. دسته‌بندی مخارج قابل کسر عبارت‌اند از:

جدول ۵-۶. کسورات

۱۴. هزینه‌های متحمل‌شده در تعمیر و نگهداری و تعمیر و نگهداری از ساختمان و محوطه متعلق به شرکت	۱. هزینه کالا و مواد خام
۱۵. هزینه‌های حمل‌ونقل	۲. هزینه کارکنان
۱۶. هزینه‌های مربوط به حمل‌ونقل و سرگرمی برای کارکنان، و هزینه‌های انبارداری	۳. هزینه اجاره محل شرکت در صورت اجاره‌ای‌بودن
۱۷. هزینه‌های پرداخت‌شده به نسبت خدمات ارائه‌شده	۴. اجاره ماشین‌آلات و ابزار
۱۸. بهره و هزینهٔ پرداخت‌شده برای انجام عملیات شرکت	۵. هزینه سوخت، برق، روشنایی، آب و ارتباط
۱۹. هزینه تعمیر و نگهداری ماشین‌آلات و تجهیزات کسب‌وکار	۶. بیمه تجاری
۲۰. مخارج اکتشاف نافرجام برای معادن احتمالی	۷. حق تألیف، عوارض، حقوق و مالیات‌های پرداخت‌شده
۲۱. عضویت و هزینه‌های اشتراک مربوط به عملیات کسب‌وکار	۸. تحقیق، توسعه و مخارج آموزش
۲۲. بد حسابی، در صورت اثبات	۹. خسارت پرداخت‌شده برای ضررهای ناشی از فعالیت‌های تجاری
۲۳. زیان نرخ ارز که به روش پذیرفته‌شدهٔ حسابداری محاسبه شده باشد	۱۰. هزینه‌های فرهنگ، ورزش، رفاه که به اداره کار و امور اجتماعی برای کارگران پرداخت شده است
۲۴. اتلاف طبیعی تولید	۱۱. ذخیره برای مطالبات مورد تردید
۲۵. ذخیره مربوط به هزینه‌های قابل قبول از دوره ارزیابی	۱۲. ضررهای اشخاص حقوقی
۲۶. هزینه‌ها برای خرید کتاب و سایر محصولات فرهنگی و هنری برای کارکنان و وابستگان آنها	۱۳. هزینه‌های اندکی که به دلیل اجاره محل شرکت ایجاد می‌شوند

هزینه‌هایی که در جدول بالا به آنها اشاره نشده است، اما مرتبط با درآمد شرکت هستند، به عنوان هزینه قابل کسر با پیشنهاد اداره مالیاتی ایران و با تأیید وزارت امور اقتصاد و دارایی، قابل قبول هستند.

۴. **ضررها**

ضرر و زیان وارده به تمام مالیات‌دهندگانِ درگیر در تجارت و فعالیت‌های دیگر، توسط مقامات مالیاتی پذیرفته می‌شود و تا سه سال در محاسبات مالیاتی سود به‌دست‌آمده در نظر گرفته می‌شود.

۵. **مالیات تکلیفی**

در گذشته پنج درصد از هر پرداخت قراردادی باید توسط پرداخت‌کننده نگهداری و به مقامات مالیاتی اختصاص داده می‌شد. چنین نگهداری مالیاتی به عنوان پیش‌پرداخت برای پرداخت نهایی مالیات در زمان مقرر بود، ولی بر اساس اصلاحات اخیر قانون مالیات‌های مستقیم، این نوع مالیات حذف شده است.

پرداخت‌کنندگان دستمزد موظف هستند، در هنگام پرداخت یا اختصاص مبلغ، مالیات موظفی را نگه داشته، و در مهلت ۳۰ روز، مالیات کسرشده به همراه فهرستی از اسامی و آدرسِ افراد دریافت‌کنندۀ حقوق و میزان پرداختی آنها، به اداره ارزیابی مالیاتی محل ارائه کنند.

۶. **استهلاک**

استهلاک دارایی‌ها در هنگام ارزیابی درآمد مشمول مالیات، قابل کسر هستند. نرخ استهلاک بین ۵ تا ۱۰۰ درصد متغیر است و مدت زمانی که یک دارایی ممکن است مستهلک شود از ۲ تا ۱۵ سال متفاوت است.

۳-۲-۵.   مالیات بر ارزش افزوده در ایران

مالیات بر ارزش افزوده در ایران بر فروش تمام کالاها و خدمات و واردات آنها، بجز ۱۷ موارد ذکرشده در ماده ۱۲ قانون مالیات بر ارزش افزوده (واتا) به عنوان مواردی که معاف هستند، اعمال می‌شود. با وجود این، قانون مالیات بر ارزش افزوده شامل صادرات کالا و خدمات از مجاری رسمی گمرکی نمی‌شود؛ بنابراین مالیات پرداخت‌شده برای صادرات کالا و خدمات با ارائه برگه مجوز گمرکی و سایر مدارک معتبر قابل استرداد است. هم‌اکنون، نرخ مالیات بر ارزش افزوده ۹ درصد است (مالیات بر ارزش افزوده برای دو کالای خاص سیگار و سوخت جت نسبتاً بالاتر است). برای کاهش وابستگی کشور به درآمدهای نفتی، قانون پنج‌ساله توسعه مقرر می‌دارد که سالانه یک درصد به مالیات بر ارزش افزوده اضافه شود تا به ۹ درصد در سال ۲۰۱۶ برسد.

فعالیت‌های اقتصادی در مناطق آزاد تجاری و مناطق ویژه اقتصادی از پرداخت مالیات بر ارزش افزوده معاف هستند.

۴-۲-۵.   توافقات اجتناب از پرداخت مالیات مضاعف

برای تسهیل همکاری ایران با اتباع کشورهای خارجی، دولت جمهوری اسلامی ایران چندین موافقت‌نامه متقابل برای اجتناب از پرداخت مالیات مضاعف دارد:

جدول ۷-۵. لیست موافقت‌نامه‌های ایران برای اجتناب از پرداخت مالیات مضاعف

جمهوری آذربایجان	الجزایر	ترکمنستان	فرانسه
افریقای جنوبی	اندونزی	ترکیه	قرقیزستان
آلمان	اوکراین	تانزانیا	قزاقستان
اتریش	بحرین	چین	قطر
اردن	بلاروس	روسیه	جرجیا
ارمنستان	بلغارستان	سریلانکا	لبنان
ازبکستان	ونزوئلا	سوییس	لهستان
اسپانیا	پاکستان	سوریه	کویت
تاجیکستان	رومانی	سودان	صربستان
عمان	کره جنوبی	کرواسی	مالزی

۵-۲-۵.   سیستم حسابرسی استاندارد در ایران

سیستم واقعی حسابرسی شرکت‌ها در ایران منطبق با معیارهای حسابرسی استاندارد بین‌المللی است. افزون بر این سیستم‌هایی مانند GAAP توسط مقامات مالیاتی پذیرفته شده است، در عین حال محدودیتی برای شرکت‌های خارجی برای استفاده از سیستم‌های خودشان وجود ندارد. پس از ثبت یک شرکت در ایران، بازرسی از اداره مالیاتی محلی به عنوان مسئول ارتباطی به شرکت معرفی می‌شود و توصیه می‌شود که گزارشی از سیستم محاسباتی شرکت برای ارجاعات بعدی، به وی ارسال شود.

۶-۲-۵.   حسابرسی گزارش‌های مالی توسط حسابرسان مستقل

حسابرسان شرکت می‌توانند گزارش‌های مالی و اظهارنامه مالیاتی را تهیه و ارائه کنند. ماده ۲۷۲ قانون مالیات‌های مستقیم بیان می‌دارد:

«در موارد حسابرسی مالیاتی توسط حسابداران خبره، محاسبه و نظر آنها توسط اداره مالیاتی قبول خواهد شد. درآمد اعلام‌شده توسط آنها مبنایی برای محاسبه مالیات خواهد بود قبل از حسابرسی مالیاتی».

بر اساس قانون مالیات‌های مستقیم، گزارش‌های مالی باید توسط اداره مالیاتی در نظر گرفته شود، یا توسط حسابداران خبره بر اساس ماده ۲۷۲ قانون مالیات‌های مستقیم تنظیم شود. همچنین باید اقدامات لازم برای تعیین درآمد مشمول مالیات و صدور فهرست پرداختی برای تعیین میزان مالیات انجام شود.

۶   فصل ششم: نیروی کار؛ اشتغال اتباع خارجی در ایران

اتباع کشورهای خارجی ممنوع به کار در ایران هستند مگر اینکه مجوز کار و اشتغال دریافت کنند؛ حتی اگر قرار باشد دستمزد خود را خارج از قلمرو ایران دریافت کنند. مجوز کار، مدرک استخدامی برای اتباع خارجی در ایران خواهد بود.

مجوز کار برای استخدام اتباع خارجی در ایران توسط «اداره کل استخدام اتباع خارجی» که اداره استخدام مهاجرین نیز نامیده می‌شود و بخشی از وزارت تعاون، کار و رفاه اجتماعی است، با درخواست کارفرمای ایرانی صادر می‌شود.

این مجوز در مراکز استان‌ها توسط بخش اتباع خارجی از اداره کل وزارت تعاون، کار و رفاه اجتماعی، صادر می‌شود. رویه کلی برای پذیرش سرمایه‌گذاری خارجی جداگانه در بخش‌هایی که در ادامه می‌آید، مطرح خواهد شد. کارفرمایان ایرانی ملزم هستند پیش از انعقاد هرگونه قرارداد که منجر به استخدام اتباع خارجی در ایران می‌شود، مجوز اداره کل استخدام اتباع خارجی را دریافت کنند.

قوانین و مقررات مربوط به اخذ مجوز کار برای اتباع خارجی در قانون کار جمهوری اسلامی ایران، مصوب ۱۹۹۰ در دسترس است (مواد ۱۲۰ تا ۱۲۹ و آیین‌نامه اجرایی ماده ۱۲۹).

اگرچه به دلیل فراوانی افراد تحصیل‌کردهٔ جویای کار در کشور و با هدف کاهش نرخ بیکاریِ افراد جویای کار متخصص و تحصیل‌کرده، هیئت فنی استخدام اتباع خارجی، قوانین و مقررات سختی (ذکرشده در ماده ۱۲۱ قانون کار) برای صدور مجوز کار دارد، قانون تشویق و حمایت از سرمایه‌گذاری خارجی (فیپا) که در سال ۲۰۰۲ تصویب شده، مقررات امیدوارکننده‌ای دربارهٔ صدور مجوز کار برای سرمایه‌گذاران، مدیران و متخصصان خارجی در ارتباط با سرمایه‌گذاری طبق فیپا، تنظیم کرده است.

۶-۱   پذیرش سرمایه خارجی بر اساس قوانین و مقررات فیپا (FIPPA)

بر اساس ماده ۳۵ از آیین‌نامه اجرایی فیپا:

«دستگاه‌های اجرایی ذی‌ربط از جمله وزارت امور خارجه، وزارت کشور، وزارت کار و امور اجتماعی (از سال ۲۰۱۱ با ادغام وزارتخانه‌ها، با عنوان وزارت تعاون، کار و امور

اجتماعی شناخته می‌شود) و نیروی انتظامی، مکلفند در خصوص صدور روادید، اجازه اقامت، صدور پروانه کار برای سرمایه‌گذاران، مدیران، کارشناسان خارجی و بستگان درجه یک آنها در ارتباط با سرمایه‌گذاری‌های مشمول قانون، براساس درخواست سازمان اقدام کنند.

وزارت امور خارجه مکلف است درخصوص روادید ورود حسب مورد به شرح زیر اقدام نماید:

الف) وزارت امور خارجه با تأیید سازمان مجوز صدور روادید کثیرالمسافره سه‌ساله، با حق ورود و اقامت سه ماه در هر بار برای هر فرد را به نمایندگی‌های جمهوری اسلامی ایران در خارج از کشور ابلاغ کند.

ب) افراد معرفی‌شده پس از ورود به کشور می‌توانند با مراجعه به اداره گذرنامه و روادید وزارت امور خارجه و ارائه تأییدیه سازمان، اجازه اقامت خود را به مدت یک سال تمدید کنند. تمدید اقامت به صورت درج مهر کثیرالمسافره با اعتبار یک‌ساله صورت می‌پذیرد تا فرد موظف به اخذ روادید رفت و برگشت نشود».

اخذ مجوز اقامت سه‌ساله توسط سرمایه‌گذار خارجی، آن‌گونه که در بالا گفته شد، آنها را از اخذ ویزا برای ورود و خروج از کشور معاف می‌کند.

۲-۶.   صدور مجوز کار خارج از چارچوب فیپا (FIPPA)

در مواردی که کارفرمایان ایرانی نیاز به تخصص فنی کارشناسان خارجی دارند، صدور ویزا با اجازه کار و همچنین مجوز کار برای اتباع خارجی با درخواست کارفرمای ایرانی انجام خواهد شد. بر اساس قوانین و مقررات مرتبط، هیچ شهروند خارجی نمی‌تواند شخصاً برای استخدام و اخذ مجوز کار در ایران اقدام کند، مگر اینکه به طور قانونی شرکتی را ثبت کرده باشد.

هنگام درخواست از اداره کل استخدام اتباع خارجی و پیش از انعقاد قرارداد با متخصصان خارجی، کارفرمایان ایرانی باید درخواست و مدارک لازم را برای تأیید به اداره کل ارائه کنند. این مدارک برای بررسی بیشتر به هیئت فنی استخدام اتباع خارجی ارائه می‌شود. تأیید یا ردّ این هیئت توسط کارشناسان مربوطه به کارفرما اعلام می‌شود.

واگذاری اختیار محدود صدور، افزایش و تجدید مجوز کار اتباع خارجی به اداره کل استانی تعاون، کار و رفاه اجتماعی: در گذشته مسئولیت صدور، افزایش یا تمدید مجوز کار اتباع خارجی

در تهران انجام می‌شد (در اداره کل استخدام اتباع خارجی)، ولی برای رفاه متقاضیان، مسئولیت این امور تا اندازه‌ای به اداره کل تعاون، کار و رفاه اجتماعی در استان‌ها واگذار شد؛ بنابراین کارفرمایان و اتباع خارجی می‌توانند به ادارات کل استانی برای صدور، تمدید و تجدید مجوز کار خود مراجعه کنند.

۶-۳.   مدت اعتبار مجوز کار

مجوز کار اتباع خارجی برای یک دوره یک‌ساله قابل صدور، تمدید و تجدید است.

۶-۴.   تمدید مجوز کار

هنگام انقضای مجوز کار، اگر کارفرمای ایرانی هنوز به تخصص کارشناس خارجی نیاز داشته باشد، می‌تواند درخواست تمدید مجوز کار کارشناس یا نیروی کار خارجی را بنماید. درخواست به هیئت فنی استخدام ارجاع می‌شود و با تأیید آنها، مجوز کار برای یک سال تمدید می‌شود.

۶-۵.   تجدید مجوز کار

اتباع خارجی که دارای مجوز کار معتبر هستند، اما قرارداد آنها با کارفرما به هر دلیلی باطل شده است، پس از تغییر کارفرمای خود تابع تجدید مجوز کار خود خواهند بود. تجدید مجوز کار ـ همزمان با تغییر کارفرما ـ توسط بخش‌های مسئول در اداره تعاون، کار و رفاه اجتماعی و پس از تأیید هیئت فنی استخدام اتباع خارجی انجام می‌شود.

۶-۶.   مجازات قانونی برای استخدام اتباع خارجی بدون مجوز کار

کارفرمایانی که اقدام به استخدام آن دسته اتباع خارجی می‌نمایند که مجوز کار آنها منقضی شده یا بدون مجوز کار هستند، یا اتباع خارجی را در شغلی به غیر از آنچه در مجوز کار ذکر شده به کار می‌گیرند، یا در صورت فسخ قرارداد کاری خود با اتباع خارجی، موضوع را به وزارت تعاون، کار و رفاه اجتماعی اطلاع نمی‌دهند، بر حسب مورد محکوم به زندان یا جزای نقدی می‌شوند.

۶-۷.   هزینه‌ها

در حال حاضر صدور و تمدید مجوز کار برای اتباع خارجی ۱/۴۰۰/۰۰ ریال هزینه دارد و هزینهٔ تمدید این مجوز ۱/۰۰۰/۰۰۰ ریال است. مهاجرانِ برخی از کشورها به دلیل توافق با کشور آنها برای ارائه امتیازات مشابه، از پرداخت این هزینه معاف هستند.

۸-۶.   امتیازات ویژه برای سرمایه‌گذاران خارجی که نیروی کار در ایران استخدام می‌کنند

سرمایه‌گذاران خارجی که افراد معرفی‌شده توسط واحدهای مرتبط با وزارت تعاون، کار و رفاه اجتماعی را استخدام می‌کنند، از تخفیف یا معافیت پرداخت بیمه‌های موظفی در موردی که واحد آنها تازه‌تأسیس باشد، یا در سال قبل در میزان استخدامیِ آنها کاهش وجود نداشته باشد، بهره‌مند می‌شوند (قسمتی از ماده ۸۰ قانون برنامه پنج‌سالۀ پنجم توسعه).

۷ فصل هفتم: حقوق مالکیت معنوی در ایران

۷-۱. علامت تجاری

بر اساس ماده ۳۰ از قانون ثبت اختراعات، طرح‌های صنعتی و علائم تجاری (۲۰۰۸):

الف) علامت یعنی هر نشان قابل رؤیتی که بتواند کالاها یا خدمات اشخاص حقیقی یا حقوقی را از هم متمایز سازد؛ ب) علامت جمعی یعنی هر نشان قابل رؤیتی که با عنوان علامت جمعی در اظهارنامهٔ ثبت معرفی شود و بتواند مبدأ یا هرگونه ویژگی‌های دیگر مانند کیفیت کالا یا خدمات اشخاص حقیقی و حقوقی را که از این نشان تحت نظارت مالک علامت ثبت شده جمعی استفاده می‌کنند، متمایز سازد؛ ج) نام تجارتی یعنی اسم یا عنوانی که معرِّف و مشخص‌کنندهٔ شخص حقیقی یا حقوقی باشد.

حق اختصاصی استفاده از یک علامت متعلق به کسی است که بر اساس مقررات این قانون، علامت خود را به ثبت رسانده باشد.

۷-۱-۱. علامت‌های غیر قابل ثبت بر اساس قانون ایران

یک علامت در موارد زیر قابل ثبت نیست:

الف) نتواند کالاها یا خدمات یک مؤسسه را از کالاها و خدمات مؤسسه دیگر متمایز سازد؛

ب) خلاف موازین شرعی یا نظم عمومی یا اخلاق حسنه باشد؛

پ) مراکز تجاری یا عمومی را به‌ویژه در مورد مبدأ جغرافیایی کالاها یا خدمات یا خصوصیات آنها گمراه کند؛

ت) عین یا تقلید نشان نظامی، پرچم، یا سایر نشان‌های مملکتی یا نام یا نام اختصاری یا حروف اول یک نام یا نشان رسمی متعلق به کشور، سازمان‌های بین‌الدولی یا سازمان‌هایی که تحت کنوانسیون‌های بین‌المللی تأسیس شده‌اند، بوده یا موارد مذکور یکی از اجزای آن علامت باشد، مگر آنکه توسط مقام صلاحیت‌دار کشور مربوط یا سازمان ذی‌ربط اجازهٔ استفاده از آن صادر شود؛

ث) عین یا به طرز گمراه‌کننده‌ای شبیه یا ترجمهٔ یک علامت یا نام تجاری باشد که برای همان کالاها یا خدمات مشابه متعلق به مؤسسه دیگری در ایران معروف است؛

ج) عین یا شبیه آن قبلاً برای خدمات غیرمشابه ثبت و معروف شده باشد؛ مشروط بر آنکه عرفاً میان استفاده از علامت و مالک علامت معروف ارتباط وجود داشته و ثبت آن به منافع مالک علامت قبلی لطمه وارد سازد؛

چ) عین علامتی باشد که قبلاً به نام مالک دیگری ثبت شده و یا تاریخ تقاضای ثبت آن مقدم یا دارای حق تقدم برای همان کالا و خدمات و یا برای کالا و خدماتی است که به لحاظ ارتباط و شباهت، موجب فریب و گمراهی شود.

۲-۱-۷.   مدارک مورد نیاز برای ثبت علامت تجاری در ایران

مدارک مورد نیاز برای ثبت یک علامت تجاری در ایران برای اشخاص حقیقی و حقوقی یکسان است؛ تنها تفاوت در هزینه‌های ثبتی است. ثبت علامت تجاری نیازمند ارائه یک اظهارنامه به مقامات ثبتی است. ثبت علامت تجاری نیازمند ارائه اظهارنامه به مقام ثبت‌کننده به ترتیب ذیل است:

الف) اظهارنامهٔ ثبت علامت باید در دو نسخه و در فرم مخصوص (ع ۱) و به زبان فارسی تنظیم شده و پس از ذکر تاریخ، توسط متقاضی یا نمایندهٔ قانونی وی امضا شود؛

ب) در صورتی‌که اسناد ضمیمه اظهارنامه و سایر اسناد مربوط، به زبان دیگری غیر از فارسی باشد، ارائه اصل مدارک مورد نیاز همراه با ترجمه عادی کامل آن الزامی است. مرجع ثبت در صورت لزوم می‌تواند در جریان بررسی اظهارنامه، ترجمه رسمی مدارک مذکور را مطالبه کند.

پ) اظهارنامه ثبت علامت باید شامل نکات زیر باشد:

- اسم، شماره ملی، نشانی، کدپستی و تابعیت متقاضی. در صورتی‌که متقاضی شخص حقوقی است، ذکر نام، نوع فعالیت، اقامتگاه، محل و شماره ثبت، تابعیت، مرکز اصلی و عنداللزوم هر شناسه دیگر آن الزامی است.

- اسم، شماره ملی، نشانی و کدپستی نماینده قانونی متقاضی در صورت وجود؛

- اسم، نشانی و کدپستی شخص یا اشخاصی که صلاحیت دریافت ابلاغ‌ها در ایران را دارند، در صورتی‌که متقاضی مقیم ایران نباشد؛

- الصاق نمونه‌ای از علامت در کادر مربوط؛

- توصیف و تعیین اجزای علامت و تعیین حروف مشخص در صورتی‌که علامت مورد درخواست ثبت مشتمل بر حروف خاص باشد؛

- ذکر کالاها و خدماتی که علامت برای تشخیص آن‌ها به کار می‌رود با تعیین طبقه یا طبقات درخواست‌شده طبق طبقه‌بندی بین‌المللی؛

- ذکر حق تقدم در صورت درخواست؛

- رشته فعالیت مالک علامت؛

- ذکر علامت جمعی در صورتی‌که ثبت آن مورد درخواست باشد؛

- در صورتی‌که علامت مشتمل بر کلمه یا کلماتی غیر از فارسی باشد، درج آوانویسی و ترجمه آن؛

- ذکر رنگ، در صورتی‌که رنگ صفت مشخصه یا ویژگی‌خاص علامت باشد؛

- ذکر سه‌بعدی بودن علامت در صورت درخواست ثبت آن؛

- تعیین ضمائم.

تبصره ۱. در صورت تسلیم اظهارنامهٔ سایر اسناد مربوط توسط اشخاص حقوقی، امضای آن‌ها از طرف اشخاص مجاز ضروری است.

تبصره ۲. در صورت تعدد متقاضی ثبت، باید شخصی که به نمایندگی از سایرین حق مراجعه و مکاتبه با مرجع ثبت و انجام سایر تشریفات اداری لازم، جز دریافت گواهی‌نامه علامت را دارد، با ذکر اقامتگاه تعیین شود.

تبصره ۳. اسم و نشانی متقاضی مقیم خارج از کشور علاوه بر فارسی باید به حروف لاتین نیز نوشته و با همان حروف نیز ثبت و آگهی شود.

تبصره ۴. در کلیه امور مربوط به ثبت و انتشار علائم، مرجع ثبت طبقه‌بندی کالا و خدمات را براساس طبقه‌بندی بین‌المللی مورد بررسی قرار می‌دهد. در صورت وجود عناصر تصویری در علامت، رعایت طبقه‌بندی مربوط الزامی و به عهدهٔ مرجع ثبت است.

ت) برای ثبت هر علامت باید از اظهارنامهٔ جداگانه استفاده شود. استفاده از یک اظهارنامه برای ثبت یک علامت جهت کالاها و خدمات مندرج در یک یا چند طبقه بلامانع است.

ث) شخصی که تقاضای ثبت چندین علامت را به طور همزمان دارد، باید برای هریک از آن‌ها مطابق مقررات این آیین‌نامه، اظهارنامهٔ جداگانه‌ای تسلیم کند. در این صورت، اگر تقاضاها توسط نمایندهٔ قانونی به عمل آمده باشد، مدرک اصلی نمایندگی باید به یکی از اظهارنامه‌ها و یک رونوشت مصدق آن به هریک از اظهارنامه‌های دیگر باید ضمیمه شود.

ج) مدارک زیر باید ضمیمهٔ اظهارنامه شود:

- نسخه اصلی نمایندگی، در صورتی‌که تقاضا توسط نماینده قانونی به عمل آید؛

- ارائه ده نمونه از علامت به صورت گرافیکی که با علامت الصاق‌شده روی اظهارنامه یکسان بوده و ابعاد آن حداکثر ۱۰*۱۰ سانتی‌متر باشد. اگر ارائه علامت به صورت گرافیکی نباشد، ده نمونه از کپی یا تصویر علامت، حداکثر در همین ابعاد و به نحوی که مرجع ثبت مناسب

تشخیص دهد، ارائه خواهد شد. چنانچه مرجع ثبت نمونه علامت ارائه‌شده را مناسب تشخیص ندهد، تسلیم نمونه مناسب را درخواست می‌کند. درهرحال، علامت باید به همان نحو که درخواست و ثبت می‌شود استفاده گردد؛

- در صورت سه‌بعدی بودن علامت، ارائه علامت به صورت نمونه‌های گرافیکی یا تصویر دوبعدی روی برگه به نحوی که از شش زاویه متفاوت تهیه و در مجموع یک نمونه واحد که همان علامت سه‌بعدی را تشکیل دهند، الزامی است؛

- مدارک مربوط به حق تقدم که باید همزمان با تسلیم اظهارنامه یا حداکثر ظرف ۱۵ روز از آن تاریخ تسلیم شود؛

- ارائه مدارک دال بر فعالیت در حوزه ذی‌ربط بنا به تشخیص مرجع ثبت؛

- نسخه‌ای از ضوابط و شرایط استفاده از علامت جمعی و ارائه گواهی مقام صلاحیت‌دار، اتحادیه یا دستگاه مرتبط، در صورتی‌که ثبت علامت جمعی مورد درخواست باشد؛

- مدارک مثبت هویت متقاضی؛

- رسید مربوط به پرداخت هزینه‌های قانونی؛

- مدارک نمایندگی قانونی، در صورتی‌که تقاضا توسط نماینده قانونی به عمل آید.

- چ) مراحل ثبت علامت تجاری از قرار ذیل است:

- جمع‌آوری اطلاعات لازم؛

- تکمیل فرم درخواست (اظهارنامه)؛

- بررسی درخواست و ضمائم آن: در این مرحله کارکنان اداره ثبت اظهارنامه و ضمایم آن را بررسی می‌کنند و یکی از سه تصمیم را اتخاذ می‌کنند: الف) اگر ایرادها و نواقصی را در اظهارنامه و ضمائم آن مشاهده کنند، مراتب را به صورت مکتوب و با قید جزئیات به متقاضی ابلاغ می‌کنند تا ظرف مهلت مقرر اقدام به رفع نقص نماید؛ ب) اگر درخواست رد شود، اعلامیه رد صادر خواهد شد؛ ج) پذیرش اظهارنامه.

- انتشار اظهارنامه: هنگامی که اظهارنامهٔ ما پذیرفته شد، اداره ثبت از ما می‌خواهد که اظهارنامه را در روزنامه رسمی منتشر کنیم؛

- درخواست شماره ثبت: یک ماه بعد از انتشار اظهارنامه، می‌توان با ارائه تصویر اظهارنامه منتشرشده در روزنامه رسمی، و پرداخت هزینه ثبت، تقاضای شماره ثبتی کرد. ثبت رسمی علامت تجاری نیز باید منتشر شود؛

- تقاضای گواهی‌نامه ثبت: یک ماه پس از ثبت رسمی علامت تجاری، می‌توان تقاضای گواهی‌نامه ثبت کرد.

۷-۱-۳   عضویت ایران در کنوانسیون بین‌المللی علائم تجاری

۱.   کنوانسیون پاریس برای حمایت از مالکیت صنعتی (۱۸۸۳)؛

ایران از سال ۱۹۹۸ عضو کنوانسیون پاریس برای حمایت از مالکیت صنعتی است؛

۲.   موافقت‌نامه مادرید (۱۸۹۱) و پروتکل مرتبط با موافقت‌نامه مادرید (۱۹۸۹) در ارتباط با ثبت بین‌المللی علائم تجاری.

در ۲۵ سپتامبر ۲۰۰۳ ایران هم موافقت‌نامه مادرید و هم پروتکل مادرید در ارتباط با ثبت بین‌المللی علائم تجاری نزد سازمان بین‌المللی مالکیت معنوی (WIPO) را پذیرفت. موافقت‌نامه مادرید و پروتکل مادرید در ۲۵ دسامبر ۲۰۰۳ در ایران اجرایی شد.

۷-۲.   حق اختراع

بر اساس ماده ۱ قانون ثبت اختراعات، طرح‌های صنعتی و علائم تجاری (۲۰۰۸) «اختراع نتیجهٔ فکر فرد یا افراد است که برای نخستین بار فرایند یا فرآورده‌ای خاص ارائه می‌کند و مشکلی را در یک حرفه، فن، فناوری، صنعت و مانند آنها حل می‌کند».

حق اختراع اساساً امتیازی دولتی است که به شخص اعطا می‌شود و وی دارای حقوق انحصاری ساخت، استفاده و فروش کشف جدید و مفید خود، طراحی، فرایند، ماشین، تولید، یا سایر ترکیبات، یا هرگونه توسعه مفید آن است.

تقاضای ثبت اختراع اجباری نیست، اما دریافت ورقه ثبت اختراع به دارندهٔ آن (مخترع) این حق و اطمینان را می‌دهد تا اقدامات قانونی را برای جلوگیری از استفاده دیگران از اختراع یا کشف ثبت‌شده بدون رضایت وی انجام دهد.

۷-۲-۱.   اختراعات و اکتشافات قابل ثبت بر اساس حقوق ایران

بر اساس ماده ۲ از قانون ثبت اختراعات، طرح‌های صنعتی و علائم تجاری (۲۰۰۸) «اختراعی قابل ثبت است که حاوی ابتکار جدید و دارای کاربرد صنعتی باشد. ابتکار جدید عبارت است از آنچه در فن یا صنعت قبلی وجود نداشته و برای دارندهٔ مهارت عادی در فن مذکور معلوم و آشکار نباشد و از نظر صنعتی، اختراعی کاربردی محسوب می‌شود که در رشته‌ای از صنعت قابل ساخت یا استفاده باشد. مراد از صنعت، معنای گستردهٔ آن است و شامل مواردی نظیر صنایع دستی، کشاورزی، ماهیگیری و خدمات نیز می‌شود».

۷-۲-۲.   اختراعات و اکتشافات غیر قابل ثبت بر اساس حقوق ایران

طبق ماده ۴ قانون ثبت اختراعات، طرح‌های صنعتی و علائم تجاری (۲۰۰۸) «موارد زیر از حیطه حمایت از اختراع خارج است:

- کشفیات، نظریه‌های علمی، روش‌های ریاضی و آثار هنری؛

- طرح‌ها و قواعد یا روش‌های انجام کار تجاری و سایر فعالیت‌های ذهنی و اجتماعی؛

- روش‌های تشخیص و معالجهٔ بیماری‌های انسان یا حیوان: این بند شامل فرآورده‌های منطبق با تعریف اختراع و مورد استفاده در روش‌های مزبور نمی‌شود؛

- منابع ژنتیک و اجزای ژنتیکی تشکیل‌دهندهٔ آنها و همچنین فرایندهای بیولوژیک تولید آنها؛

- آنچه قبلاً در فنون و صنایع پیش‌بینی شده باشد.

۷-۲-۳.   مدارک مورد نیاز برای ثبت اختراع در ایران

مخترع یا کشف‌کننده ملزم است تقاضانامه کتبی را به اداره مالکیت صنعتی تهران (اداره ثبت اختراع) ارائه نموده، و همراه با پرداخت هزینه‌های لازم، آنچه را به عنوان «اظهارنامه» شناخته می‌شود، تکمیل نماید. ثبت اختراع نیاز به ارائه اظهارنامه به مقامات ثبتی به ترتیب زیر دارد:

الف) اظهارنامه ثبت اختراع باید در سه نسخه و در فرم مخصوص (الف ـ ۱) و به زبان فارسی تنظیم شده و پس از ذکر تاریخ، توسط متقاضی یا نماینده قانونی وی امضا شود.

ب) در صورتی‌که اسناد ضمیمه اظهارنامه و سایر اسناد مربوط، به زبان دیگری غیر از فارسی باشد، ارائه اصل مدارک مورد نیاز همراه با ترجمه عادی کامل آنها الزامی است. اگر ترجمه کامل این مدارک برای متقاضی میسر نباشد، می‌تواند خلاصه آنها را به فارسی ضمیمه نماید. مرجع ثبت در صورت لزوم می‌تواند در جریان بررسی اظهارنامه، ترجمه رسمی مدارک مذکور را مطالبه کند. چنانچه اصطلاحات فناوری و علمیِ به‌کاررفته در اسناد مذکور، معادل فارسی نداشته باشند، ذکر همان اصطلاحات کفایت می‌کند.

ت) متقاضی باید اظهارنامه ثبت اختراع را به صورت حضوری یا با پست سفارشی و یا در چارچوب ماده ۱۶۷ این آیین‌نامه به مرجع ثبت تسلیم نماید. تاریخ وصول اظهارنامه یا تاریخ داده پیام، تاریخ اظهارنامه تلقی می‌شود.

پ) اظهارنامه ثبت اختراع باید حاوی نکات زیر باشد: ۱) اسم، شماره ملی، نشانی، کدپستی، تابعیت و سمت متقاضی. در صورتی‌که متقاضی شخصی حقوقی است، ذکر نام، نوع فعالیت، اقامتگاه، محل و شماره ثبت، تابعیت، مرکز اصلی و عندالزوم هرگونه شناسه دیگر آن الزامی

است؛ ۲) اسم، شماره ملی، نشانی و کدپستی نماینده قانونی متقاضی در صورت وجود؛ ۳) اسم، اقامتگاه و کدپستی شخص یا اشخاصی که صلاحیت دریافت ابلاغها در ایران را دارند، در صورتی‌که متقاضی مقیم ایران نباشد؛ ۴) اسم، نشانی و شغل مخترع، در صورتی‌که متقاضی شخص مخترع نباشد؛ ۵) عنوان اختراع به نحوی که اختراع ادعایی را مشخص سازد و مشتمل بر کلماتی مثل «بهتر» و غیره نبوده و ترجیحاً بین سه تا ۱۰ کلمه باشد؛ ۶) تاریخ، محل و شماره اظهارنامه یا گواهی‌نامه اختراع در خارج، در صورت درخواست حق تقدم؛ ۷) اطلاعات مربوط به اظهارنامه اصلی در صورت تکمیلی‌بودن اختراع؛ ۸) تعداد صفحات توصیف، ادعاها، خلاصه توصیف اختراع و نقشه‌ها؛ ۹) تعیین طبقه اختراع براساس طبقه‌بندی بین‌المللی اختراعات؛ ۱۰) تعیین ضمائم؛ ۱۱) در صورت تسلیم اظهارنامه و سایر اسناد مربوط توسط اشخاص حقوقی، امضای آن‌ها از طرف اشخاص مجاز ضروری است؛ ۱۲) اسم و نشانی متقاضی مقیم خارج از کشور، علاوه بر فارسی باید به حروف لاتین باشد و با همان حروف نیز ثبت و آگهی شود.

ث) مدارک زیر باید ضمیمه اظهارنامه شود: ۱) توصیف اختراع؛ ۲) ادعا یا ادعاهای اختراع؛ ۳) خلاصه‌ای از توصیف اختراع؛ ۴) نقشه یا نقشه‌ها، در صورت لزوم؛ ۵) مدارک مثبت هویت متقاضی و مخترع؛ ۶) درخواست کتبی مبنی بر عدم ذکر اسم مخترع، چنانچه مخترع نخواهد اسم وی ذکر شود؛ ۷) مدارک مربوط به حق تقدم که باید همزمان با تسلیم اظهارنامه یا حداکثر ظرف ۱۵ روز از آن تاریخ تسلیم شود؛ ۸) رسید مربوط به پرداخت هزینه‌های قانونی؛ ۹) مدارک نمایندگی، در صورتی‌که تقاضا توسط نماینده قانونی به عمل آید.

تبصره ۱) چنانچه اظهارنامه در زمان تقاضا فاقد شرایط مقرر در ماده ۱۱ قانون باشد، مرجع ثبت از متقاضی دعوت خواهد کرد تا از تاریخ ابلاغ ظرف ۳۰ روز اصلاحات لازم را انجام دهد و تاریخ تقاضا همان تاریخ دریافت اصلاحات مذکور خواهد بود. اگر در مهلت تعیین‌شده اصلاح صورت نگیرد، اظهارنامه کان لم یکن تلقی خواهد شد. این مهلت برای اشخاص مقیم خارج از کشور ۶۰ روز است.

تبصره ۲) اگر در اظهارنامه به نقشه‌هایی اشاره شود که در آن درج یا ضمیمه نشده است، مرجع ثبت از متقاضی دعوت می‌کند تا نقشه‌ها را ظرف ۳۰ روز ارائه دهد. در صورت ارائه، تاریخ دریافت نقشه‌ها، تاریخ تقاضا تلقی خواهد شد. در غیر این صورت، مرجع ثبت تاریخ تقاضا را همان تاریخ دریافت اظهارنامه قید نموده و اشاره به نقشه‌ها را کان لم یکن تلقی خواهد کرد. این مهلت برای اشخاص مقیم خارج از کشور ۶۰ روز است.

هر صفحه از توصیف، ادعا، خلاصه توصیف و نقشه اختراع باید توسط متقاضی یا نمایندهٔ قانونی او امضا شود.

اظهارنامه باید فقط به یک اختراع یا به دسته‌ای از اختراعات مرتبط که یک اختراع کلی را تشکیل می‌دهند مربوط باشد. در غیر این صورت، متقاضی می‌تواند اظهارنامهٔ مربوط به اختراع خود را به دو یا چند اظهارنامهٔ مجزا و مستقل تقسیم کند.

ج) مرجع ثبت پس از دریافت اظهارنامه و ضمائم مربوط، آن را ظرف شش ماه از حیث انطباق با شرایط شکلی و ماهوی مندرج در قانون و این آیین‌نامه بررسی می‌کند.

تبصره ۱) مرجع ثبت در صورت ضرورت می‌تواند از مراجع ذی‌ربط اعم از خصوصی یا دولتی و یا از متخصصان و کارشناسان امر برای احراز شرایط ماهوی اختراع، استعلام و کسب نظر نماید. مهلت پاسخ به استعلام و اعلام نظر حداکثر ۳ ماه خواهد بود.

تبصره ۲) اظهارنظر مراجع و اشخاص مذکور جنبه مشورتی داشته و عدم پاسخ به استعلام و کسب نظر، مانع از بررسی و اتخاذ تصمیم مرجع ثبت نیست.

تبصره ۳) استعلام و کسب نظر از مراجع و اشخاص مذکور می‌تواند بر اساس قراردادهای منعقده با آن‌ها صورت گیرد.

چ) چنانچه پس از بررسی اظهارنامه و ضمائم آن، انجام اصلاحات یا تکمیل اظهارنامه و ضمائم آن ضرورت داشته باشد، مرجع ثبت با تعیین مواردی که نیاز به اصلاح یا تکمیل دارند کتباً از متقاضی می‌خواهد تا ظرف ۳۰ روز از تاریخ ابلاغ نسبت به انجام اصلاحات یا تکمیل مدارک اقدام نماید. در غیر این صورت اظهارنامه کان لم یکن تلقی خواهد شد. مهلت تعیین‌شده در این ماده برای اشخاص مقیم خارج از کشور ۶۰ روز است. تصمیم مرجع ثبت مبنی بر اعطای گواهی‌نامه اختراع کتباً به متقاضی اعلام شده و متقاضی باید ظرف مدت ۳۰ روز پس از اعلام جهت پرداخت هزینه‌های مربوط به ثبت اختراع و انتشار آگهی موضوع ماده ۳۲ این آیین‌نامه اقدام کند. در صورت عدم پرداخت هزینه‌ها در مهلت مقرر فوق، اظهارنامه کان لم یکن تلقی می‌شود. این مهلت برای متقاضیان مقیم خارج از کشور ۶۰ روز است.

ح) اختراع با قید مراتب زیر طبق فرم (الف ـ۲) در دفتر ثبت اختراع ثبت می‌شود: ۱) شماره و تاریخ اظهارنامه با قید ساعت و روز و ماه و سال؛ ۲) شماره و تاریخ ثبت اختراع؛ ۳) اسم و نشانی و تابعیت مالک اختراع؛ ۴) اسم و نشانی و تابعیت مخترع در صورتی‌که متقاضی شخص مخترع نیست مگر اینکه مخترع کتباً تقاضا نموده باشد که نامش در گواهی‌نامه اختراع ذکر نشود؛ ۵) اسم و نشانی نمایندهٔ قانونی مخترع، اگر ثبت اختراع توسط وی تقاضا شده باشد؛ ۶) عنوان اختراع؛ ۷) طبقه‌بندی بین‌المللی اختراع با ذکر زمینه علمی‌ای که اختراع در آن طبقه قرار می‌گیرد؛

۸) در صورت ادعای حق تقدم و پذیرش آن، تاریخ، شماره و محل تسلیم اظهارنامه مقدم؛ ۹) مدت حمایت.

تبصره ۱) در دفتر ثبت اختراع، برای هر اختراع دو صفحه اختصاص می‌یابد و هر تغییر و اصلاح و همچنین نقل و انتقال‌هایی که جزئاً یا کلاً نسبت به موضوع اختراع صورت می‌گیرد، در صفحات مزبور قید می‌شود.

تبصره ۲) درج مراتب فوق پس از تکمیل باید به امضای مالک اختراع یا نمایندۀ قانونی وی و همچنین رئیس اداره ثبت اختراعات برسد.

خ) پس از ثبت اختراع، آگهی مربوط به ثبت ظرف ۳۰ روز با قید مراتب مذکور در ماده ۳۱ این آیین‌نامه، در روزنامه رسمی منتشر می‌شود. آگهی مزبور به امضای رئیس اداره ثبت اختراعات رسیده و برای انتشار تسلیم روزنامه رسمی می‌شود.

د) پس از انتشار آگهی ثبت اختراع و تحویل نسخه منتشرشده یا منعکس در سایت روزنامه رسمی به مرجع ثبت، گواهی‌نامه اختراع صادر و به متقاضی یا نماینده قانونی وی تسلیم خواهد شد. گواهی‌نامه اختراع باید با استفاده از فناوری روز تهیه و مشتمل بر نسخه‌ای از توصیف ـ ادعا ـ خلاصه توصیف و نقشه بوده و منگنه و مهر شده و به امضای رئیس اداره ثبت اختراعات برسد. گواهی‌نامه اختراع طبق فرم (الف ـ۳) باید حاوی نکات زیر باشد: ۱) شماره و تاریخ اظهارنامه؛ ۲) شماره و تاریخ ثبت اختراع؛ ۳) اسم، نشانی و تابعیت دارندۀ اختراع؛ ۴) اسم، نشانی و تابعیت مخترع، مگر اینکه مخترع کتباً از مرجع ثبت، درخواست عدم ذکر نام خود را نماید؛ ۵) عنوان اختراع؛ ۶) طبقه‌بندی بین‌المللی اختراع؛ ۷) ذکر تاریخ، شماره و محل تسلیم اظهارنامۀ مقدم، در صورت ادعای حق تقدم و پذیرش آن؛ ۸) مدت حمایت.

ذ) طبق ماده ۱۶ قانون ثبت اختراعات، طرح‌های صنعتی و علائم تجاری (۲۰۰۸) «اعتبار گواهینامه اختراع با رعایت این ماده، پس از بیست سال از تاریخ تسلیم اظهارنامه اختراع منقضی می‌شود. به منظور حفظ اعتبار گواهینامه یا اظهارنامۀ اختراع، پس از گذشت یک سال از تاریخ تسلیم اظهارنامه و پیش از شروع هر سال، مبلغی که به موجب آیین‌نامۀ این قانون تعیین می‌شود، توسط متقاضی به اداره مالکیت صنعتی پرداخت می‌شود. تأخیر در پرداخت حداکثر تا شش ماه در صورت پرداخت جریمه مجاز است. درصورتی‌که هزینۀ سالانه پرداخت نشود، اظهارنامۀ مربوط مستردشده تلقی و یا گواهینامۀ اختراع، فاقد اعتبار می‌شود».

۷-۲-۴.   عضویت ایران در کنوانسیون‌های بین‌المللی ثبت اختراع

کنوانسیون پاریس برای حمایت از مالکیت صنعتی (۱۸۸۳)

ایران از سال ۱۹۹۸ عضو کنوانسیون پاریس برای حمایت از مالکیت صنعتی است. طرفین این موافقت‌نامه تعهد نموده‌اند که به اتباع یکدیگر، حق اختراع و علائم تجاری را مشابه با آنچه به اتباع خود می‌دهند، اعطا نمایند. حق اولویت یکی از مهم‌ترین مزایای کنوانسیون پاریس است. این حق به شخصی که در یکی از کشورهای عضو تقاضای ثبت اختراع نموده است، اجازه می‌دهد در مدت یک سال برای حمایت از حق خود، در سایر کشورهای عضو کنوانسیون نیز تقاضای ثبت اختراع کند.

چنین تصور می‌شود که این تقاضانامه، در همان روز تقاضانامهٔ اول ارائه شده است. این مقرره یک مزیت مهم برای اتباع خارجی است که قصد دارند اختراع خود را در چندین کشور از جمله ایران، ثبت و حمایت کنند.

معاهده همکاری ثبت اختراع (PCT)

در ۴ جولای ۲۰۱۳، ایران ابزار تأیید را به PCT ارائه نمود و صد و چهل‌وهشتمین کشور امضاکنندهٔ این معاهده شد، و در ۴ اکتبر ۲۰۱۳ ملزم به اجرای آن شد. بدین ترتیب، هر تقاضانامهٔ بین‌المللی که در، یا پس از ۴ اکتبر ۲۰۱۳ ارائه شده باشد، خودبه‌خود مشمول شناسایی جمهوری اسلامی ایران نیز خواهد بود.

همچنین چون ایران ملزم به رعایت فصل دوم PCT است، در هر درخواستی به طور خودکار به عنوان کشور مورد بررسیِ بین‌المللی تقاضاشده انتخاب می‌شود. افزون بر این، اتباع و افراد مقیم جمهوری اسلامی ایران از ۴ اکتبر ۲۰۱۳، حق خواهند داشت بر اساس PCT تقاضای ثبت بین‌المللی کنند.

۸ فصل هشتم: ضمیمه

جدول ۱-۸. وب‌سایت‌های مهم ایرانی

وزارت اقتصاد و دارایی	www.mefa.gov.ir
وزارت صنعت و معدن	www.min.gov.ir
وزارت بازرگانی	www.iranministryofcommerce.com
اتاق بازرگانی، صنایع و معادن	www.iccim.org
گمرک جمهوری اسلامی	www.irica.gov.ir
وزارت امور خارجه	www.mfa.gov.ir
وزارت نفت	www.nioc.com
وزارت کار	www.irimlsa.ir
سازمان مدیریت و برنامه‌ریزی	www.mpzog.ir
سازمان مالیات بر ارزش افزوده	www.vat.ir
جامعه حسابداران رسمی ایران	www.iacpa.ir
سازمان بورس اوراق بهادار تهران	www.tse.or.ir
بانک مرکزی ایران	www.cbi.ir
سازمان امور مالیاتی کشور	www.intamedia.ir
سازمان خصوصی‌سازی ایران	www.ipo.ir
سازمان سرمایه‌گذاری و کمک‌های اقتصادی و فنی ایران	www.investiniran.ir
شرکت سرمایه‌گذاری‌های خارجی ایران	www.ific.org.ir
سازمان حسابرسی	www.audit.org.ir
ویزای الکترونیکی برای ایران	wvisa.mfa.gov.ir

سلب مسئولیت

در نوشتن این کتاب راهنما، تلاش شده تا اطلاعات شفاف، درست و به‌روز ارائه شود. با وجود این، اطلاعات ارائه‌شده در متن کتاب، تنها بیان‌کنندهٔ راهنمای قانونی و کلی هستند. این کتاب با درک این موضوع منتشر و پخش شده است که نویسندگانْ مسئول هرگونه اقدام انجام‌شده بر اساس این کتاب یا هرگونه اشتباه یا کمبود در آن نیستند. نویسندگان با نوشتن این کتاب در صدد ارائه مشاوره حقوقی یا مالی نبوده‌اند. به خوانندگان عزیز توصیه می‌شود پیش از اتخاذ هرگونه تصمیمی در مورد موضوعات خاص با مشاوران حرفه‌ای مشورت نمایند.

نمایه

Printed by Printforce, the Netherlands